The Question of Law

The Question of Law

Young Kim

LEXINGTON BOOKS
Lanham • Boulder • New York • London

Published by Lexington Books
An imprint of The Rowman & Littlefield Publishing Group, Inc.
4501 Forbes Boulevard, Suite 200, Lanham, Maryland 20706
www.rowman.com

86-90 Paul Street, London EC2A 4NE

British Library Cataloguing in Publication Information Available

Library of Congress Cataloging-in-Publication Data

Names: Kim, Young, 1949- author.
Title: The question of law / Young Kim.
Description: Lanham : Lexington Books, 2024. | Includes bibliographical references and index. | Summary: "The Question of Law offers an original theory of law, stated as two normative principles. Law is seen having a political foundation, with the question of law thus becoming a question of obedience - whether and in what circumstances it is appropriate to obey the law. Kim further maintains that law should serve the demands of justice"-- Provided by publisher.
Identifiers: LCCN 2023048859 (print) | LCCN 2023048860 (ebook) | ISBN 9781666938272 (cloth) | ISBN 9781666938289 (epub)
Subjects: LCSH: Law--Philosophy. | Obedience (Law) | Political obligation. | Legal positivism. | Liberalism.
Classification: LCC K231 .K56 2024 (print) | LCC K231 (ebook) | DDC 340/.1--dc23/eng/20231019
LC record available at https://lccn.loc.gov/2023048859
LC ebook record available at https://lccn.loc.gov/2023048860

This book is dedicated to my wife Jane, of course, and to my family and many friends in the legal profession—this is my take on what we've been engaged in all these years.

Contents

Acknowledgments ix

Introduction 1

PART I: A THEORY OF LAW 3

Chapter 1: What Is Law? 5

Chapter 2: Obligations 13

Chapter 3: Values and Norms 23

PART II: EARLY THEORIES OF LAW 33

Chapter 4: Classical Views 35

Chapter 5: Natural Law 51

Chapter 6: Legal Positivism 57

PART III: POLITICAL FOUNDATIONS OF LAW 65

Chapter 7: Political Society and Civil Government 67

Chapter 8: Liberalism 77

Chapter 9: Group Rights 87

Chapter 10: International Relations 103

PART IV: CONTEMPORARY THEORIES OF LAW 115

Chapter 11: Natural Law 117

Chapter 12: Social Facts 125

Chapter 13: Legal Positivism 135

Chapter 14: Contemporary Theories of Justice 149

PART V: JUSTICE AND LAW 163

Chapter 15: Justice and Law 165

Conclusion: Normative Principles of Law 169

Works Cited 185

Index 193

About the Author 197

Acknowledgments

My gratitude to SunHee Kim Gertz, Professor Emerita of Clark University, for her careful and thoughtful review of the manuscript. It was a pleasure working again with my editors at Lexington Books, Joseph Parry, Sara Noakes, Emily Kasprzyk, and Megan Murray. I'm thankful for their useful comments, which helped make this a better book.

Introduction

Practicing lawyers often engage the question of what law is applicable to a given set of circumstances. This study addresses a somewhat different inquiry, namely, what is law. Many contemporary accounts of the nature of law focus on the interplay between morality and politics, often in the area of norms, and thus they develop normative theories of law.

Further, while it has been argued that the task of justice is to develop a moral framework for political interaction, I argue for an inverse relationship between law and morality; that is, that law articulates attempts to make authoritative political pronouncements that regulate human behavior, and these pronouncements, embedded as they are in societal mores, sometimes overlap with moral and normative concerns.

Fundamentally, I believe that law should serve justice. The particular concept of justice that I have in mind is a relational one, justice as right actions, which is led by moral concerns. While arising from a political foundation, law is thus connected to morality at the top level, with justice providing the moral framework within which rules of law are articulated.

What is law? In my view, law comprises social and normative rules of behavior imposed by a political authority, and thus, the foundation of law is political, including the power to enforce rules. Accordingly, at the ground level, the question of law is primarily a question of obedience—whether and in what circumstances it is appropriate to obey the law. Since the question of obedience to the law is a normative question, it thus follows that the answer is dependent on the contingent content of a society's conventions, and also the relevance and strength of morality in the legal system.

In developing a theory of law in Part I of this study, my working assumption is that law and the legal system consist of rules and duties that depend for their legal validity on the values and norms of society. Further, this study's theory of law rests upon two principles of law that I present and describe in operation. Thus, the nature of obligation—especially legal and moral obligations—is explored here, along with the concept of moral responsibility. Finally, as they are at the core of any normative theory of law, I discuss critical questions of values and norms.

I investigate early theories of law in Part II, including the classical views of Plato and Aristotle, and how their accounts relate to their respective theories of justice. The natural law theories of Thomas Aquinas, Thomas Hobbes, and John Locke are then examined, and followed by a review of the 18th century legal theories of Jeremy Bentham and John Austin.

I turn then to the political foundations of law in Part III, to probe concepts such as: natural rights, the state of nature, and the social contract; civil government, constitutions, and political legitimacy; political liberalism; international relations and war; and the term rule of law (which some use to designate law and order), to focus upon societal and political stability and thereby test the margins between democratic and authoritarian rule.

The theories of prominent contemporary legal theorists are reviewed in Part IV, including a range of debates between natural law theorists on the one hand—who advance the thesis that the moral content of putative norms bears on their legal validity—and legal positivists on the other hand—who argue that the conditions of legal validity are purely a matter of social facts.

In Part V, to articulate the distinction between the questions of justice and law, I review contemporary distributive and relational theories of justice, arguing that a relational approach to the question of justice provides a superior method for examining the question of law. I argue that the question of justice involves a search for the moral right thing to do in given circumstances, while law, with its political foundations, should serve the demands of justice. I then proceed to examine the fit of a theory of justice as right actions to the normative legal theory developed in this study. I conclude this study with a summary of the investigation into the nature of law and the normative theory of law presented in these pages.

PART I

A Theory of Law

Chapter 1

What Is Law?

The inquiry into the nature of law, or more recently, into normative legal theory, has been pursued in the Anglophone world through three separate paths of analysis: legal theory, jurisprudence, and the philosophy of law. While these terms may be lodged in scholarly conventions and/or the specific training or proclivities of educators and theorists, for my purposes here, the term legal theory combines all three approaches in order to delineate a deep approach that takes into account multiple perspectives.

Anglophone scholarship generally assesses theories of law by measuring how they fit the facts, thereby tending to the empirical. The debates emerging from this focus often take place in the arena of social norms. Clearly, debates can only be productively engaged when social norms are shared to some degree, and thus, they comprise common standards with respect to acceptable or appropriate behavior in differing social circumstances. While social norms vary by community, as do the strength or weakness of such norms within different communities, they also change over time. In other words, social norms represent contingent circumstances.

Fueling this empirical perspective in contemporary times is a hermeneutic approach to legal theory, engaged in by disparate contemporary theorists, like H.L.A. Hart, Joseph Raz, Ronald Dworkin, and John Finnis. Linking their hermeneutic arguments is their contention that theories of law would be better served by presenting an account of the attitudes of citizens who view the law as providing them with reasons for action. For instance, in the legal positivist tradition, H.L.A. Hart uses a somewhat complex interpretive strategy to argue that sanction-oriented theories of law, like John Austin's, ignore an essential feature of law: that law is not merely about threatened sanctions, but that the law also imposes obligations. Thus, a hermeneutic strategy may proffer the practical attitude of rule acceptance, as seen in Hart's theory of social rules, in comparison with social habits, which are central to Austin's command theory and the latter's concepts of sovereignty and legality.[1]

Such approaches reflect a grounding in the social sciences. That is, acceding that knowledge of social institutions and participants in them is different from knowledge in the physical sciences, the social sciences avoid only chronicling and outlining behavior. Rather, they place a primary focus in capturing the motivations and purposes of participants and their understanding.

AN APPROACH TO THE QUESTION

In this study, I take an analytic approach to the inquiry into the character of law, one that recognizes the conventions, thought and richness of the different moral traditions of various cultures, and thus making law a matter of cultural contingency.

By evoking an analytic approach, I reference the Enlightenment project of methodological investigation that proceeds with certain assumptions, including that of ascertaining the relevant facts to the situation at hand.[2] Moreover, I recognize that the facts or circumstances in a given situation are often not hard and nubby items, but rather may be open to various shades of interpretation and characterization, which may then affect the determination of what actions to take in any given event.

Such variety of interpretation and characterization inexorably link law to concepts of politics and morality. Consequently, in pursuing the normative character of the question of law, I construct a deontological theory of law. That is, I argue for the priority of the right over the good. Further, it is my view that any normative theory of law should serve the demands of justice in society, and thus I conclude this study by discussing concepts of justice and the fit of the theory of law developed here with the demands of justice.

Rules or Duties

I contrast this deontological perspective with teleological or consequentialist perspectives. For instance, the classic utilitarianism of Jeremy Bentham, Henry Sidgwick, and James Mills propounds that the moral worth of an action is judged solely by its utility in providing happiness or pleasure to human beings.[3] Classic utilitarianism thus presents, as a moral theory, a consequentialist perspective,[4] since the moral worth of an action is measured by its outcome.

In stark contrast to Bentham's utilitarianism is Immanuel Kant's position on the will to universal law, a concept fundamental to many deontological theories that look to rules or duties for determining what moral choices should be made, as is the case with this study as well. Kant's various formulations in his *Groundwork of the Metaphysic of Morals* represent attempts to present a Supreme Principle of Morality, by famously presenting the Categorical Imperative. Just as well known, Kant foregrounded rational and autonomous moral agency and action-guiding principles in his Formula of Universal Law (which he viewed as fundamental), whereby one should: "Act only on the maxim through which you can at the same time will that it should become a universal law."[5] By universal law, I take Kant to mean a law which is not self-defeating, that is reversible, and that may be consistently applied.

Rationality and Autonomy

While I follow Kant's view that the concept of moral agency includes the constituent elements of rationality and autonomy, I diverge from his view that rationality entails autonomy. In this much debated arena, some, including John Rawls, interpret Kant's stance as a constructivist account, in which autonomy and independence of reason are seen to produce objective moral ends. Notably, the particular constructivist account that Rawls attributes to Kant argues for a conception of objectivity that is not metaphysical, but political. That is, Rawls develops a foundation that hosts objective standards in reasoning and is aimed at solving practical problems of what to do in society, including principles of justice that govern the basic structure of society, as defined by major social institutions.[6]

Critics of this interpretation, however, point out that the basic argument for constructivism in Kant's account arises from the analysis of obligation in the *Groundwork* and that there are realist strands in the *Critique of Pure Reason*, where Kant refers to our consciousness of the moral law as the "fact of reason."[7] The debate, on metaethical grounds, raises the question of whether morality is grounded on rationality. For example, one of the battles fought queries the correctness of moral judgments based on non-ontological grounds. Rather than enter the metaethical fray directly, I suggest that for purposes of developing a legal theory that comprises both moral and political aspects, the questions raised by Kant's conception of rational agency are best met on the grounds of normative ethics.

In taking this normative view, I thereby reject Kant's position that rationality entails autonomous agency. Rather, as I see it, rationality requires autonomy, since rational deliberation requires freedom to enact it. Thus, while I support the view that moral agency requires the elements of reason and autonomy, I loosen the linkage between autonomy and reason from a directly dependent relationship. In doing so, I also acknowledge that I have a more than instrumental view of rationality, whereby rationality guides agents to take those actions necessary in relation to given ends. Further, I recognize that instrumental rationality provides an incomplete explanation for evolving independent standards of evaluation of those ends.

Additionally, instrumental rationality does not, in itself, generate reasons for action. Thus, I arrive at the conclusion that instrumental rationality functions as a structural component of one's attitudes. Necessarily, in order to map out the nature and scope of practical reason, instrumental rationality must be seen as one of various structural requirements of rationality.[8]

Obligations

The normative character of law orchestrates obligations, especially moral and legal obligations. By obligation, I mean an act, course of action, or condition which, given a defined set of societal expectations, generates conditions by which a person is morally or legally bound. I use the word obligation interchangeably with duty in the following discussion to explore normative reasons for action, and thus also to initiate an inquiry into questions of intention and psychological motivation.

A moral obligation arises when an individual questions what actions should or should not be taken under given circumstances. In posing the question, established concepts of right and wrong behavior, along with those of good and bad actions are foregrounded. And in gathering such concepts to make a judgment, the question of moral responsibility is evoked, whereby the responsibility for actions and the consequences of actions define the axes that will diagram responses.

With respect to legal obligation, while it could be argued that a person has a prima facie duty to obey the law (a legal obligation), if the law in question offends societal norms and customs, then the question of obedience to the law becomes critical. It follows that political obligation may be seen as the extent to which legal obligations, simply because they are legal obligations, give rise to moral obligations. Otherwise stated, is a citizen of a nation obliged to obey the legal norms of the society where he or she lives?

Values and Norms

Clearly, underlying many discussions of normative legal theory are questions of value, as they undergird the framework for moral decision-making. Importantly, questions of value tend to crosscut classifications of moral theory as metaethical and normative inquiries. For instance, both Plato and Aristotle are moral realists who believe in the pursuit of The Good; however, their individual theories of foundational forms and virtue ethics lead to quite different normative approaches to questions of value.

Basic questions informing value theory include definitions of goodness as well as views of what define good, better, and bad. Further, value theory treats the shape of morality, as, for example, articulated in debates of value monism vs. value pluralism or the issue of incommensurability. Emerging from such questions are teleological or consequentialist approaches to moral decision-making as well, which contrast with deontological approaches, thereby additionally including disputes such as the right vs. the good.

One problem in these explorations is that the rational authority of moral norms often proves difficult to pinpoint.[9] One approach, inspired by Aristotle, centers on practical reflection, based in the question of what it means to act well.[10] Another strategy maximizes rationality in various ways (e.g., decision theory).[11] Not surprisingly, some scholars approach values and theories of values as an important focus for practical reflection.[12]

Legal Validity

When exploring normative aspects of law, it also becomes necessary to explain how legal norms can give rise to actions as well as what kinds of reasons are involved. Thus, many contemporary legal theories focus on what general conditions make a putative legal norm valid. Otherwise stated, this is the question of legal validity, discussed later in this study.

A THEORY OF LAW

For the legal theory articulated here, two principles provide normative guidance with regard to questions of lawful actions. Deontological in approach to the question of law, the theory attempts to be value-neutral acknowledging, however, an underlying thin theory of the good, including concepts of rationality, autonomous moral agency, equal concern and respect for others, and the plurality of values.

More specifically, the normative character of law may be stated as two principles in lexical priority, as follows:

> *First Principle*: One should obey those laws of legal-rational political authority that do not otherwise violate societal norms and customs.
>
> *Second Principle*: Governments should only enforce rules of human behavior of legitimate legal-rational political authority.

Underlying these two principles of law is the Kantian notion of due respect and concern for persons. Moreover, the legal theory I develop here includes both moral and political aspects. That is, the *First Principle* engages moral considerations, as based on the individual and is further designed to provide normative guidance to a person's actions. In designating the individual as responsible for her or his own actions, the first principle creates a relation to political aspects as articulated in the *Second Principle*.

That is, to engage in moral considerations, an individual relies upon the external world and experience for limits on appropriate actions. In this manner, the first principle sets the ambit of proper actions for persons in society, based in the caveat that norms and customs need to be taken into account, thus making the determination a culturally contingent matter. Hence, the first principle also points to the political foundation of law, and the question of obedience—whether and in what circumstances it is appropriate to obey the law.

In keying on the individual for this first principle, I express my view of the importance of responsible actions by individuals based on rational and autonomous moral agency. That is, I view persons as responsible, in the sense of accountability, for their intentional actions. The sense of agency that I pursue includes elements of rationality and autonomy although, as mentioned above, I diverge from Kant's view that rationality entails autonomy. In other words, for rational, autonomous individuals, the first principle states a normative rule for obeying laws in society.

As just described, the *First Principle* sets the parameters for the *Second Principle*, which is political and which accedes in lexical priority to the first principle. It corresponds to the first principle in that it sets the proper ambit of societal response to an individual's lawful actions. It directly addresses government and the political foundation of law, addressing the proper treatment of citizens in society.

Obedience to Laws

In attempting to determine whether and in what circumstances the law should be obeyed under the first principle, the norms and customs of the relevant society should be taken into account, thus making the determination a culturally contingent issue. As an example, it may be useful to consider that, for Kant, the operation of the Categorical Imperative resulted in the absolute prohibition against murder, theft, and lying. While the operation of the Two Principles of Law articulated here also results in a prohibition against murder, it does in contradistinction to Kant's Categorical Imperative by taking an empirical view of the external world and experience through the first principle and allowing for sanctions through the second principle.

The functioning of these two principles becomes perhaps more evident with regard to theft and lying. That is, depending on the circumstances, such actions may or may not be actionable (under the law) or excusable (by custom) and, in fact, may even be praiseworthy, again, given the circumstances, as for example, portrayed in Victor Hugo's *Les Misérables*.[13] That is, in the novel, Jean Valjean steals a loaf of bread to feed his sister's seven starving children and is sent to prison for five years for violating the law, but eventually serves nineteen years, an extreme sanction. Given that Hugo depicts a fictional world, yet his example corresponds with established norms so much so that his novel has been readily accepted as a masterpiece.

How would Valjean's actions fare under this study's first principle? Telling is Inspector Javert's decision-making process. Although devoted to the law, the Inspector does not arrest Valjean for a later violation of the law. Instead, he surmises that following a lawful course in the circumstances would be immoral and possibly unjust, as he determines of the applicable law itself. In Part V of this study, I explore the underlying issues in Javert not pursuing Valjean by examining the interplay of justice with concepts of the law.

Norms and Customs

As Hugo suggests, the cultural contingency implied in the first principle may be ameliorated by its reference to the external world and experience. For instance, there are moral resources and constraints contained in Tim Scanlon's concept of "parametric universalism," which seeks to identify certain deeply embedded, culturally universal concepts that exclude genocide, murder, and totalitarian rule from morally acceptable behavior.[14] While Scanlon's views may be seen as relativistic, they are nonetheless grounded on certain universal, cross-cultural concepts, making external analyses possible while minimalizing intuition as a standard.

In further searching for action-guiding moral resources referenced in the first principle of this theory of law, it proves useful as well to identify morally thick concepts. For instance, Bernard Williams in his benign treatment of moral relativism identifies four concepts that can bear a substantial amount of cross-cultural weight, including cowardice, truthfulness, brutality, and gratitude.[15]

Finally, for those situations in which a conflict of values is identified under the first principle, the value that best adheres to or promotes the notion of equal respect and concern for persons embedded in this principle is the one that should prevail as a priority rule.

NOTES

1. See H.L.A. Hart, *The Concept of Law*, ed. Leslie Green (Oxford: Oxford University Press, 2012), particularly 55–60 and John Austin, *Lectures on Jurisprudence*, or *The Philosophy of Positive Law*, 2 vols., ed. R. Campbell (London: John Murray; reprinted, Bristol: Thoemmes Press, 2002).

2. See Philip Petit, "The Contribution of Analytical Philosophy," in Robert Goodin and Philip Petit, eds., *A Companion to Contemporary Political Philosophy* (Malden: Blackwell Publishers, 1995) 7: "1. There is a reality independent of human knowledge of which we human beings are part. 2. Reason and method, particularly as exemplified in science, offer us the proper way to explore that reality and our relationship to it. 3. In this exploration traditional—in particular, traditional evaluative preconceptions—should be suspended and the facts allowed to speak for themselves."

3. See Jeremy Bentham, *The Works of Jeremy Bentham* (Edinburgh: William Tait, 1843).

4. G.E.M. Anscombe, "Modern Moral Philosophy," *Philosophy* 33;124 (1958): 1–19.

5. Immanuel Kant, *Groundwork of the Metaphysic of Morals*, trans. H. J. Paton (New York: HarperCollins, 2009), I. 88.

6. See John Rawls, *A Theory of Justice* (Cambridge: Harvard University Press, 1971), ch. 2.

7. E.g., see R. M. Hare, *Moral Thinking* (Oxford: Oxford University Press, 1981), ch. 9. See Immanuel Kant, *Critique of Pure Reason*, trans. and eds. Paul Guyer and Allen Wood (Cambridge: Cambridge University Press, 1997).

8. I use the term *practical reason* to address the normative question of what one is to do in given circumstances, thus leading to a consideration of matters of value. In contrast, *theoretical reason* addresses facts and their explanations.

9. See Christine Korsgaard, *The Sources of Normativity* (Cambridge: Cambridge University Press, 1996), for a strong Kantian approach to the question of norms, their sources, and authority.

10. For Aristotle, practical wisdom proves foundational to his ethical views as well as to his views of human nature and virtue, with well-being (*eudaemonia*) belonging to those living virtuous lives. See Aristotle, *The Nicomachean Ethics of Aristotle*, trans. D. Ross, rev. Leslie Brown (Oxford: Oxford University Press, 2009); also see Philippa Foot, *Natural Goodness* (Oxford: Clarendon Press, 2001).

11. See Philip Pettit and Michael Smith, "Parfit's P," in *Reading Parfit*, ed. Jonathan Dancy (Oxford: Blackwell, 1997), ch. 5.

12. E.g., Joseph Raz, *The Morality of Freedom* (Oxford: Oxford University Press, 1986).

13. See Victor Hugo, *Les Miserables*, trans. Norman Denny (London: Penguin Books, 1982).

14. T. M. Scanlon, *What We Owe to Each Other* (Cambridge: Harvard University Press, 2000): 328–361.

15. See Bernard Williams, *Ethics and the Limits of Philosophy* (Cambridge: Harvard University Press, 1985), ch. 9.

Chapter 2

Obligations

The following discussion of obligations explores normative reasons for action and initiates an inquiry into questions of intention and psychological motivation. In examining these matters, I review concepts of practical reason, due concern and respect, responsibility, moral luck, and moral relativism.

LEGAL OBLIGATION

At a broad level, laws may be seen as rules of conduct or action regulating behavior which are created and enforced by a controlling authority, often social institutions or government. While one may argue that a person has a prima facie duty to obey the law, if the law at issue offends societal norms and customs, then the question of obedience to the law is evoked. The main question here is often presented as the extent to which legal obligations, simply because they are legal obligations, give rise to moral obligations. Is there a general duty to obey the legal norms of the society in which a person lives?

MORAL OBLIGATION

Morality is seen as concerning principles of right and wrong, and of good and bad behavior. Among classical views of morality, Plato bases individual morality on knowledge of foundational forms as metaphysically conceived in terms of universals, and especially the form of the Good. He characterizes these forms as immaterial and unchanging, whether mortals intellectually apprehend them or not. Within this metaphysical framework, Plato theorizes that to apprehend the good, the individual must keep the three constitutive parts of the soul in balance, the three parts comprising: reason, spirit, and appetite. Morality on the individual level is the basis for morality on the societal level, for when the souls of individuals are in balance, the good of the state will be furthered, as an orderly, hierarchal society can emerge.[1]

Rather than taking a metaphysical approach, Aristotle dramatically moves the discussion of morality to the secular and pragmatic. In doing so, he develops a teleological approach to ethics, in which he derives moral obligation from what is good as an end or what is desirable to be achieved, thereby underscoring the proper purpose, goals and ends of the human enterprise. The character of an individual, with character traits as learned dispositions, is paramount to Aristotle, and living well (*eudaemonia*) is his answer to an individual leading a moral life.[2]

Practical wisdom proves foundational to Aristotle's ethical views as well as to his views of human nature and virtue. Consequently, Aristotle posits that an individual's powers of reason bifurcate into practical reason, the intellectual faculty central to ethical life, and theoretical reason, the intellectual faculty deployed in philosophy and the sciences. Identifying the intellectual faculty governing *ethos* as practical, Aristotle further links an individual's practical reason to certain excellences of character, or virtues, which he treats as internalized dispositions of action, desire, and feeling.[3]

Aristotle accordingly defines the concepts of well-being, virtue, and practical wisdom with and against each other, and in developing a theory of virtue (*arête*), he depicts ethical life in *The Politics* as essentially a social matter concerning an individual's coming to terms with the laws, rules, norms, and customs of political community. Certainly, classic utilitarianism shares Aristotle's teleological approach to ethics, and in contemporary times, there has also been a revival of virtue ethics.[4]

PRACTICAL REASON

I rely on a moderate view of rationality rather than on a more extreme Platonic or Cartesian view, as a precedential method of acquiring knowledge. Thus, theoretical reason comprises reflection on questions of explanation and prediction. I also enlist knowledge of practical experience, as grounded in a particular society, to execute the conclusions of theoretical reason. That is, practical reasoning is the general capacity of human beings to resolve, through reflection, the question of what should be done.

Thus, the contrast between practical reason and theoretical reason addresses two different systems of norms: those for the regulation of action (practical reason), and those for the regulation of belief (theoretical reason). Importantly, though, even proponents of instrumental rationality—which holds that an individual is rationally required to take the means that are necessary her/his ends—agree that instrumental principles do not generate reasons for action. As such, the instrumentalist mode basically rests upon a consequentialist account of the relation of action to value.[5] An ethical gap becomes discernible when practical reason drives intentional action, thereby eliciting the question of psychological motivation, which could possibly drive an extreme set of circumstances, which Hume had designated with the phrase, "slave to passions."

Rather than posing an instrumental view of rationality, Immanuel Kant challenged doctrines of his time by focusing on the individual. Concomitantly, in positing the importance of an individual's free will, he underscores the necessity of its being rational. The reach of this concept of reason extends into practical affairs beyond that of a Humean "slave to passions" and directly addresses the normative question. Critically, it is the presence of this self-governing reason in human beings that Kant offers as decisive grounds for viewing each person as possessed of equal worth and deserving of equal respect, the grounds, that is, for acting as a moral agent.

When practical reason weighs such issues as to whether and how deliberative reflection gives rise to action, and what norms are binding upon us as moral agents, moral responsibility is evoked. That is, moral responsibility, treated in more detail later in this chapter, depends upon a rational and autonomous individual to judge, act, and deliberate about norms in such a manner that a particular type of reaction—generally speaking, praise or blame—is elicited. It is important to underscore here, that in deliberating the requisite reaction (e.g., praise or blame), the conditions and objects of moral responsibility intrinsically require analyses that consider norms to some degree.

DUE CONCERN AND RESPECT

A concept of due respect and concern for others undergirds both principles of the legal theory articulated in this study. I believe that legal theorizing involves a moral inquiry, based on a rational and autonomous view of moral agency, pertaining to beings who are capable of acting with reference to some notion of right and wrong. In other words, human beings as moral agents are rational, free, and responsible agents.

This view accords with the Kantian notion of treating persons with respect derived from his Formula of the End in Itself, "Act in such a way that you always treat humanity, whether in your own person or in the person of any other, never simply as a means but always at the same time as an end."[6] Kant's view, then, is that we must treat others with respect, as rational persons formulating their own maxims, principles that propel one's actions.

Important to note here is that a maxim represents a subjective principle of action and should be distinguished from an objective principle—namely, practical law. In this light, Kant's subjective principle of action contains a practical rule determined by reason in accordance with the conditions of the subject (often the agent's ignorance or inclination), formulated as the principle upon which the subject acts. A law for Kant, on the other hand, is an objective principle valid for every rational being, and it is consequently a principle upon which an agent ought to act—that is, an imperative. Kant thus expresses his fundamental principle of morality as the Categorical Imperative, which may be seen as the law of an autonomous will.[7]

RESPONSIBILITY

In Aristotle's view of moral responsibility, he states that it is sometimes appropriate to respond to an agent with praise or blame on the basis of the individual's actions and/or dispositional traits of character.[8] He continues to argue that only agents who qualify as moral agents are properly subject to ascriptions of responsibility, namely, those who possess a capacity for decision. This narrowing of the field to moral agents stems from his view that a decision represents a certain kind of desire resulting from deliberation, one that expresses the agent's conception of what is good.[9] In addition, an agent is a likely candidate for praise or blame if and only if his action or disposition is voluntary.

Marginalizing autonomy to qualified moral agents, however, poses the possible threat to the concept of moral responsibility identified as causal determinism. That is, causal determination proffers the view that everything that happens or exists is caused by antecedent conditions, making it impossible for anything to happen or exist other than as it does or is. Scientific determinism, for example, may be viewed as a variety of causal determinism, whereby the antecedent conditions identified are a combination of the prior states of the universe and laws of nature.

P. F. Strawson attempts to alter the traditional debate by asserting that judgments about responsibility should be understood in relation to the role social "reactive attitudes" play in the practice of holding persons responsible. That is, according to Strawson, the attitudes expressed when holding persons morally responsible should include a wide range of attitudes that derive from their participation in personal relationships (attitudes such as resentment, indignation, hurt feelings, anger, gratitude, reciprocal love, and forgiveness).[10] These attitudes represent reactions to the perception of another's good will, ill will, or indifference, and further, they are expressed from the stance of a person involved in interpersonal relationships, who regards the agent held responsible as a participant in such relationships as well.

Strawson's emphasis on the social aspects of responsibility points to where my views differ from Kant's. That is, Strawson's emphasis reflects my interest in metaphysical treatments of freedom and moral responsibility. That is, I agree with Strawson that the place and role of reactive attitudes in human lives may be accommodated in a theory of moral responsibility, one that draws a distinction between responsibility understood as attributability and responsibility understood as accountability.[11] In other words, while my views on moral responsibility may be classified similarly to Kant's as those of a merit-based incompatibilist, I nonetheless accommodate Strawson's insights regarding reactive attitudes by viewing responsibility as accountability rather than as attributability.[12]

MORAL LUCK

My views as to moral responsibility differ from Kant's not only in the integration of social reactive attitudes, but also with regard to the problem of moral luck in the correlation of moral responsibility with voluntary action. This difference further delineates the proposed ambit of the second principle of law in the legal theory presented here.

With regard to moral luck, Plato raises the question in *Laws* in the context of laws and punishment, by exploring how moral luck should affect punishment.[13] In contrast, luck enters Aristotle's account of eudaimonia in Book V of *Nicomachean Ethics* in at least two ways: (1) whether one receives the upbringing and training, creating dispositions, to lead a virtuous life; and (2) whether the external world cooperates for an individual to be virtuous, and so truly happy, since "happiness needs the external goods as well; for it is impossible, or not easy, to do noble acts without proper equipment."[14]

Unlike both Plato and Aristotle, Kant's discussion of good will stimulated the view that matters of morality are immune from luck.[15] In contemporary times, however, Bernard Williams and Thomas Nagel have powerfully raised the question of whether we should be morally responsible for only those matters that are within our control, and further, whether individuals should be morally assessed in different manner, if the only differences between them are outside of their control.[16]

Although Williams had initially intended the term "moral luck" to be an oxymoron, he has nonetheless addressed the seemingly contradictory term in correlating moral responsibility with voluntary action and exploring the phenomenon whereby a moral agent is assigned moral blame or moral praise for an action or its consequences, even when it is clear that the agent did not have full control over the act or its consequences.

To illustrate the problem of moral luck, the following is a rendition of the familiar traffic accident example: Two people drive cars down a road, Driver A and Driver B. They are alike in every way. Driver A, in a moment of inattention, runs a red light as a child is crossing the road and slams on the brakes in an attempt to avoid hitting the child, but unfortunately, s/he hits and kills the child. Driver B, in the meantime, also runs a red light in a moment of inattention, but since no one was crossing the road at the time, s/he merely gets a traffic ticket. The only difference between the drivers is the occurrence of an external uncontrollable event, a child walking onto the road. The question, then, is: are both Drivers A and B equally worthy of moral blame?

Kant would answer yes, since in his rationalist view, moral luck does not play into the calculus of whether an agent has done her or his duty. That is, for Kant equal fault equates with equal blame.

To address the problem of moral luck, I combine the rationalist approach with the consequentialist approach, by constructing an internal/external view of the problem. Thus, in the above example, if both drivers failed to check their brakes, from an external perspective, they should be equally at fault and equally blameworthy. If both drivers did everything correctly, including checking the brakes of their cars, then externally (and rationally), they should again be equally blameworthy. In the latter variation, however, if Driver A hits and kills the child, then internally, Driver A may view her-/himself as deserving of more blame than Driver B, in whose case, no child crossed the road.

This view accords with Williams's observation that Driver A, who may have done nothing wrong, s/he nonetheless has "reasonable regret" for the consequences of her/his actions. In Strawson's terms, this view also incorporates reactive attitudes into the notion of accountability. On the other hand, Nagel might classify the traffic accident as resultant (or consequential) moral luck; both drivers were affected by moral luck in that a particular set of circumstances resulted in two different ways.[17]

Thus, the traffic example illustrates how this study's first principle of law, in which the moral agent is responsible for her/his actions, is constrained by the second principle of law in its view of the role of government, and in so doing, adopts the internal/external approach to moral luck and the "reasonable regret" of the internal/consequentialist view of Driver A.

MORAL RELATIVISM

In his epistemological work *Theaetetus*, Plato introduces a fragment attributed to Protagoras, "Of all things the measure is man, of the things that are, that [or 'how'] they are, and of things that are not, that [or 'how'] they are not," using it to discuss the *homomesura* concept.[18] This passage has been interpreted to endorse a form of relativism, but as moral realists, Plato, and Aristotle as well, deny moral relativism on metaethical grounds. Aristotle further argues that human nature is such that virtues such as courage, temperance and justice are necessary for any plausible conception of a good life.

Metaethically, then, relativism is an anti-realist account, since moral realism holds that there is in some sense an objective moral reality. As a theory, relativism should nonetheless be amenable to testing per se against other moral theories, for its validity, coherence, as well as its explanatory and predictive power. It is important to note in this regard, that as a method of moral theorizing, relativist accounts are coherentist, in that they especially look to the internal consistency of an account.

In his defense of moral relativism, for example, Gilbert Harman develops the concept of "moral frameworks" in a coherentist manner, whereby through a process of continuing rational reflection, an individual refines an original set of values until s/he arrives at a coherent set of "corrected values" in a stable equilibrium, and hence, a moral framework.[19] With this relativist, coherentist approach, obviously, the question must be posed: of what probative value are an individual's corrected values?

Ultimately, the question emerges from how moral relativism foregrounds social reactive attitudes and is assumed to deny the existence of universal moral truths to the extent that right and wrong must be defined variously, based on differences in cultural norms and mores. What is seen as morally right is relative, then, to an individual's society, as well as to its time and place in history. Some versions of moral relativism, multiculturalism, for instance, not only justify individual actions based upon a particular group's cultural norms and mores, but also award rights to groups, thus denying or abrogating, in effect, individual moral agency.[20]

As stated above, I have a deontological approach to the question of law, one in which the development of normative, action-guiding principles proves useful. Thus, my approach conflicts not only with consequentialist views, but also with various forms of moral relativism. With an empirical outlook, however, some moderate forms of moral or cultural relativism may be seen as providing constraints, albeit thin constraints, as well as resources, for moral decision-making.

With respect to ethical decision-making, Williams proffers another approach. That is, he develops the concept of real and notional confrontations for ethical disagreements, whereby he understands that for relativism to be true, there must be a real confrontation between two moral systems such that at any given time there is a group for whom two moral systems meeting a "condition of exclusivity" are a real option. In contrast to Harman's stronger precondition to moral judgments of "shared motivational attitudes," Williams' formulation of a real confrontation precondition results in an approach that has a broader reach for the proper extent of moral judgments.[21] Williams further provides some moral resources for moral decision-making, as he identifies morally thick concepts (cowardice, lying, brutality, and gratitude), that are able to bear a substantial, culturally conditioned, ethical load. As such, they succeed in articulating action-guiding concepts for members of a particular culture as well as providing what can be reasonably viewed as ethical knowledge to members of that culture.

Tim Scanlon treats what may be categorized as moral relativism by arguing that morality is a question of what we owe each other to develop a theory of "parametric universalism." While his theory may indeed be viewed as relativistic, it is nonetheless grounded on certain universal, cross-cultural concepts, making external analyses possible while minimalizing intuition as a standard.[22] In identifying these concepts, Scanlon states that they should be deeply embedded culturally and sufficient to exclude genocide, murder, and totalitarianism. Thus, in Scanlon's account, as well as in Williams' benign treatment of relativism, there are empirical constraints formulated, as well as resources provided, that may be used in moral decision-making.

NOTES

1. See Plato, *The Republic*, trans. Desmond Lee (London: Penguin Books, 2003) and Plato, *The Statesman*, trans. J. B. Skemp (London: Bristol Classical Press, 2002). For various views on Plato's concept of the tripartite soul and moral psychological aspects in *The Republic*, see *Plato and the Divided Self*, eds. Rachel Barry, Tad Brennan, and Charles Brittain (Cambridge: Cambridge University Press, 2012), Part II.

2. Aristotle, *The Politics*, trans. Ernest Baker (Oxford: Oxford University Press, 2009), Book V.

3. Accordingly, Aristotle treats the opposite trait of practical irrationality as *akrasia*, to underscore incontinence or weakness of will.

4. E.g., see Jeremy Bentham, *An Introduction to the Principles of Morals and Legislation,* eds. J. H. Burns and H.L.A. Hart (Oxford: Clarendon Press, 1996) regarding utilitarianism; also see Phillipa Foot, *Virtues and Vices* (Oxford: Oxford University Press, 2002); and Alasdair MacIntyre, *After Virtue* (Notre Dame: University of Notre Dame Press, 2007) with respect to contemporary virtue ethics.

5. See David Hume, *A Treatise of Human Nature*, eds. David Fate Norton and Mary J. Norton (Oxford: Oxford University Press, 2001), II; 3, ch. 1, 399, "Reason is, and ought only to be the slave of the passions."

6. Immanuel Kant, *Groundwork of the Metaphysic of Morals*, trans. H. J. Paton (New York: HarperCollins, 2009), 96.

7. Ibid. Underscoring how the Categorical Imperative differs from the Golden Rule ("So in everything, do to others what you would have them do to you"), the Categorical Imperative is based not on what an individual desires to do (or have done to her- or

himself), but rather, what is necessary for any being to act rationally and *universally*, without consideration of self-interest.

8. Aristotle 2009: 1190b30–35, following the customary Bekker format.

9. Ibid., 1111b–1113b3.

10. P. F. Strawson, "Freedom and Resentment," in *Freedom and Resentment and Other Essays* (New York: Routledge, 2008), 1–28.

11. See, generally, Andrew Eshleman, "Moral Responsibility," ed. Edward N. Zalta, *The Stanford Encyclopedia of Philosophy* (2014), http//plato.stanford.edu/archives/sum.2014/entries/roal-responsibility.

12. Some have made distinctions between responsibility as attributability, answerability, and accountability; see David Shoemaker, "Attributability, Answerability, and Accountability," *Ethics* 121 (2011): 603–632; while others have argued that all three concepts are just one, answerability; see Angela Smith, "Attributability, Answerability, and Accountability," *Ethics* 122 (2012): 575–589.

13. Plato, *The Laws*, trans. Trevor Saunders (London: Penguin Books, 1970), IX, 876–877, following the customary Stephanus format.

14. Aristotle 2009: 1099a 31–33. A third way that luck may enter Aristotle's account of *eudaimonia* is through the provision, or not, of minimum external goods such as health, security, access to resources. See Terence Irwin, *Classical Thought* (Oxford: Oxford University Press, 1988), 445.

15. See Kant 2009: 62.

16. See Thomas Nagel, *Mortal Questions* (New York, Cambridge University Press, 1979), ch. 3; and Bernard Williams, *Moral Luck* (Cambridge: Cambridge University Press, 1981).

17. Nagel 1979: ch. 3. Further refining the concept of moral luck, Nagel develops three additional categories in his work: circumstantial moral luck, focusing on the environment of the moral; constitutive moral luck, emphasizing the personal character of the moral agent; and, more controversially, causal moral luck, which some interpret as an alternative presentation of the problem of free will.

18. Plato, *Theaetetus*, ed. Bernard Williams, trans. M. J. Levett, rev. Miles Burnyeat (Indianapolis: Hackett Publishing Company, 1992), DK 80b1, using the Diels-Kranz numbering system. Further, see 151d7–e3, ff.

19. Gilbert Harman, "Moral Relativism and Moral Objectivity," in eds. Gilbert Harman and J. J. Thompson, *Moral Relativism and Moral Objectivity* (Cambridge: Blackwell Publishers, 1996), 3–64.

20. See Will Kymlicka, *Multicultural Citizenship* (Oxford: Oxford University Press, 1995), regarding group rights; compare with Brian Barry, *Culture and Equality* (Cambridge: Polity Press, 2001) and his rejection of group-based rights as antithetical to the universalist liberal project, which he views as based on the individual; also see discussion of group rights in chapter 9 *infra*.

21. Bernard Williams, *Ethics and the Limits of Philosophy* (Cambridge: Harvard University Press, 1985), ch. 9.

22. See T. M. Scanlon, *What We Owe to Each Other* (Cambridge: Oxford University Press, 2000), 328–361; also see Scanlon's discussion of Williams' "all external reasons are false" argument in the Appendix.

Chapter 3

Values and Norms

In this chapter I explore critical questions of values and norms, since they underpin normative legal theories: What is the source of values? What shape should a theory of values have? Should there be one overarching value or a plurality of values? If a plurality of values may exist, without any overarching value or hierarchal ranking of values in a value theory, what should be made of incommensurable values? What defines the right and the good? What is the rational authority of norms?

While I consider some interpretations of religious commands, rules and laws in this study for their normative significance, I do so without delving into their ontological contexts. Likewise, in examining some metaphysical arguments on the nature of law, I do so not for their ontological significance, but with respect to their normative characteristics. More specifically, religious approaches often stipulate starting points that require an initial leap of faith and are thereby unsatisfying as neutral rational vantage points for exploring questions of morality and the normative character of law. Similarly, metaphysical approaches start with top-down theoretical assumptions, that hinder an analysis and study of the question of law. Consequently, I exclude ontological considerations of religious and metaphysical approaches to the question of law.

To clarify, I do not intend to shrug off the often robust debate about the relationships between law and religion. Certainly, many nations throughout history have attempted to ground law on religion or the divine. Since modern times, however, I believe that the world can no longer be viewed as an integrated, meaningful whole under a comprehensive religious or metaphysical worldview. Consequently, law can no longer be legitimized by apparent religious or metaphysical foundations. This position can be seen as well, for example, in how Jürgen Habermas develops his critical theory of communication-oriented reason and discourse theory of law. That is, although coming from a platonic tradition, Habermas explicitly accommodates the modern consensus that law must be legitimized independently of a religious or metaphysical worldview.[1]

SOURCE OF VALUE

Aristotle views contemplative activity as the source of value. In the *Nicomachean Ethics*, he observes that a hierarchical array of three types of life seem to define happiness: (1) the life of enjoyment; (2) the political life; and (3) the life of contemplation. The highest is contemplation, which consists of understanding and leads to Aristotle's definition of true happiness as an activity of the soul that follows a rational principle in accordance with excellence.[2] Consequently, Aristotle's argument that contemplation is the final good is grounded on the claim that only contemplation can serve as a source of value.

Kant reverses Aristotle's argument regarding contemplation as the final good and source of value—that is, the final purpose for human beings must be also regarded as the final purpose of the world. Since whatever is chosen with a good will is good, Kant argues that we can construct the ideal of a totality of all good things. That is, Kant does not agree with Aristotle's putting unconditional value on contemplation since, on metaphysical grounds, Kant articulates the only value as what human beings give to their own lives; Q.E.D. individuals must be the source of value.[3]

Again, in contrast to Plato and Aristotle, in the *Critique of Practical Reason*, Kant claims that good is a rational concept. For Kant, this means that if the ends are to be good, they must be determined by reason, not merely by inclination or pleasantness.[4] To be determined good in the judgment of every reasonable man, the reasons for calling a thing good must be universal. Again, for Kant, specifically the rational nature of human beings confers value on the objects of its choices and is itself the source of all value.

VALUE MONISM

In value theory, instrumental values are excluded, since it is evident that instrumental values clearly number more than one. Value theory, however, does address the central question of whether there is more than one fundamental intrinsic value. Value monists say no.

In his metaphysical theory of multiple forms, Plato may be seen as a value pluralist, but also as a value monist when he maintains that all foundational forms are sustained by the form of the Good.[5] Some also view Aristotle as a value monist in respect to his theory of eudaimonia (which differs from

Plato's account) and his teleological orientation to human well-being—a life worth living as the proper goal of human beings.[6] Kant may be understood as a value monist as well, insofar as he embraces one overarching principle, arising from practical reason, and to which all other principles are derived. While Kant does not deny happiness, in the Groundwork, Kant's moral theory is grounded on duty, whereby the rightness or wrongness of actions depends not on their consequences, but rather, on whether they fulfill moral obligations as formulated in his Categorical Imperative.

Classic utilitarianism, as espoused by Jeremy Bentham, Henry Sidgwick, and James Mills, presents a teleological or consequentialist moral approach as well, since classic utilitarianism propounds that the moral worth of an action is judged solely by its utility in providing happiness or pleasure to human beings. Thus, Bentham links happiness and utility in a formula of "the greatest happiness of the greatest number."[7] Further, classic utilitarianism theorizes the maximizing of pleasure as a sensation, pleasures which may persist comprise quantitative utiles, useful entities, and hence, are scientifically measurable. Thus, in placing one value above all others, classic utilitarianism may thus be seen as being value monist.

VALUE PLURALISM AND INCOMMENSURABILITY

By value pluralism, I specify here moral pluralism rather than political pluralism. As indicated above, value pluralism questions whether values (such as freedom, happiness, and welfare) are plural or monist, while engaging in discussions concerning the shape of morality, as, for example, probing how many values can or should be included in a moral theory.

Not surprisingly, the debate between pluralists and monists often focuses on the complexity of moral choice and whether values can be better explained by monists or by pluralists. Notably, since morality is often viewed as action-guiding, pluralists must navigate the additional tensions between explaining how comparisons among values are made and/or defending widely dispersed value incommensurability.

In a thin theory of the good, the idea of plural values—where there may be several values that are equally fundamental and correct and yet in conflict with one another—is one of the goods underlying the deontological approach of the theory of law presented here.[8] That is, value pluralism enters this theory of law through the reference to the external world in the first principle (one should obey those laws of legal-rational political authority that are not otherwise violative of societal norms and customs), and which provides moral resources and normative guidance for decision-making, making provision for persons holding different values. While I embrace plural values as one of the tenets underlying this theory of law, my approach cannot be said to represent a strong value pluralist account and certainly not one afflicted by the problem of incommensurability.

That is, while value monists believe that all goods are somehow commensurable, what proves controversial in the argument of value pluralists is that they believe that some values may conflict and in fact be incommensurable. For instance, the moral life of a nun is incompatible with that of being a mother, but there is no rational measure for determining which is preferable. Having said that, not all value pluralists are committed to the view that all ways of life are good, and some would allow for hierarchal value rankings.[9]

With respect to the problem of conflicting moral values, for example, Brian Barry suggests that fundamental values may be compared, even when they are incommensurable. His view is that deliberative argument can provide reasons for choices among qualitatively different claims, even when no common measure of value is available.[10] Another method of dealing with the problem of incommensurability is simply to accept that there may be situations in which a reasoned choice among plural values cannot be made. Bernard Williams, for instance, believes that occasionally there are genuinely irresolvable conflicts among values and to expect a rational resolution in such situations is wrong-thinking. Williams does, however, suggest that there are methods of comparison, even when a common scale is not shared (e.g., ethical or aesthetic considerations against economic ones), but he does not go further to suggest how such weighting may occur.[11]

For a strong value pluralist, however, the problem of incommensurability is especially keen, as may be exemplified by a brief look into the work of Joseph Raz, particularly with regard to his central notions of personal autonomy and social forms.[12] Raz situates his theory of value pluralism in a liberal perfectionist regime, one in which the good trumps the right.[13] Oddly for a perfectionist concerned with goods, however, Raz's approach poses no theory of values, nor does he make an ontological inquiry into the existence of values, let alone determine their hierarchy.

On first blush, Raz appears to make a functional argument for the overriding principle of personal autonomy in modern life, based on fast-moving technology and the free movement of labor. Given this impression, the question surfaces as to whether Raz views autonomy as an intrinsic good or not.[14] The problem emerges more clearly when examining Raz's notion of social forms—the particular social practices and institutions in a given society—and whether they create value. In his 1994 essay collection, *Ethics and the Public Domain*,[15] Raz deals with some of these issues in the first set of essays, emphasizing the importance to the individual's well-being of belonging to a cultural group and of the good life configured as an active rather than a passive life. Moreover, in his 2003 essay, "The Practice of Value,"

Raz further argues for the social dependence of values, but without relativism.[16] Caught in a conundrum, Raz's strong value pluralism precludes him from deploying his concept of autonomy (as well as the various social goods that constitute his perfectionist regime) for purposes of ranking or lexical priorities when making moral decisions.[17]

Raz's solution to the problem of incommensurability therefore balances upon the claim that when there are no further reasons for favoring X over Y, it can be rational (in a weak sense) to choose X over Y. This may be a plausible approach when faced with a non-moral choice, as exemplified by Raz's own example of choosing between a banana and a pear. In the context of making moral choices, however, the proposal does not suffice. For Raz, when reasons have run their course, individuals should take the object of desire as the preferred choice, opting for a mere appeal to basic preferences; in choosing without reasons, the slide into subjectivity vitiates any credible decision-making process.

THE RIGHT AND THE GOOD

Joseph Raz joins John Stuart Mill in the debate of the right and the good, by making the argument for the good over the right. By contrast, Immanuel Kant and John Rawls profess the view of the priority of the right over the good.

Mill approaches the political debate of the good over the right with a vision of the good life defined as that which allows an individual freedom from governmental interference, subject to the constraints of what he developed as his harm principle, which provides that "the sole end for which mankind are warranted, individually or collectively, in interfering with the liberty of action of any of their number, is self-protection."[18]

Theoretically, his "one simple principle," the harm principle, operates in two steps: (1) the inquiry is made as to whether liberty is restricted, and if so, (2) a calculus of harms is developed. Standing alone, the principle's restrictions on liberty do resemble the kind of deontological rule proposed by Aristotle rather than forming part of a utilitarian happiness calculus. They also seem very much like a statement proposing liberty as an intrinsic good, reminiscent of Plato, rather than a simpler instrumental justification. If this is the case, again, the problem indeed emerges of whether this principle may subsist in a value monist view of utilitarianism.[19] Much criticized, Mill's harm principle can in these ways be faulted for indeterminacy.

Although Mill intends the harm principle not to be morally dependent (and in this sense, anti-perfectionist), many judgments concerning harm depend on a rich, context-dependent concept of the good. That is, what constitutes harm is seen as socially contingent and not, importantly, as a morally neutral idea, making the harm principle much more complex than it at first appears. Here, John Gray correctly observes that "determining when restraint of liberty is justified turns out to be an intractably difficult business, since it hinges on assessments of the relative severity of harms that, in their dependency on disputed conceptions of the good life, are inherently controversial."[20]

In contrast to Mill, Raz argues that government may engage in coercive action to protect a vision of the good life and the underlying personal autonomy of individuals, thereby making values the ultimate determining factor in his vision of liberalism as he creates a liberal perfectionist regime in which the good trumps the right.

For Raz, then, the development of a liberal perfectionist state committed to protecting and promoting personal autonomy proceeds from the value of individual well-being. An individual's well-being, moreover, depends on success in the pursuit of valuable goals, and such valuable goals in turn are largely determined by the social conventions of an individual's community. Fundamentally, he argues that the social conventions characterizing modern liberal states reflect the pervasiveness of autonomy.

The critical question, consequently, is to what extent liberal societies should promote autonomy as a way of life. If autonomy is as pervasive a fact of life of modern liberal societies as Raz asserts, then a case may be made for its further promotion. On the other hand, if autonomy has a more limited role, then perhaps a less interventionist state may be appropriate. In either event, in Raz's view, there is no sacrosanct "self-regarding" sphere that political authority need protect; indeed, success in making goals based in social conventions requires the effective exercise of autonomy, using coercion where government deems necessary. In fact, Raz believes that strict adherence to state neutrality would "undermine the chances of survival of many cherished aspects of our culture."[21]

By contrast, in the *Groundwork*, Kant presents a classic deontological moral theory, one in which the right takes priority over the good, and whereby the rightness or wrongness of actions depends not on their consequences, but rather, on whether they fulfill moral obligations. To determine what these moral duties are, Kant formulated the Categorical Imperative, one version of which is found in the Formula of Universal Law, that articulates a version of the Supreme Principle of Morality, referred to earlier: "Act only on that maxim through which you can at the same time will that it should become a universal law."[22]

His duty-for-duty's sake ethical theory has met many challenges, in addition to utilitarian accounts. For instance, one approach criticizes Kant's theory since it has individuals adjudicate out of duty a priori, thus denying the importance of individual experience when working out what is right and thereby relying perhaps too heavily on certain socially accepted norms, which may not necessarily represent a majority of individuals. In addition, a question of motivation remains in his account. Realizing that something is irrational, that is, does not always motivate individuals to do the right thing. If it did, of course, we would have less need for law and legal systems.

Further, due to its universal nature, the application of the Categorical Imperative cannot easily provide assistance in choosing between conflicting duties nor in addressing the practical difficulty of formulating maxims, especially with respect to social interactions. For instance, an individual may adopt a maxim that can indeed be universalized in favor of pacifism and consequently act accordingly. However, if others do not adopt the same maxim, then Kantian pacifists could be challenged by non-Kantians, or even Kantians, who do not adopt pacifist maxims.

Aligned with Kant in arguing for the right over the good, Rawls makes vigorous attempts to present a neutral liberal account in his *A Theory of Justice*. Yet, questions remain as to whether he successfully re-affirms the priority of right over the good. Although Rawls asserts that his theory of justice as fairness is deontological in approach, the outcome-orientation of Rawls' second principle of justice, the difference principle, moves his theory outside a comfortably deontological framework. Also, while reason plays a critical role in justice as fairness, Rawls' four other concepts of the good require judgments or publicly accessible and reasoned decisions that are not likely to be in accord in a pluralistic society.[23] Further, the various permissible comprehensive conceptions of the good embedded in his account is especially problematic in a deontological approach.

Rawls further fails to establish the priority of the right over the good, even when he takes the discussion into the political realm. More specifically, Rawls must foray into the political realm since his last four concepts of the good require publicly reasoned discussion, as introduced in his notion of the "congruence of the right and the good." Here, he argues that right and goodness are congruent, since doing what is right contributes to each person's good. This argument, however, seems to diminish the privileging of the right over the good. Ultimately, he strains and confuses the concept of the priority of the right over the good when moving from a moral view to a political one and in doing so, conflates the political into the moral. That is, the individual as moral agent tends to disappear from his account.

I do not share Rawls' views on the congruence of the good and the right. Rather, in adopting a right-over-good approach, I understand attendant theoretical problems that emerge from such an approach. Fundamentally, the communitarian challenge to a liberal neutral view must be viewed as relevant, since communitarianism holds that a society may not exist in a vacuum and must, as well as should, be framed by a larger vision of the good.[24]

NORMS

A social norm may be seen to result from a conditional preference for conforming to a relevant behavioral rule. Such preferences are conditional on two different kinds of beliefs: empirical and normative expectations. As previously discussed, the rational authority of moral norms often proves difficult to pinpoint.[25] One approach, inspired by Aristotle, centers on practical reflection, based in the question of what it means to act well.[26] Another strategy to address this problem has been to maximize rationality in various ways (e.g., decision theory).[27] Yet another approach has been to look to values and theories of values as an important focus for practical reflection.[28]

In the question of law, the issue of norms goes to the political foundation of law. That is, norms are critical in determining whether and under what circumstances an individual should obey the law. Obviously, then, norms, including a plurality of values, need to be taken into account, whether foregrounding reason, values, or actions.

NOTES

1. In theories of law, legitimation or justification often addresses the question of what makes a law valid. Habermas claims that "[in] the legal mode of validity of the facticity of the *enforcement* of law is intertwined with the legitimacy of a *genesis* of law claims to be rational because it guarantees liberty" (emphasis original). Jürgen Habermas, trans. W. Rehg, *Between Facts and Norms* (Cambridge: Polity Press, 1996), 28.

2. Aristotle, *Nichomachean Ethics of* Aristotle, trans. D. Ross, rev. Lesley Brown (Oxford: Oxford University Press, 2009), I: 5 and 7.

3. See Christine Korsgaard, "Aristotle and Kant on the Source of Value," *Ethics* 96;3 (1986): 486–505, particularly 502–505.

4. Immanuel Kant, *Critique of Pure Reason*, trans. and eds. Paul Guyer and Allen Wood (Cambridge: Cambridge University Press, 1997), 62–64.

5. Plato, *The Republic*, trans. Desmond Lee (London: Penguin Books, 2003), VI: 508e–509b.

6. There is a tautology here, however, in Aristotle's relation of a life worth living to his concept of character, comprising learned dispositions and virtues. That is, we know the right thing to do because that is what a person of good character would do. But how does one know whether a person has good moral character because of what one does?

7. *A Comment on the Commentaries and A Fragment of Government*, eds. J. H. Burns and H.L.A. Hart, in *The Collected Works of Jeremy Bentham* (London: University of London Press, 1977), 393.

8. The four concepts that I refer to as comprising the thin theory of the good underlying this theory of law include: (1) rationality, (2) autonomous moral agency, (3) equal concern and respect for others, and (4) plurality of values.

9. See John Gray, *Two Faces of Liberalism* (Cambridge: Polity Press, 2000), 92.

10. See Brian Barry, *Political Argument* (Berkeley: University of California Press, 1990), 3–8.

11. See Bernard Williams, *Ethics and the Limits of Philosophy* (Cambridge: Harvard University Press, 1985), 17.

12. See Joseph Raz, *The Morality of Freedom* (Oxford: Oxford University Press, 1986), ch. 14.

13. Ibid., 133: "Moral pluralism asserts the existence of a multitude of incompatible but morally valuable forms of life. It is coupled with an advocacy of autonomy. It naturally combines with the view that individuals should develop freely to find for themselves the form of the good which they wish to pursue in their life. . . . But there is nothing here which speaks for neutrality. For it is the goal of all political action to enable individuals to pursue valid conceptions of the good and to discourage evil or empty ones."

14. Is autonomy a supervening value or a component of other values? Further, for Raz, is autonomy an intrinsic good and/or instrumental in determining good choices? See John Gray, *Mill on Liberty* (Oxford: Routledge, 1996), 96–104.

15. Joseph Raz, *Ethics in the Public Domain* (Oxford: Clarendon Press, 1994).

16. Joseph Raz, "The Practice of Value," in ed. Grethe B. Peterson, *Tanner Lectures on Human Value* (Salt Lake City: University of Utah Press, 2003), vol 11: 113–150.

17. See Gray 2000: 96–99, regarding the conflict between the central role of personal autonomy in Raz's theory and value pluralism.

18. John Stuart Mill, "On Liberty," ed. John Gray, in *John Stuart Mill on Liberty and Other Essays* (Oxford: Oxford University Press, 1998), 14.

19. As Gray notes (2000: xix): "the principal paradox of Millian utilitarian liberalism is that the Principle of Liberty actually disqualifies utility-promotion as a reason for restraint of liberty, unless such restraint also prevents harm to others."

20. Gray 1996: 140; Gray's emphasis.

21. Raz 1986: 162.

22. Ibid., 88.

23. In his essay revisiting the question of liberal neutrality of justice as fairness, Rawls continues to assert the priority of right in his theory of justice, but understands that five ideas of good are embedded in his account: "(1) the idea of goodness as rationality, (2) the idea of primary goods, (3) the idea of permissible comprehensive conceptions of the good, (4) the idea of the political virtues, and (5) the idea of the good of a well-ordered (political) society." John Rawls, "The Priority of the Right and Ideas of the Good," *Philosophy and Public Affairs* 17;4 (1988): 251–276; also see chapter 14 *infra* regarding Rawls' theory of justice as fairness.

24. Michael Sandel believes that one version of the liberal-communitarian debate remains interesting, namely, the debate taken up as the right vs. the good. See Michael Sandel, *Liberalism and the Limits of Justice* (Cambridge: Cambridge University Press, 1998).

25. See Christine Korsgaard, *The Sources of Normativity*, ed. Onora O'Neill (Cambridge: Cambridge University Press, 1996), for a strong Kantian approach to the question of norms, their source and authority.

26. See Aristotle 2009; also see Philippa Foot, *Natural Goodness* (Oxford: Oxford University Press, 2001).

27. See Philip Pettit, "The Contribution of Analytical Philosophy," in eds. Robert Goodin and Philip Pettit, *A Companion to Contemporary Political Philosophy* (Malden: Blackwell Publishing, 1993), ch. 5.

28. E.g., Raz 1986.

PART II

Early Theories of Law

Chapter 4

Classical Views

In the classical accounts of Plato and Aristotle, concepts of law are subsumed under their views of justice, positioning law in service of justice. While both Plato and Aristotle believed in a moral universe, Plato constructed a metaphysical framework with his theory of forms, while Aristotle focused on character development as leading to the good life.

PLATO

Under Plato's metaphysical theory of forms, his concept of justice includes both individual and social morality. Politically, Plato considers laws in the context of the constitution of the city-state, which constitution may be seen as lawful or unlawful, and with laws that may be just or unjust.

While Plato places laws in the service of justice, his theory of forms characterizes forms as unchanging in an intelligible realm—whether mortals in their corporeal existence ever apprehend them or not—and that these forms represent what is ultimately real.[1] Humans, who are born into, live, and die in the sensible world, nonetheless have immortal souls and by means of reason may come to recognize, contemplate, and remember forms from prior times when earlier their incorporeal souls came into contact with the eternal forms. In other words, by exercising their rational faculties, humans may intellectually apprehend forms, see the eternal and hence true reality, and thereby come to understand how to live a good life. This metaphysically driven epistemology proves critical here, because Plato's account of justice, of *dikaiosune*—of individual and social morality—is defined by his theory of forms.[2]

Law

Plato's theory of law is intertwined with his concept of justice, which he views as the most important and essential virtue.[3] As an extreme rationalist,

Plato extends his emphasis on reason into his definition of law as reasoned thought (*logimos*) embodied in the decrees of state.[4] Indeed, his metaphysical approach rejects the view that the authority of the law rests on the mere will of the governing power, as argued, for example, in the last dialogue of *The Laws*.[5]

In the same section, Plato further attempts to formulate a systematic code to govern the whole of social life, as he undertakes to create a good city and provide a detailed description of many branches of law. In contrast with the ideal *polis* in *The Republic* with a true constitution under the rule of a philosopher-king, in *The Laws*, Plato appears to concede that law and order under an imitative constitution are necessary for Magnesia, a new Cretan colony.[6]

Here, a brief overview of *The Laws* may prove useful. While Books 1 and 2 explore the purpose of government and provide a preliminary account of education and virtue, Book 3 examines the origins of government and the merit of different constitutions and refers to the development of a legal code for Magnesia.[7] Moving then a somewhat pragmatic vein, Book 4 analyzes the correct method of legislation, and Book 5 contains moral lessons before outlining the proper distribution of land. Continuing to explore societal institutions, Book 6 details various political and legal offices, and then examines the institution of marriage, while Books 7 and 8 discuss musical and physical education, sexuality, and economics. After thus examining governance per se and considering a society's constituent elements, Plato articulates necessary safeguards. Thus, Book 9 deals with criminal laws and punishment; Book 10 presents theological matters, in a somewhat surprising accommodation to his own metaphysical theory of forms, as well as laws against impiety; and finally, Books 11 and 12 continue the development of a legal code, ending with an account of the Nocturnal Council, the "anchor of the city."

The good city created in *The Laws* elicits comparison with the ideal city created by Plato in his earlier treatise, *The Republic*.[8] For instance, in contrast to the ideal polis in *The Republic*, where there would be little need for legislation, in *The Laws* Plato appears to accept "law and order, which are second best."[9] In perhaps the most famous passage of this dialogue, Plato has the Athenian announce that citizens are to engage in the construction of a "second-best city":

> Anyone who uses reason and experience will recognize that a second-best city [*deuterôs . . . pros to beltiston*] is to be constructed. . . . That city and that constitution are first, and the laws are best, where the old proverb holds as much as possible throughout the whole city: it is said that the things of friends really are in common.[10]

Some have interpreted this passage to signify that Plato endorsed the city outlined in *The Republic* as the best possible city, with its high political and ethical demands of its inhabitants and that the city described in *The Laws* is second-best, since it more likely accords with his views of human nature and its defects. Others, though, have argued that *The Laws* also presents an ideal city-state, one in which all citizens are subject to the same high ethical demands. This latter argument is based on Plato's concept of rational eudaimonism; that is, Plato believes that each individual's goals, insofar as the individual is rational, is one's own happiness or well-being (*eudaimonia*).[11]

Another important contrast emerges when Plato specifies in *The Statesman* that the ideal city in *The Republic* is to be ruled by a philosopher-king, chosen from the class of guardians.[12] In *The Laws*, however, ruling officially belongs to a Nocturnal Council consisting of the ten eldest guardians, the supervisor of education (and predecessors), examiners, citizens who have won awards of honor, and certain citizens who have traveled abroad. This Nocturnal Council seems to have great political power and authority: "If this divine council should come into being for us, dear friends, the city ought to be handed over to it [*paradoteon toutôi tên poulin*]."[13]

Justice

In *The Republic*, Plato transforms the apparently simple question, "What is justice?" by means of the Greek term *dikaiosune*—a term for "justice" that captures both individual justice and the justice that informs societies, by mirroring the individual in the cosmic universe. His use of *dikaiosune* thus allows Plato to wed ethics to politics and therewith moor the central question epistemologically, in order to inquire, "What is the basis of moral and social obligation?"[14] Plato's well-known answer rests upon the fundamental responsibility to seek wisdom, wisdom which leads to an understanding of the Good. Importantly here, good politics and justice depend on the knowledge of such eternal forms.

Based in this wisdom, Plato argues that a just society is one that is well-ordered, with laws subordinate to the demands of justice. He postulates three classes in society (philosophers, auxiliaries, and producers), with each providing a necessary function to society as a whole, and which mirror an individual's tripartite soul (reason, spirit, and appetite). In order for a society to be stable, and thereby provide one of the conditions still considered necessary for a just society, the society should not only be stratified, it should also be hierarchical. In this same treatise, Plato presents Thrasymachus as articulating a dangerous position insofar as he refuses to recognize that laws apply to him, thereby posing a threat to the political stability of a well-ordered society.[15]

Thrasymachus does not present an amoral position such as that articulated in the seventeenth century by Thomas Hobbes' in the *Leviathan*; rather, he proves to be an immoralist, believing not only in self-interest, but also in the dictum that might makes right. On the individual level, Thrasymachus appears to be a hot-headed individual, an unnatural man, whose tripartite soul is out of balance.[16] It is for these reasons that Plato presents Socrates as obliged to launch an attack on Thrasymachus' arguments, and on the sophist's own terms, in order to affirm that, by nature, men are mutual benefactors, cooperators rather than natural perpetrators of harm, that, in other words, justice does pay and that the just individual is a happy individual.

Given Thrasymachus' position on justice, the obvious question that emerges is "why should a person be just?" Plato answers this individually-situated question: for one's psychological health and pleasure. In taking up Thrasymachus' conventional immoralist challenge to justice, whose purpose he asserts is to have the weak serve the interests of the strong, Plato argues that justice as a virtue allows the soul to perform its function well. That is, justice allows the tripartite soul to be balanced, so that a person who performs his function well is "blessed and happy." His metaphysically-lodged argument is at once both deontological as well as teleological in its claim that justice belongs "in the highest category, which anyone who is happy welcomes for its own sake and for the sake of its consequences."[17] Thus, Plato constructs an account of happiness insofar as he argues that a just person is always happier than an unjust person.[18]

Epistemologically, Plato tries to show that Thrasymachus' view of interest rests on ignorance, a lack of understanding of the form of the Good. From a secular point of view, that is, Plato appears to be arguing that virtue is its own reward, a stance that may obtain epistemologically and metaphysically, but one that falls short when measured in knowledge of the visible world and its worldly goods. Indeed, for centuries, it is along this moral-political continuum that tensions concerning justice have emerged, for justice per se mandates a view greater than the individual and the concrete with ideas nonetheless situated, as I argue, in societal norms.

Constitutions

Plato expresses what just relations between persons and classes are in the phrase: "doing one's own work and not meddling with what isn't one's own."[19] Complying with this vision, Plato delineates six imitative constitutions in *The Statesman*, which he arranges in a hierarchy proceeding from most to least tolerable forms of governance.[20] First, he notes the three most tolerable law-abiding societies: kingship, aristocracy, and democracy. If, in contrast, a society is not law-abiding, again proceeding from most to least tolerable, governance finds articulation in democracy, oligarchy, and tyranny.[21] The seventh constitution is the true constitution under the rule of the philosopher-king.

Critically, law-abiding constitutions are involved in the pursuit of knowledge whereby rulers are motivated to seek the common good. In contrast, constitutions which are not law-abiding are characterized by ignorant self-interest. In this framework, democracy has some limited purchase on the Good since it at least has the common good as its stated object. However, it remains categorized as not law-abiding, since, as Plato argues, democracy is an unstable form of rule dependent upon chance and must be held together with competent leadership.[22] In fact, Plato criticizes unchecked democracy because of its dominant features, freedom and equality.[23]

By contrast, in Plato's law-abiding *polis*, rulers would be chosen from a military elite, the guardians, because they excel at shepherding and caring for the interests of the community. For his purposes, the middle class of auxiliaries may be seen as guardians in training. As Plato further explains in *The Statesman,* there is an art or technique (*techne*) of ruling and its best practice is engaged in by the statesman, the familiar philosopher-king with knowledge of forms as well as insights into the use of due measure—the unchanging standards of what is right—insights that he applies to particular circumstances.

The *techne* of the statesman, then, comprises political theorizing and furthers the skills of both thinking and ruling. The rational statesman has the collective well-being and common good of each citizen as his disinterested main interest—he is the released prisoner who returns to the Cave in order to help his fellows.[24] The success of his project (and its proper object) is the harmonious fellowship of different individual types and *technai* in society; he artfully weaves the warp and weft, the courageous and the moderate types found in society, into a harmonious whole. Hierarchically, he also orchestrates the different *technai* of individuals, the functional specialists, to serve a balanced society.

The Noble Lie

In creating a harmonious whole, Plato would have rulers convince the people of the Noble Lie—that the categories of rulers, auxiliaries, and producers obtain not due to circumstances within the people's control, upbringing, or education, but rather, because of God's intervention. God, as the myth goes, had put certain metals in each person's blood and these metals determined their stations in life: rulers have gold, auxiliaries have silver, and producers have bronze. Most children of philosophers also have gold in their blood, but some may have silver or bronze and would be demoted to a lower class, whereas auxiliaries and producers born with gold in their blood may be promoted.[25]

Plato viewed the Noble Lie as necessary to keep a stable social structure; he claims that this fictional account, though false, if believed by the people would result in an orderly and harmonious society.[26] The so-called Noble Lie is "noble," then, by reason of its purpose of keeping the masses under control and happy with their lots in life. Of course, in developing the Noble Lie, Plato reveals his belief that most people either are not intellectually capable of looking after their own and society's best interests or, perhaps, in contrast to the true guardians, belong to Thrasymachus' camp and thus would be too unbalanced to apprehend the need for a stable social structure. Of course, another response to the Noble Lie's faith in the true guardians is represented in the retort made popular by Juvenal's cynical question regarding the deficient faithfulness of wives, "Who will guard the guardians?"[27]

The question of whether good and effective politicians can be completely truthful and still achieve the necessary ends of society has been raised by, among others, Leo Strauss, who asks his readers whether noble lies have a positive role in uniting and guiding the *polis.* That is, are myths needed to give people meaning and purpose and to ensure a stable society or can individuals relentlessly examine, in Friedrich Nietzsche's words, those "deadly truths" and still flourish freely? In effect, the question becomes one of whether there are limits to the political, and concomitantly, what can be known absolutely.

More specifically, in *The City and Man,* Strauss discusses the myths in *The Republic* that he believes are essential to all governments. These include the myth that the state's land belongs to it, even if it had been illegitimately acquired, and that citizenship is rooted in something more that accidents of birth. In this sense, Strauss himself may be seen as endorsing noble lies, suggesting that dissembling and deception comprise "the peculiar justice of the wise."[28] The difference in their approaches is found in their foundations. That is, Plato bases his belief in the Noble Lie on a moral good, while Strauss presents the superiority of ruling philosophers as intellectually, not morally, defined, thereby interpreting Plato in a rather cynical manner.

More typically, contemporary commentators have also rejected the Noble Lie, mainly as devious and fundamentally antidemocratic. Thus, Karl Popper accuses Plato of trying to establish religion on a noble lie as well. In *The Open Society and Its Enemies,* Popper writes, "It is hard to understand why those of Plato's commentators who praise him for fighting against subversive conventionalism of the sophists, and for establishing a spiritual naturalism ultimately based on religion, fail to censure him for making a convention, or rather an invention, the ultimate basis of religion."[29]

ARISTOTLE

Aristotle wrote the *Nicomachean Ethics* as a preliminary discussion to his *Politics,* and in both treatises, he examines virtue (*arête*) and human well-being (*eudaimonia*) as the foundation of the ethical and political questions raised in them.[30] Like Plato, Aristotle also views law as subsumed under his concept of justice, although he frees justice from the metaphysical constraints of Plato's utopian views. Instead, Aristotle locates the concept as a virtue in societally-situated individuals, said virtue including both intellectual virtues and moral virtues.[31] More specifically, he argues that virtues (*arête*) are learned dispositions of individuals that formulate a mean between extremes; courage, for example, is the mean positioned between cowardice and recklessness.

Law

Aristotle views the concept of law as deeply embedded in his political philosophy.[32] Nowhere, though, does he provide a formal definition. His main term for law is *nomos*, and he variously identifies it with order, with reason, and with agreement. Thus, he refers to law as "a sort of order, and good law is good order"; "reason unaffected by desire"; and "the mean."[33] For Aristotle, the purpose of law is, as it is for Plato, contextual and must be understood in relation to his concept of justice and the constitution of the city-state.[34]

Although he never presents a systematic theory of law, Aristotle does state that laws must uphold just principles, such that "true forms of government will of necessity have just laws and perverted forms of government will have unjust laws."[35] The primary source of law for Aristotle is embodied in a human legislator. He recognizes, however, that for a legal order to exist, citizens must be law-abiding, thus characterizing law as a kind of common agreement (*homologia*) and a sort of convention.[36] Furthermore, "[t]he law has no power to command obedience except that of habit."[37] Rejected are rival claims of the rule of law, as well as the rule of a supremely virtuous person, since absolute kingships are actually a limiting case of aristocracy.

In *Politics*, Aristotle further makes the case that laws should be changeable.[38] Nonetheless, since the law derives its force from citizens' habit of obedience, great care should be exercised in making any changes to it, and it may sometimes be better to leave defective laws in place rather than encouraging lawlessness by changing the law too frequently, an argument that is certainly contestable.

Universal Justice

In Book V of the *Nicomachean Ethics*, Aristotle presents justice as a moral virtue, and in so doing, he applies the doctrine of the mean to various aspects and types of justice. In the process, he abandons the simple location of virtue as between two extremes by asserting that justice is *a kind* of mean, in that "it relates to an intermediate amount, while injustice relates to the extremes," and that "injustice is both excess and deficiency."[39] This is not the only equivocation in his discussion of justice.[40]

Further, Aristotle claims that in its broad sense, or on the societal level, universal justice effects the characteristic of lawfulness, while on the individual or particular level, in the narrow sense, particular justice defines through the principle of equality.[41] In adumbrating universal justice, Aristotle expands the term "lawfulness" (*nomos*) to include not only the enactments of a lawgiver or legislature, but also the norms, customs, and traditions of a polity. In other words, the societal virtue of lawfulness is far greater than being law-abiding; it possesses every other ethical virtue. In the same vein, a just person who is just in the broad sense is more than a just individual in that the individual possesses every other ethical virtue as well.[42] This view appears to commit Aristotle to the proposition that whoever is just in the broad sense of lawfulness also possesses the virtue of justice in the narrow sense. That is, a just individual in the narrow sense is one who aligns with the virtue of equality, or of being fair. Put another way, justice in the universal sense of lawfulness is the whole of justice, while justice in the particular sense of equality is only one portion of the whole.[43]

As to the question of whether an individual may treat him- or herself unjustly, in Book VII of the *Nicomachean Ethics*, Aristotle investigates the matter of *akrasia* (incontinence).[44] In doing so, he adopts Plato's tripartite model of the soul to develop the idea that an *akratic* person goes against reason as a result of some *pathos* (emotion, feeling), a *pathos* for either pleasure or anger and which can lead to two possible types of *akrasia:* impetuosity and weakness. Consequently, there are four forms of *akrasia*: (1) impetuosity caused by pleasure, (2) impetuosity caused by anger, (3) weakness caused by pleasure, and (4) weakness caused by anger. Interestingly, his analysis of *akrasia* is rather more complicated than a conflict between reason and feeling.[45]

In order to make sense of the equation of Aristotle's various applications to universal justice as lawfulness, it may be best to view lawfulness as a goal, an aspiration, so that a just man is seen as a person who not only abides by the laws, but who also serves his community by means of its legal system and its established pattern of norms. This may be the more effective way to approach Aristotle's definition of justice in the broad sense of lawfulness since he does not, in fact, provide any criteria for how to act in particular cases. Indeed, none of his definitions of the virtues provides action-guiding principles. Rather, they are intended as prescriptive formulations for the kind of person an individual ought to become.

Political Justice

As a form of universal or broad justice, political justice is justice in a state under the rule of law and not under the rule of a tyrant.[46] A state ruled by law is one in which citizens "share the life with a view to self-sufficiency," are free and have equal shares, or have shares which are proportionate and fair, in "ruling and being ruled."[47] Political justice, in other words, governs the relationships among members of a political community. Deeply anti-platonic in this regard, Aristotle's conception of political justice rests upon the thesis that justice requires active participation in the political affairs of one's society, even if only limited opportunities for reform exist. Rather than idealistically remaining aloof to the mundane business of politics, Aristotle argues that, actually, the approximate forms of justice negotiated by hostile factions are important: one way to lead a worthwhile life is to promote some measure of legality and justice in defective regimes.[48]

Further, Aristotle bifurcates political justice into natural justice and legal or conventional justice. Natural justice "has the same force and does not depend on what is thought to be so or not so";[49] that is, natural justice seems to consist of the laws, norms, and rules that would ideally govern relationships in a political community. This allows Aristotle to appeal to the concept of natural laws as an authority and thereby to override the view that universal justice consists of lawfulness in the sense of merely abiding by society's laws and conventions, which could prove less than perfect. The second aspect of universal political justice—legal or conventional justice—comprises the principles or rules that fall short of an ideal community, rules that may accord with human nature and conditions of human happiness as expressed *in vivo,* in the mutable world.

Although the generality inherent to laws, particularly in Plato's analyses, evince analytical strength, their generality also harbors weaknesses insofar as laws are inevitably too general, and potentially too rigid, for all particular cases. Aristotle recognizes the difficulty and formulates equity (*epiekeia*) as a gap-filler to meld the spirit of the law and legislator. Thus, treating justice in a patently more pragmatic manner than Plato does, Aristotle formulates the concept of equity in the narrow arena of political justice as "a sort of justice and not a different state of character."[50] In a sense, equity thereby provides a pragmatic margin of error or escape valve conceived in order to support legal or conventional justice. The equitable is "what the legislator himself would have said had he been present and would have put into his law if he had known."[51]

In this regard, equity seems to safeguard the law from adhering too rigidly to its own rules and principles, especially when these rules and principles produce injustice. In other words, judges are allowed to depart from legal principles in order to promote justice. Problematically, this conclusion is somewhat inconsistent with some of Aristotle's other claims about justice, raising rival conceptions of what is just as well as creating ambiguity about who or what is just in a particular instance, let alone who determines "what the legislator himself would have said had he been present."

Particular Justice

In shifting focus from individual virtue to relations within a political community, Aristotle's primary concern with regard to what he terms particular justice, based on the underlying concept of equality, seems to be what some may term "social justice" nowadays.[52] In the particular or narrow sense, for example, injustice is motivated by greed, by an individual's particular desire to have more than his or her share.[53] Indeed, when addressing injustice in the narrow sense, Aristotle uses the term "greedy" (*pleoneketes*) to underpin his analysis of that which is "unequal."[54] Importantly, the greed that Aristotle refers to is not greed in an individual per se, but rather, a pernicious desire to have more at the expense of others, thereby looking at the ramifications an individual trait has on societal relationships.

Aristotle further distinguishes among various kinds of particular justice: (1) justice that "plays a rectifying part in transactions between man and man," also known as rectificatory or corrective justice;[55] (2) reciprocal justice; and (3) justice in the distribution of goods or distributive justice.

Thus, Aristotle's category of particular justice is grounded in equality, on the individual level or in the particular sense, and includes rectifying or correcting wrongs committed in either voluntary or involuntary transactions. More specifically, voluntary transactions include such matters as promises, sales, or loans, while involuntary transactions include such matters as theft, assault, and adultery. A second kind of individual justice in the particular sense of equality is reciprocal justice. In his treatment of this topic, Aristotle focuses on commercial activities such as buying, selling, lending, and the like. In doing so, not surprisingly, Aristotle's basic notion is that goods should be exchanged for goods on an equal basis. With regard to the third kind of particular or individual justice, distributive justice, Aristotle understands that different kinds of equality and inequality prove fundamental to his concept. Distributive justice may thus be seen as concerned with the ethical appropriateness of who receives benefits and burdens in society and to what extent they receive them.

Of course, the question of equality in the distribution of benefits and burdens in society has preoccupied contemporary political theorists, as seen in the work of John Rawls, Ronald Dworkin, and Charles Beitz, discussed later in this study. As to Aristotle, although he begins with the proposition that such benefits and burdens should be allocated equally among members in society, this initial paradigm undergoes a significant alteration based upon the merit of the recipients. If recipients are of equal merit, they should receive equal shares. If they are of unequal merit, they should receive unequal shares.

Yet, Aristotle does not articulate guiding principles for ethically just distributions such as may be required for contribution, need, desert, and such factors, the very defining of which would likely result in a high degree of rigidity. How should the distributive principle of merit be applied, for example, to a situation in which scarce food is to be shared? Should larger amounts be distributed to those who have greater need, that is, who are starving, or to those who carry out critical state functions? Aristotle remains silent on such scenarios.

Instead, the principal question Aristotle addresses in his discussion of distributive justice is political: who should have power in society? His answer is that those better qualified to hold office should have greater power. In positing this solution, Aristotle recognizes that criteria for determining who is better qualified—for determining merit—are contestable. Again, he makes no further attempt to resolve the issue in the *Nicomachean Ethics,* although he does take up the discussion in his *Politics.*[56] There, his conclusion seems to be that in choosing among various criteria for determining merit, consideration should focus on what it takes for citizens to live well. That is to say, the kind of merit to hold as a standard is that which best serves the common good of the whole community. This explanation, of course, appeals to Aristotle's belief in the ultimate goal of political society which, for him, is to create and to sustain those conditions under which the pursuit of the good life can best be achieved by all citizens.

Various contemporary distributive theories of justice (whether focused on the distribution of social goods, wealth, or natural resources) have their foundation in Aristotle's distributive account of particular justice based on merit. Notably, such distributive theories have formed the predominant contemporary approach to the question of justice and thereby respond to some of the complexities of today's societies. Although akin to Aristotle's approach, such theories largely fail to take into account the individual's moral responsibility to act,[57] which, Aristotle argues, is subordinate to the constitution of the city-state.[58] Accordingly, he recognizes that legal order may be achieved only if citizens are law-abiding.[59] Further, in his view of virtue ethics, law is seen as a necessary instrument for educating individuals to virtue.[60] Nonetheless, Aristotle rejects the rule of law, as well as the rule of a supremely virtuous person, as the optimal correct constitution, in favor of rule by the *aristoi*, the best persons.[61]

Constitutions

In *Politics*, Aristotle considers the ideal state, one in which the common good of all citizens is achieved, as well as the question of a constitution or the manner in which a city-state is organized.[62] He views the model political community as a city-state composed of citizens who have the right to participate in deliberative or judicial office, with a more direct involvement of citizens in governance than in the representative democracy model.[63] Still restricted from citizenship, however, are women, slaves, foreigners, those of the working class, and others.

In addition to more direct involvement in governance, Aristotle's model constitution provides a method to organize the offices of the city-state. Addressing the question of a sovereign office, he adapts six possible constitutional forms from Plato's *Statesman*. Thus, the three correct forms of constitution are kingship, aristocracy, and polity, while the three incorrect forms are tyranny, oligarchy, and democracy.[64] In distinguishing between correct and incorrect constitutions, Aristotle claims that "constitutions which aim at the common advantage are correct without qualification, whereas those which aim only at the advantage of rulers are deviant and unjust, because they involve despotic rule which is inappropriate for a community of free persons."[65]

Having accepted Plato's guide to types of constitutions, Aristotle further claims that oligarchs mistakenly think that those superior in wealth should have superior political rights, while democrats mistakenly believe that those who are equal in birth should have equal political rights. Both these perspectives of political justice are mistaken in his account, since they both assume a false conception of the ends of the city-state. That is, the city-state is neither a business association to maximize wealth (oligarchy), nor is it an agency to promote liberty and equality (democracy). Rather, Aristotle contends that "the good life is the end of the city-state."

For Aristotle, the correct conception of justice is aristocratic, assigning full political rights to those who make a full contribution to the political community, that is, to those with virtue as well as property and freedom. The rule of the *aristoi,* the best persons, then, fulfills the aristocratic, the ideal, constitution, one in which the citizens are fully virtuous.

NOTES

1. Plato uses the word *eidos*, or "idea," and *paradeigma*, or "standard" or "pattern," for what we have come to term *form*. For these translations, as well as for a translation of *The Republic*, generally, I rely on Desmond Lee's text (London: Penguin Books, 2003).

2. See Nicholas White, "Plato's Metaphysical Epistemology," in Richard Kraut, ed., *The Cambridge Companion to Plato* (Cambridge: Cambridge University Press, 1992), 277–310.

3. Plato 2003: 540e. See Part V *infra* regarding Plato's and some other theorists' various concepts of justice and of law.

4. Plato, *The Laws*, trans. Trevor Saunders (London: Penguin Books, 1970), 644d.

5. Ibid., 644d.

6. Ibid., 875d.

7. For Plato, the constitution of a city state supersedes and should inform the laws of the city state.

8. Compare Plato 1970 with Plato 2003.

9. Plato 1970: 875d.

10. Ibid., 793A3–740C3.

11. Ibid., 662C–E.

12. See Plato, *The Statesman*, trans. J. B. Skemp (London: Bristol Classical Press, 2002).

13. Plato 1970: 969B2–3; cf. 960B5–E11 and 961C3–6.

14. See Plato 2003; also see Young Kim, *Justice: Classical Foundations and Contemporary Debates* (Lanham: Lexington Books, 2018), ch. 2.

15. Thrasymachus is portrayed as an immoralist rather than as a Hobbesian amoralist. See Plato 2003.

16. See Richard Kraut, "The Defense of Justice in Plato's *Republic*," in Richard Kraut, ed., *The Cambridge Companion to Plato* (Cambridge: Cambridge University Press, 1992), 311–337; Julia Annas, *An Introduction to Plato's Republic* (Oxford: Oxford University Press, 1981), 153–169.

17. Plato 2003: 358a1–2.

18. See Terence Irwin, *Plato's Ethics* (Oxford: Oxford University Press, 1995), 244–261.

19. Plato 2003: 433a.

20. The two concepts of freedom and equality form the basis of modern political liberalism. See chapter 8 *infra*.

21. The following chart is derived from Plato, *The Statesman*, trans. J. B. Skemp (London: Bristol Classical Press, 2002), 291d–e and 301b–c:

Table 1

	Law Abiding	Not Law-Abiding
One Ruler	Kingship	Tyranny
Few Rulers	Aristocracy	Oligarchy
Many Rulers	Democracy	Democracy

22. Ibid., 501b.

23. Ibid., 557a–564a; the same two features, freedom or liberty and equality, constitute the basic elements of most definitions of political liberalism.

24. The generalized referencing of individuals in this discussion reflects the conventions of various authors. As to his views concerning women, interestingly, in Book V of *The Republic*, Plato states that the function of guardianship is to be performed by men and women alike (451c–457b); since the major distinctions between male and female guardians is that women give birth to children and are physically weaker than men, there is no justification for barring women from the guardian class. Further, for guardians, the private household along with the institution of marriage is to be abolished (457b–466d) since guardians do not own property, and the care of children is to be a communal responsibility. See discussion regarding guardians later in this chapter; also see Julia Annas, "Plato's 'Republic' and Feminism," *Philosophy* 51;197 (1976): 307–321; Gregory Vlastos, "Was Plato a Feminist?," in ed. Richard Kraut, *Plato's Republic* (Lanham: Rowman & Littlefield Publishers, Inc., 1997).

25. Plato 2003: 414–415.

26. Desmond Lee takes issue with the translation of "noble lie" (414b) and states that the proper translation should be "magnificent myth." This mistranslation, in his view, has led to the criticism that Plato countenances manipulation by propaganda. In Lee's more benign view, the magnificent myth is meant "to replace the national traditions which any community has, which are intended to express the kind of community it is, or wishes to be, its ideals, rather than to state matters of fact." Plato 2003: 112.

27. "Sed quis custodiet ipsos custodies." Juvenal, *Satire* 6, ed. Lindsay Watson and Patricia Watson (Cambridge: Cambridge University Press, 2014), II. 347–348.

28. Leo Strauss, *The City and Man* (Chicago: University of Chicago Press, 2002), 108.

29. Karl Popper, *The Open Society and Its Enemies* (Princeton: Princeton University Press, 1971), vol. 1: 142.

30. Aristotle, *The Nicomachean Ethics of Aristotle*, trans. D. Ross, rev. Lesley Brown (Oxford: Oxford University Press, 2009). Aristotle, *The Politics*, trans. Ernest Baker (Oxford: Oxford University Press, 2009).

31. Aristotle 2009, II V.

32. See Aristotle 1992.

33. Ibid., 1326a; 1287a; and 1287b.

34. Another approach to understanding Aristotle's approach to the nature of law and the reason for its binding force is articulated by von Leyden as: (1) its general nature, (2) its rationality, (3) its moral nature, and (4) its antiquity, habits of obedience. See W. von Leyden, "Aristotle and the Concept of Law," *The Journal of the Royal Institute of Philosophy* XLII;159 (1967): 1–19.

35. Aristotle 1992: IV, VII.

36. Ibid., I.6.1255a6; cf. III.9.1280b10–11.

37. Ibid., II.8.1269a20–21.

38. Ibid., II8.

39. Aristotle 2009: V.1133b–11234a and 1134a8–9.

40. See Kim 2018: ch. 3.

41. Aristotle 2009: 1130a, ff.
42. Ibid., 1129b25–1130a10.
43. Ibid., 1130b–14.
44. See *Aristotle's Nicomachean Ethics, Book VII,* ed. Carlo Natali (Oxford: Oxford University Press, 2009).
45. See Richard Kraut, "Aristotle on Becoming Good: Habituation, Reflection and Perception," in *The Oxford Handbook of Aristotle,* ed. Christopher Shields (Oxford: Oxford University Press, 2013), 529–557.
46. Aristotle 2009: 1134135–b1.
47. Ibid., 1134126–28, b15.
48. See Aristotle 1992: IV.
49. Aristotle 2003: 1134b19–20.
50. Ibid., 1138a2–3.
51. Ibid., 1137b22–24.
52. "Social justice" is a somewhat controversial term, variously defined in contemporary usage. In a narrow sense, it refers to the distribution of wealth, opportunities, and privileges within a society, thereby articulating an egalitarian distributive approach. In this sense, it has similarities to Aristotle's view that particular justice is based on the concept of equality. But see Friedrich August von Hayek's famous charge asserting confusion in category error when applying notions of justice (which refer to actions of individuals) to relative holdings of people across a free society. F. A. von Hayek, *Law, Legislation and Liberty* (Chicago: University of Chicago Press, 1978), vol. II, ch. 9.
53. Aristotle 2003: 1129a–b11.
54. Ibid., 1129a32033.
55. Ibid., 1130b30–1131a9.
56. See Aristotle 1992: IV.
57. E.g., see John Rawls, *A Theory of Justice* (Cambridge: Harvard University Press, 1971); and Ronald Dworkin, *Sovereign Virtue* (Cambridge: Harvard University Press, 2000).
58. Aristotle 2009: I.1289a13–20.
59. See ibid., IV.
60. Aristotle 2009: X10.
61. Aristotle 1992: III.
62. Ibid., VII and VIII.
63. Ibid., I.1252a1–7.
64. Ibid., VII.
65. Ibid., I.1279a17–21.

Chapter 5

Natural Law

In this chapter, I discuss the natural law theories of Thomas Aquinas, Thomas Hobbes, and John Locke. While the term natural law covers a broad range of views, for this discussion I start with the classic view of natural law: (1) natural law is given by God; (2) it is naturally knowable and authoritative over humans; and (3) it holds that the good is prior to the right, although this last proposition has raised controversy as applied to Hobbes' and Locke's theories.

THOMAS AQUINAS

In the discussion of early natural law theories, the moral theorizing of Thomas Aquinas often serves as a traditional starting point.[1] Aquinas defines law as "an ordinance of reason for the common good, made by him who has care of the community, and promulgated."[2] Thus, practical reason of the Aristotelian sort plays an important role in the promulgation of laws for Aquinas. Further, political rulers should aim these laws at the common good and make them public.

In *Summa Theologiae*, Aquinas describes four kinds of law in hierarchical order, as follows: (a) eternal law, (b) divine law, (c) natural law, and (d) human law. Eternal law is God's perfect plan, not fully knowable by humans, but determinative of how inanimate objects and animals behave and how humans should behave. Divine law is drawn primarily from the Bible and guides humans beyond the world to eternal happiness and St. Augustine's City of God. Regarding natural law, Aquinas states, "natural law is nothing else than the rational creature's participation of the eternal law." Further, the "light of reason is placed by nature (and thus God) in every man to guide him in his acts."[3] Consequently, humans should thus use reason to lead their lives. Finally, contrary to natural law, human law is a contingent matter which could vary with time, place, and circumstance, leading Aquinas to define human law as "an ordinance of reason for the common good," made and enforced by a ruler or government.[4]

For Aquinas, then, the master principle of natural law is that "good is to be done and pursued and evil avoided,"[5] and its two key features are: (1) God's role as the giver of natural law and (2) human beings as the recipients of natural law. As Aquinas argues, natural law consists of principles of practical rationality by which human action may be judged as reasonable or unreasonable. Consequently, the precepts of natural law are universally binding and universally knowable.

Traditionally, Aquinas' natural law theory is interpreted to position human nature itself as the basic moral criterion. Aquinas states that "every human law has so much of the nature of law as is derived from the law of nature. But if in any point it deflects from the law of nature, it is no longer a law but a perversion of law."[6] Actions are morally permissible, then, if they conform to the teleologies inscribed within human nature, morally wrong if they do not. Since the standard for what is morally right is what fulfills human nature, an individual must first determine by a theoretical procedure what end or ends genuinely fulfill human nature. In his account, the list of basic goods includes: (a) life, (b) procreation, (c) social life, (d) knowledge, and (e) rational conduct. That is, these goods provide reasons for action, which lead to a theoretical good over right approach to actions. However, as chapter 11 argues, Aquinas' natural law theory goes beyond traditional interpretations, insofar as the basic moral criterion of natural law demands that we choose in line with an openness to and respect for all basic human goods, both in ourselves and in others.

THOMAS HOBBES

Thomas Hobbes is viewed by some as a natural law theorist, and his moral and political philosophy is seen by some to fit within the tradition of Aristotelian-Thomistic natural law theory.[7] In the *Leviathan*, Hobbes states that laws of nature are divine law, that all humans are bound by them, and that it is obvious to know the basics of natural law.[8]

However, as some scholars point out, epistemologically, Hobbes observes that the Bible should be seen as a source of beliefs, not of knowledge. Further, civil science (including, for Hobbes, the consideration and promulgation of laws) is separate from theology, including "the nature and attributes of . . . the incomprehensible God."[9]

As to natural laws, Hobbes holds them as mere precepts of prudence rather than literal laws; that is, they "are but theorems . . . and therefore not properly laws." Thus, Hobbes redefines natural law:

> A Law of Nature is a precept or general rule, found out by reason, by which a man is forbidden to do that which is destructive of his life or which takes away the means of preserving the same. . . . For though they that speak of this subject used to confound jus and lex (right and law), yet they ought to be distinguished, because Right consists in liberty to do or forbear, whereas Law binds to one of them; so that law and right differ as much as obligation and liberty.[10]

While the natural law view of Aquinas posits that the natural end of human beings is the good life of virtue in a just community, Hobbes rejects such a teleological view of human nature. He states that the fundamental good is self-preservation and that the laws of nature are directed to this good; as such, his view is situated in the natural rights tradition.[11] Hobbes sees human beings as restlessly striving for power, and he insists that, contrary to natural law theory, there is no *summum bonum* or *finis ultimus* which Aristotelian reason dictates.[12] Rather than reason imposing a necessary end by itself, Hobbes' discussion of reason identifies it as "nothing but . . . a calculative faculty," that operates on definitions to "add and subtract names in our affirmations." That is, reason discovers the means to ends, as provided by passions.[13]

Hobbes' underlying view of the state of nature, then, is anarchic. There is no recognized authority to resolve disputes and enforce its decisions, and left to their own devices, individuals would be in a "state of war," a war of "all against all."[14] With this perspective, Hobbes may well be viewed as an opponent of both natural law and divine law, in that they do not undergird the political sovereign.

Despite his insistence on self-preservation as a fundamental good, subjects have a "right to refuse" a sovereign's commands that carry capital punishment rather than act dishonorably. In other words, the claim that goodness is self-preservation is challenged by Hobbes' own definition of good: "good and evil are names . . . of what is conformable or disagreeable to reason in the actions of common life." With this view, Hobbes may further be seen as a proponent of a natural rights theory as the concept of natural rights gained prominence through his writings, as well as through those of Hugo Grotius, and Samuel Pufendorf. Whereas natural law emphasizes duties, accounts of natural rights normally emphasize privileges or claims to which an individual was entitled.[15]

JOHN LOCKE

Well-known for his empirical theory of knowledge as well as for his liberal political theory, the bridge between these two sets of doctrines has been variously argued to reside in his views of natural law or in his views of individual rights and limited government.[16]

In the *Two Treatises of Government*,[17] Locke defended the claim that men are by nature free and equal against claims that God made all people naturally subject to a monarch. He argued that people have rights, such as the right to life, liberty, and property, rights that comprise a foundation independent of the laws of any particular society. Locke used the claim that men are naturally free and equal as part of the justification for positing legitimate political government as the result of a social contract by which people in the state of nature conditionally transfer some of their rights to the government in order to better ensure the stable, comfortable enjoyment of their lives, liberty, and property. Since governments exist by the consent of the people in order to protect the rights of the people and promote the public good, governments that fail to do so can be resisted and replaced with new governments.

Central to Locke's political philosophy is his theory of natural law and natural rights. For Locke, natural law allows that certain moral truths apply to all people, regardless of the particular place where they live or the agreements they make. As such, natural law is distinct from divine law in the Christian tradition, which refers to those laws that God had directly revealed through prophets and other inspired writers. In other words, natural law can be discovered by reason alone and applies to all people, while divine law can be discovered only through special revelation and applies only to those to whom it is revealed and to whom God designates.

Eliding natural and divine law, Locke bases his views of natural law on moral obligations, while he also affirms that there is a "rule of morals, or law of nature given to us," because God exists. More specifically, in Locke's *Essays on the Law of Nature*,[18] two predominant features of natural law are developed: rationalism and legalism. Here, reason serves as the primary avenue by which humans come to understand moral rules, and it is via reason we can draw two distinct but related conclusions regarding the grounds for our moral obligations: we can appreciate the divine, and thereby righteous, nature of morality, and we can perceive that morality is the expression of a law-making authority.

Rather than following Aquinas' approach to the role of reason ("Since reason is the universal rule and measure of action then becomes an obligation prescribed by reason"), Locke views law as the will of a superior, one who has the right to command.[19] For him, the proper function of law is to legislate,[20] and the legislator who decrees the law is rightly obeyed as a superior power.[21] Fundamental to interpreting his views on who possesses the right to legislate, Locke suggests that there are ways to determine the content of the law of nature: by sense experience, of limited relevance here, and by the light of nature.

The light of nature points to an exercise of reason and the intellectual faculties.[22] In a manner similar to Hobbes, Locke conceptualizes a state of nature, as characterized by individuals not having agreed to establish a common political authority, a state in which there is no government with real political power. In this respect, Locke defines political power as

> a right of making laws with penalties of death, and consequently all less penalties, for the regulating and preserving of property, and of employing the force of the community, in the execution of such laws, and in the defence of the common-wealth from foreign injury; and all this only for the public good.[23]

Unlike Hobbes, however, Locke does not view a state of nature as leading to a state of war; he prefers a view of the state of nature as pacific, rather than ceding to the absolute sovereignty of an arbitrary ruler as would Hobbes.

Some scholars have adopted the view that natural law, not natural rights, is primary. They hold that when Locke emphasized the right to life, liberty, and property, he was primarily making a point about the duties we have toward other people: duties not to kill, enslave, or steal. Most scholars also argue that Locke recognized a general duty to assist with the preservation of humankind, including a duty of charity to those who have no other way to procure their subsistence.[24] These scholars regard duties as primary in Locke because rights exist to ensure that we are able to fulfill our duties.

I agree with another group of theorists, however, who take rights to be paramount for Locke, some going so far as to portray Locke's position as essentially similar to that of Hobbes. They point out that Locke defended a hedonist theory of human motivation and claim that he must agree with Hobbes about the essentially self-interested nature of human beings.[25] Locke, they claim, recognizes natural law obligations only in those situations where our own preservation is not in conflict, further emphasizing that our right to preserve ourselves trumps any duties we may have.

NOTES

1. See Thomas Aquinas, *Summa Theologica*, trans. Fathers of the English Dominican Province, ed. Paul A. Boer Sr. (New York: Benziger Brothers, 1920), I–II, QQ. 90–108.
2. Ibid., I–II, Q. 90.a.4.
3. Ibid., I–II, Q. 91, a.2.
4. Ibid., I–II, Q. 90, a.4.
5. Ibid., I–II, Q. 94.
6. Ibid., I–II, Q.95, a.2.

7. E.g., see Kody Cooper, *Thomas Hobbes and the Natural Law* (Notre Dame, IN: University of Notre Dame, 2018).

8. Thomas Hobbes, *Leviathan*, ed. J. C. A. Gaskin (Oxford: Oxford University Press, 1998), xv. 35, 36, 41.

9. Ibid., xiv.

10. Ibid., xiv.3.

11. Ibid., xiii. 14; xiv. 3. See chapter 7 *infra* regarding a more complex view of Hobbes, natural law, and natural rights.

12. Hobbes 1998: xi. 1–2.

13. Ibid., v. 1–2. This view is reminiscent of Hume's "Reason is, and ought only to be the slave of the passions." David Hume, *A Treatise of Human Nature*, T II.3.3 415.

14. See Hobbes 1998: xiii.

15. See chapter 7 *infra* regarding the tension between concepts of natural law and natural rights.

16. Editions used: John Locke, *Essays on the Law of Nature*, ed. W. von Leyden (Oxford: Oxford University Press, 2002); John Locke, *An Essay Concerning Human Understanding*, ed. Kenneth Winkler (Indianapolis: Hackett Publishing, 1996); John Locke, *Two Treatises, Two Treatises on Government*, ed. Peter Laslett (Cambridge: Cambridge University Press, 1988).

17. John Locke, T*wo Treatises on Government*. Ed. Peter Laslett (Cambridge: Cambridge University Press, 1998).

18. John Locke, *Essays on the Law of Nature*. Ed. W. von Leyden. Oxford: Oxford University Press, 2002).

19. Locke 2002: 111–113.

20. Ibid., 113.

21. Locke 1988: Treatise 2.

22. Locke 2002: II:123.

23. Locke 1988, Treatise 2, II, 1, 3.

24. Ibid., Treatise 2, 1.42.

25. Locke 1996, 2.20.

Chapter 6

Legal Positivism

While there are differences in their legal theories, both Jeremy Bentham and John Austin starkly distinguished positive law and natural law. That is, as 18th century advocates of legal positivism, Bentham and Austin marginalize natural law theory as comprising a series of propositions derived from nature that closely connects legal and moral normativity, based in the supposition that there is a moral determinant to legality. In both their views, however, legal positivism denies a necessary connection between law and morals. Moreover, they both posit that the validity of any law can be traced to an objectively verifiable source.

JEREMY BENTHAM

Perhaps best known for his moral theory of classic utilitarianism, Jeremy Bentham propounds that the moral worth of an action is judged solely by its utility in providing happiness or pleasure to human beings, thereby basing his ethical theory in a hedonistic account of motivation and value. That is, what ultimately motivates individuals is pleasure and pain.[1] Thus, in the beginning of his *Introduction to the Principles of Morals and Legislation*, Bentham states:

> Nature has placed mankind under the governance of two masters, pain and pleasure. It is for them alone to point out what we ought to do, as well as determine what we shall do. On the one hand the standard of right and wrong, on the other the chain of causes and effects, are fastened to their throne. They govern us in all we do, in all we say, in all we think: every effort we can make to throw off their subjection, will serve but to demonstrate and confirm it.[2]

In other words, Bentham's underlying account of human nature does not require social relationships. He remarks that "the community is a fictitious body," and that it merely represents "the sum of the interests of several members who compose it." Clearly, for Bentham there is no inconsistency between his moral greatest happiness principle and his view of psychological hedonism and egoism.

Accordingly, Bentham posits a "negative" view of law, somewhat similar to that of Thomas Hobbes in the sense that it is a sanction-oriented legal theory, but without Hobbes' concept of a single unified sovereign. While rejecting the Hobbesian idea of sovereignty based on simple command and obedience in which the sovereign is a single unified supreme power,[3] Bentham's underlying political views nonetheless center on a theory of sovereignty, making the case for limited government and a sanction-oriented legal theory. By "sovereignty" Bentham means the power to legislate (legal sovereignty) and the power of people to limit control of government officials (political or popular sovereignty). Consequently, he requires that power be located in the hands of the legislator, however constituted, and stipulates that all laws are imperative and depend for their enforcement on coercive sanctions.[4]

More specifically, Bentham holds that law is not rooted in natural law. Rather, he argues, rights are created by the law, and that law itself simply executes the will of the sovereign. That is, Bentham rejects the notion that there can be rights not based upon sovereign command and which pre-exist the establishment of government.

For Bentham, then, liberty is not a natural state of being existing prior to a social life; on the contrary, he holds that people have always lived in societies, and consequently, there can be no "state of nature" and no theoretical "social contract." Nonetheless, while law, by its very nature, involves a restriction of liberty, Bentham does recognize that law is necessary for social order, and that good laws are essential to good government. That is, the existence of law, and rights, requires government.

In denying that such matters as liberty or rights exist independently of government, Bentham may be seen as an early proponent of legal positivism, in that his concept of law is what humans posit that it is. As a political check on the legislator, for example, Bentham posits a "public opinion tribunal" that would scrutinize the actions of public officials and impose penalties, generally moral sanctions, when applicable. Critically, the dissemination of information and liberty of the press would be vital to the functioning of this public opinion tribunal.[5]

In detailing his view, Bentham's *A Fragment of Government* attacks the legal theory of William Blackstone and Blackstone's defense of tradition in law. In doing so, he also repudiates many of the concepts underlying the political philosophies of Thomas Hobbes and John Locke, including the concepts of natural rights, the state of nature, and the social contract.[6] Instead, Bentham advocates for the rational restructuring of legal systems, a restructuring of the process of determining guilt and of punishment, and a more extensive freedom of contract.

Moreover, Bentham's legal theory closely links civil law and penal law. He sees the primary purpose of civil law as economic and national security. Thus, the threat of punishment should provide protections afforded persons and their property. With regard to constitutional law, Bentham seems to argue that utilitarian principles should be adopted in representative democracies. Near the beginning of the Constitutional Code, he announces that,

> Of this constitution, the all-comprehensive object, or end in view, is, from first to last, the greatest happiness of the greatest number; namely, of individuals, of whom, the political community, or state, of which it is the constitution, is composed.[7]

JOHN AUSTIN

As with Jeremy Bentham, John Austin's concept of law articulates a system of coercive social rules. Austin's command theory thus holds that law consists of the commands of a sovereign backed by force. More specifically, he argues that the task of law is to promote an orderly society in which commands are issued by the state to regulate the conduct of its citizens, the violation of which would be subject to punishment. A law, then, is "a rule laid down for the guidance of an intelligent being by an intelligent being having power over him."[8]

Austin's command theory of law poses two central concepts: command and the sovereign. A command involves an expressed desire that something be done, combined with the willingness and ability to impose a sanction if that desire is not complied with. A sovereign is a person (or a determinate body of persons) who receives habitual obedience from citizens, but who does not habitually obey any other person or institution; all independent political societies, by their nature, have a sovereign. Legality in Austin's account is determined by the source of a norm (the sovereign), rather than the merits of its substance. A social rule is legally valid (a law) if and only if the rule is commanded by the sovereign and is backed up with the threat of a sanction.

Austin describes his work as offering a "science" of law and he attempts to approach the theory of law analytically, emphasizing the analysis of certain key concepts such as law, (legal) right, (legal) duty, and legal validity. In doing so, he rejects much of the reliance in English common law on custom, societal values, and morality. Rather, in his version of legal positivism, Austin asserts that it is both possible and valuable to have a morally descriptive theory of law.

Austin's view of positive law thus consists of commands of the sovereign and denies other law-givers, such as God's general commands and religious law and rules. He states his version of legal positivism (man-made law), as follows:

> The existence of law is one thing; its merit or demerit is another. Whether it be or be not is one enquiry; whether it be or not conformable to an assumed standard, is a different enquiry. A law, which actually exists, is a law, though we happen to dislike it, or though it vary from the text, by which we regulate our approbation and disapprobation.[9]

As various commentators have pointed out, Austin's work also concerns the role of coercion in the nature of law. Austin's command theory, then, is essentially about power. Some commentators also point out that, for Austin, law is best understood as a top-down institution, with norms imposed by government on its citizens, rather than a bottom-up institution, an approach taken, for instance, by classical commentators on English common law. Also implied in Austin's approach is the concept that every legal system has some entity whose power is effectively unconstrained.[10]

In identifying law with the commands of the sovereign, Austin develops a rather elaborate taxonomy of law and related phenomena. Laws are descriptive (laws of nature) or prescriptive (expressing the desire of one person that others behave in a certain way). Further, there are non-command prescriptive commands (requests) and positive law (law made by humans for humans). Positive law itself includes positive morality (rules of conventional morality, etiquette, international law) and positive law proper (a command by the sovereign to subjects whereby the sovereign is defined in terms of habits of obedience).

As did Bentham, Austin also criticizes Blackstone and his defense of natural law which views adequate moral content as a necessary condition of positive law,[11] including the notion of custom in law, along with theories based on common law reasoning. In contrast, Austin insists in the command theory of law that law supports legal positivism. He argues that a sovereign may issue commands which are morally acceptable or not. As cited above, "[t]he existence of law is one thing, its merit or demerit another."[12]

The command theory may serve absolute monarchies as well as criminal and tort law, where such laws regulate behavior by imposing duties. By contrast, a number of critics, including H.L.A. Hart, point out that other kinds of law (for instance, contract law, probate law and family law) actually confer legal powers. In his criticism of the command theory of law, Hart further makes a distinction between public and private power-conferring rules. Public power-conferring rules define official positions, responsibilities, and prerogatives. Private power-conferring rules, on the other hand, confer powers to private citizens, investing them with responsibilities and rights. While public power-conferring rules may sync with the command theory of law, private power-conferring rules do not.[13]

Hart raises other issues with Austin's command theory, which may be presented by questions and possible responses, as follows:

1. Is the sovereign above the law? Austin seems to argue that either the sovereign commands himself, which seems absurd, or that the sovereign is two people, the sovereign and a citizen. In the latter case, Hart argues that it seems to strain logic to claim that the sovereign-independent public power-conferring rules delimit the sovereign's powers.[14]
2. How are customary laws explained? Austin seems to aver that courts can be said to recognize custom as law insofar as judicial enactments are tacit or indirect commands of the sovereign.[15] Yet, as Hart posits, rather than equating custom with law, perhaps courts themselves recognize custom as law.
3. There is an authority problem: How is the orderly transition of sovereign power explained? Assuming an orderly transition, as Hart points out, a successor sovereign may not actually realize his first commands as law, since there is as yet a habit of obedience to the successor sovereign established.
4. How does a law persist after the sovereign who commanded the law is gone? To this question, Hart poses the question: are a predecessor sovereign's commands still law?[16]
5. Must sanctions be part of the concept of law? Here, other questions can challenge the underlying assumption. Thus, are there laws which do not include a sanction, or is there a legal system that does not regularly threaten and apply sanctions for noncompliance? What about private power-conferring rules? Further, regarding this last point, may the command theory of law properly fit under a superseding theory of justice?[17]

Hart used his criticisms of Austin's command theory of law to build a platform upon which to develop his own positivist theory of law, one which does not attempt to reduce all legal rules to one kind of rule, but rather one which emphasizes various types and functions of legal rules. His social facts legal theory thus attempts to be objective and neutral by means of a distinction between obligation and being obliged. Thus, some participants in a legal system may accept legal rules as reasons for actions without the threat or fear of sanctions. As such, Hart's hermeneutic approach takes a path sharply divergent from Austin's command theory of law.[18]

In the positive, normative theory of law developed in this study, I have also used the command theory of law as a platform, diverging, however, from the approach taken by H.L.A. Hart, Ronald Dworkin's responses to Hart's social facts legal theory, and various other contemporary positivist accounts, such as those of Hans Kelsen and Joseph Raz. Further, I have placed this study's theory of law under, and serving, a concept of justice.[19]

I emphasize here that the focus of the succeeding chapters in part III of this study is to examine the political foundations of law; and not to engage in a discussion of contemporary politics, partisanship, autocracy v. democracy, and the like, and the relationship of such topics to law (domestic and international). I do touch on some of these matters, especially in chapters 8, 9, and 10, but they are incidental to my comments on the political foundations of law.

NOTES

1. See Jeremy Bentham, *The Works of Jeremy Bentham* (Edinburgh: William Tait, 1843), vol. 1.

2. Jeremy Bentham, *An Introduction to the Principles of Morals and Legislation,* eds. J. H. Burns and H.L.A. Hart (London: The Athlone Pres, 1970), ch. 1.

3. See Bentham 1977.

4. See Jeremy Bentham, *Constitutional Code*, eds. F. Rosen and J. H. Burns (Oxford: Oxford University Press, 1983), vol. I.

5. Ibid., 399; Bentham 1983: 35–39. Also see Jeremy Bentham, *Securities Against Misrule and Other Constitutional Writings for Tripoli and Greece*, eds. P. Schofield and F. Rosen (Oxford: Clarendon Press, 1990), 23–73.

6. See chapter 5 *infra* for further discussion of Hobbes' and Locke's legal accounts and Bentham's views in opposition to them.

7. Bentham 1983: 1983b: 18.

8. John Austin, *The Province of Jurisprudence Determined,* ed. Wilfred Rumble (Cambridge: Cambridge University Press, 1995), 18–20.

9. Ibid., Lecture V: 157.

10. See John Austin, Lectures on Jurisprudence, or The Philosophy of Positive Law (London: John Murray, 1879; reprinted Bristol: Thoemmes Press, 2002), 2 vols.

11. Blackstone writes of natural law, "This law of nature, being coeval with mankind and dictated by God himself, is of course superior in obligation to any other. It is binding overall the globe in all countries, and at all times: no human laws are of any validity, if contrary to this, and such as them are valid derive all their force, and all their authority, mediately or immediately, from this original." William Blackstone, *Commentaries on the Laws of England,* ed. David Lemmings (Oxford: Oxford University Press, 2016), Book I.ii.41.

12. Austin 1995: 157.

13. See H.L.A. Hart, *The Concept of Law*, ed. Leslie Green (Oxford: Oxford University Press, 2012), 27–33.

14. Ibid., 42–44.

15. Austin 1995: 86.

16. Ibid., 61–66.

17. See chapter 15 *infra* regarding the fit of distributional and relational theories of justice with various theories of law.

18. See chapter 12 *infra* concerning Hart's social facts theory of law and inclusive legal positivism.

19. See chapters14 and 15 *infra* with respect to the theory of justice as right actions, the theory of law presented here, and the fit of the theory of law with and under the theory of justice as right actions.

PART III

Political Foundations of Law

Chapter 7

Political Society and Civil Government

As I argue here, I view law as consisting of social and normative rules of behavior imposed by a legitimate political authority, together with legal principles for interpreting such rules. This view understands the foundation of law to be political, including the power to enforce rules; thus, the question of law is primarily a question of obedience—whether and in what circumstances it is appropriate to obey the law.

Granting that the foundation of law is political, in this chapter I proceed to examine the tensions between the concepts of natural rights and natural law, justifications of political rule, modern concepts of rights, and political legitimacy and civil government. In exploring the question of political legitimacy, I examine the broad contemporary concept of rights, since rights drive discussions of permissible actions and institutions, as well as underlie the concept of political legitimacy.

NATURAL RIGHTS

The concept of individual rights in contemporary political society is often traced to the natural rights theories of Thomas Hobbes and John Locke. Indeed, according to the contemporary sense, neither Plato nor Aristotle consider the concept of individual rights in political society. Plato's discussion may nonetheless be seen to foreshadow the possibility in his functional argument about individuals working in society as appropriate to their class. Further, some scholars link Aristotle to the natural rights tradition, while additionally claiming that Aristotle's teleological view of human nature and his ethical theory of *eudaimonia* can serve as a foundation for a theory of individual rights akin to Locke's.[1]

While an early version of natural law theory has been attributed to Thomas Hobbes, he may also be seen as a progenitor of the concept of natural rights. Typically, natural law theory recognizes a type of higher law that lays out universal truths for the moral ordering of society based on a rational understanding of human nature. On the other hand, Hobbes' view of natural law may be characterized as a negative one insofar as he claims that anarchy and civil war are caused by appeals to natural and divine laws above the will of the sovereign. Thus, he accepts positive law, that is, man-made law, as the only reliable guide to political authority.

There is a contradiction here. How can Hobbes' view of natural law as intolerant and anarchial be reconciled with his understanding of natural rights as leading to what we now call social justice? One answer may rest in his view of human nature and humans' desire for power: "So that in the first place, I put for a general inclination of all mankind, a perpetual and restless desire for power after power, that ceaseth only in death."[2] As described above, Hobbes also denies the teleological views of both Aristotle and Aquinas, stating that, "There is no *Finis Ultimus* (utmost aim) nor *Summum Bonum* (greatest good) as is spoken of in the books of the old moral philosophers. . . . Felicity is a continual progress of the desire, from one object to another."[3]

In his later account found in the Leviathan, Hobbes' description of the way in which individuals become subjects to a sovereign authority deviates from his earlier accounts in *Elements* and *De Cive*.[4] In the earlier two treatises, individuals relinquish their rights (of self-government and to pursue all things they judge useful or necessary for their survival and commodious living) in favor of one and the same sovereign person (whether a natural person as a monarch or a rule-governed assembly in effect acting as a monarch). That is, sovereigns alone retain their right of nature to act on their own private judgment in all matters and to apply the transferred rights of subjects. Whether exercising its own retained right of nature or the subjects' transferred rights, a sovereign's action is attributable to the sovereign itself and bears moral responsibility for such action.

In contrast, in Hobbes' *Leviathan*, each individual covenants to "own and authorize" all of the sovereign's actions, to accede to whatever the sovereign does as a public figure or commands that subjects do. Herein lies an apparent inconsistency: if in "owning and authorizing" all their sovereign's actions, subjects become morally responsible for all that the sovereign does and all that they do in obedience to its commands, Hobbes cannot consistently maintain his position that merely obedient actions in response to sovereign commands are the moral responsibility of the sovereign alone. One resolution of this apparent inconsistency denies that Hobbes' idea of authorization carries responsibility for the act authorized, as our contemporary approach to authorization generally does.

Another seeming contradiction in Hobbes' political account puts his view of the sovereign with absolute authority over citizens at odds and against the subjects' rights to disobey or resist when their lives or honor are at stake, their natural rights. Formulated as a question, what are the limits of political authority?

While Hobbes insists that we should regard our governments as having absolute authority, he allows subjects the liberty of disobeying some of their government's commands. That is, he argues that subjects retain a right of self-defense against the sovereign power, giving them the right to disobey or resist when their lives are in danger. He further extends to subjects seemingly broad rights to resistance, when their families or their honor are at stake. These exceptions are puzzling: Hobbes' ascription of apparently inalienable rights—what he calls the "true liberties of subjects"—seems incompatible with his defense of absolute sovereignty. Moreover, if the sovereign's failure to provide adequate protection to subjects extinguishes their obligation to obey, and if it is left to individual subjects to judge the adequacy of that protection, it seems that people have never really exited his fearsome, anarchic state of nature.

Similar to Hobbes, the political account of John Locke is also based on the notion of natural rights: we all equally have rights to life, liberty, health, and property, even in a state of nature before the introduction of civil government. That is, Locke explains that there is a law of nature, based upon reason, the Golden Rule, interpreted in terms of natural rights: "The state of nature has a law of nature to govern it, which obliges everyone: and reason which is that law, teaches all mankind who will but consult it, that being equal and independent, no one ought to harm another in his life, health, liberty or possessions."[5]

Controversy has arisen, however, concerning Locke's view of property as a fundamental natural right. Locke appears to argue that since persons own their own labor, when they mix their labor with what has been previously unowned, it becomes their property. That is, Locke argues that property may be acquired "at least where there is enough, and as good left in common for others." Later, he repeats that the acquisition of unowned property should be "enough and as good," although this phrase has led to a number of different interpretations.

In contemporary times, Robert Nozick has taken the concept of natural rights to an extreme, as he develops a libertarian view of civil government, provocatively beginning *Anarchy, State, and Utopia* with the statement that, "Individuals have rights . . . so strong and far-reaching . . . that they raise the question of what, if anything, the state and its officials may do."[6]

Influenced by Locke, he constructs a natural rights theory arguing not only that the individual is inviolable, but also that a person's property rights become non-negotiable.[7] As Locke asserted "every man has a 'property' in his own 'person.' This nobody has any right to but himself. The 'labour' of his body and the 'work' of his hands, we may say, are properly his."[8] For Nozick, natural rights are "natural" in the sense that they are not legal rights established by legislation, but rather, they constitute moral rights, which legislation and government should respect.[9]

In spite of his adaptation of Locke's concept of self-ownership, whether the notion of natural rights is actually compatible with privately-held property, as Nozick claims, is questionable, especially in situations where the property is a natural resource and not produced by persons, by the work of their hands. In fact, Locke viewed natural resources, initially unprotected by any property rule (no consent is needed for use or appropriation), as protected by a compensation liability rule. Further, his original formulation itself goes beyond the measure articulated by Nozick to suggest that a limit be placed upon the amount of a resource that may be extracted from nature by any individual. Those who use natural resources or claim rights over them owe compensation to others for any wrongful costs imposed. Defining what is "enough and as good," however, is to be left to others.[10]

Notably, Nozick's fundamental view of ownership and exchange seems to emerge from marginalizing the human dignity at the core of Kantian principles which he professes,[11] whereby an individual is not to be used simply as a means for others—or put another way—from ignoring, as Jerry Cohen has argued, that given an individual's impoverished circumstances, coercion may exist beyond what the law defines.[12] That is, what Nozick treats as normatively axiomatic presents problems not only with respect to the ownership of natural resources and the use of one's own property, but also with respect to his fundamental view of ownership and exchange.[13]

POLITICAL JUSTIFICATION

Thomas Hobbes is well-known for his development of social contract theory, a method of justifying political principles by appeal to the putative agreement that would be made among suitably situated rational, free, and equal persons. He has been much criticized for using the social contract theory to arrive at the conclusion in the *Leviathan* that we ought to submit to the authority of an absolute sovereign power.[14]

John Locke also looks to social contract theory to justify government, and he further draws the distinction between legitimate and illegitimate civil government. While he advocates universal consent to the establishment of civil government, he draws an important distinction between universal consent on the one hand and, on the other hand, majority consent, defined as duty to society and duty to government. From this perspective, Locke formulates the aim of legitimate government to preserve, so far as possible, the rights to life, liberty, health, and property of its citizens; to prosecute and punish those of its citizens who may violate the rights of others; and to pursue the public good even when it may conflict with the rights of individuals.[15]

CONTEMPORARY RIGHTS

In contemporary times, a broad concept of rights dominates discussions of permissible actions and political institutions in analyzing: the form of civil government, the shape of morality, and the content of laws. In analyzing the form of rights, I look first to the Hohfeldian analytical system. Next, I examine the function of rights by means of the will theory vs. the interest theory.

For Wesley Hohfeld, the four basic elements of rights include: privilege, claim, power, and immunity,[16] which he arranges in tables of opposites and correlatives. The first pair of "Hohfeldian incidents" involve the obligation of duty. Thus, the first basic element of rights is identified as privilege or liberty, for which an individual has no duty to comply. The second element, a claim, includes a duty to at least one duty-holder. Examples of the basic elements of privilege and claim include bodily rights, property rights, and contract rights. These privileges and claims comprise what H.L.A. Hart describes as "primary rules," whereby rules require persons to perform or to refrain from performing particular actions.[17]

The last pair of Hohfeldian incidents defines what Hart calls "secondary rules," rules that specify how agents can introduce and change primary rules. Thus, the third basic element of power may alter the authority of others, as when an owner of a business has the power to countermand an officer's directive to other employees. The last Hohfeldian incident is immunity, a basic element exemplified in the American legal system, which guarantees that a witness has the right not to incriminate herself.

Given what Hart categorizes as Hohfeld's primary and secondary rules, it follows that the function of rights should be examined, as they are in the two main theories of the will theory and the interest theory. A will theorist asserts that the function of a right is to give the holder of the right control over another's duty. Thus, according to Hart, the right-holder is "a small scale sovereign."[18] In this camp, the views of Immanuel Kant and Hans Kelsen link rights and normative control. That is, for will theorists, this link between rights and authority (the authority to control what others may do) is a matter of definition.

By contrast, interest theorists maintain that the function of a right is to further the right-holder's interests. An owner has a right not because owners have choices, but because ownership makes the owner better off, advancing her interests. An individual's rights, claims the interest theorist, are Hohfeldian incidents which benefit the person involved. Jeremy Bentham, John Austin, Joseph Raz, and Matthew Kramer may be included in this camp.

There are weaknesses in both accounts. With regard to will theory, there may be no such thing as an unwaivable right (for instance, a right not to be enslaved). Under the will theory, it is impossible for incompetents to have rights; yet, the concept contradicts what is ordinarily perceived as what should be the case. Further, bare privilege rights (e.g., in a Hobbesian state of nature), do not represent the right of authority over others.

The interest theory also fails what ordinarily would be understood as rights. On the one hand, a person may have an interest in something without having a right to that object. On the other hand, a judge may have an interest in sentencing a convict to life in prison, but the judge's interests cannot justify ascribing such power to affect a convict's normative situation. Raz, for instance, admits that such important rights such as freedom of expression or freedom of contract are not justified by the interests of the citizens who hold them; rather, such rights advance the common good.[19]

I find the Hohfeldian approach to be useful in analyzing rights in the broad sense. In this sense, natural rights would then appear to be a subset of moral rights, and for the legal theory presented in these pages, the will theory proves helpful for the function of rights with its focus on such concepts as power and duty.

POLITICAL LEGITIMACY

At this point, it may prove helpful to reiterate the two principles of law that undergird my approach to the theory of law.

> *First Principle*: One should obey those laws of legal-rational political authority that are not otherwise violative of societal norms and customs.

> *Second Principle*: Government should only enforce rules of human behavior of legitimate legal-rational political authority.

For these two principles, I reference Max Weber's widely known descriptive typology defining the three sources of political legitimacy in his *The Theory of Social and Economic Organization*: charismatic, traditional, and rational-legal.[20]

Weber's general political project developed two intertwining themes: the resuscitation of certain character traits he saw lacking in modern society on the one hand, and, on the other hand, the promotion of a classic liberal political theory, one which emphasizes liberty or freedom of the individual and rationality in a society he saw as increasingly bureaucratic and value fragmented.[21]

By political legitimacy, I mean the justification of coercive power and the creation and/or sanctioning of political authority, the right to rule. Under Weber's typology, rational-legal authority is seen as a source of political legitimacy and the basis of modern democracies. Examples of this type of authority include: officials elected by voters, rules that are expressed in a constitution, and policies that are written in a formal document. For Weber, rational-legal authority derives its power from a system of bureaucracy and legality.

Weber views the state is as "a human community that (successfully) claims the monopoly of the legitimate use of physical force within a given territory."[22] Thus, the political question for Weber becomes one of orderly domination and management within a given territory. He believes that "the merely external fact of the order being obeyed is not sufficient to signify domination in our sense; we cannot overlook the meaning of the fact that the command is accepted as a valid norm."[23] Weber also suggests that in answering the question of obedience to the law, even without coercive power or expectations of benefits for obedience, such factors as identity, role, habit, and convention may play a part in explaining obedience or compliance to the law.[24]

Rather than emphasizing moral goals as such, like justice (e.g., Kant) or freedom (e.g., Hegel), Weber accepts a Hobbesian outlook on politics, or what Bernard Williams much later identifies as the "First Political Question," which poses that a state ensure conditions that legitimatize authority. That is, Weber accepts the Hobbesian-infused idea of agonistic value pluralism—and in doing so also fulfills Williams' criterion for the First Political Question—by accepting the potentially positive outcomes stemming from conflicts. In doing so, Weber further accepts that liberalism may well support a foundation based in natural law. Further, Williams argues that the theoretical construction of a workable political order needs to also satisfy the "Basic Legitimation Demand," whereby state power can be justified for all subjects. That is, a legitimate political order comprises an institutionalized modus vivendi for collective life that "makes sense as an intelligible order" in the eyes of the beholder.[25]

Restated, the three ideal types of legitimate domination Weber identified are based on charisma, tradition, and legal rationality. The first type of legitimacy claim, charisma, depends largely on how persuasively the leaders prove their qualities, for which they receive personal devotions and emotive investment from those ruled. The second kind of claim, tradition, can be made successfully when certain practices, customs, and mores are institutionalized to produce a stable pattern of domination over a long duration of time. In contrast to these crucial dependences on personality traits and the passage of time, the third type of authority, legal rationality, is unfettered by time, place, and other contingencies as it derives its legitimacy from adherence to impersonal rules and general principles that can only be found by suitable legal-rational reasoning.

It seems, though, that Weber is uncertain of the proper place of democracy in his analysis. At one point, he deems democracy as a fourth type of legitimacy because it should be able to embrace legitimacy from below, whereas his three ideal types are all top-down models. At other times, Weber seems to argue that democracy is simply non-legitimate, rather than another type of legitimate domination, since it aspires to an identity between the ruler and the ruled (i.e., no domination at all), but without assuming a hierarchical and asymmetrical relationship of power. Here, his concept of legitimate domination hardly takes off the ground.

Thus, according to Weber's realist outlook on democracy, if genuine self-rule of the people is impossible, the only choice is between leaderless and leadership democracy. The primary concern for Weber in designing democratic institutions, then, has less to do with the realization of democratic ideals—such as freedom, equality, justice, or self-rule—than with the cultivation of certain character traits befitting a robust national leadership.

In this respect, however, it should be noted that in its democratic theory of partisanship Weber's take on civil society is quite different from a communitarian-Tocquevillean outlook. Like recent advocates of partisanship, that is, Weber remains critical of the conventional communitarian view that simply equates civil society with voluntary associational life itself. Not all voluntary associations are conducive to democracy; in fact, some are detrimental to its viability. While even in a civil society, associative practices may cultivate civil virtues that regulate our private lives, nonetheless, such social capital cannot be automatically transferred to the public realm as a useful set of civic virtues and skills for democratic politics. This realization led Weber as well as a number of contemporary democratic theorists to call for the politicization of civil society with not less, but better, partisanship, making Weber's politics of civil society crucially different from that of a communitarian-Tocquevillean model.

Weber's political outlook is also quite different from a liberal-Habermasian "public sphere," which provides for a rational-communicative shelter in which the open exchange and fair deliberation of impartial opinions can take place until reasonable consensus emerges. By contrast, Weber's civil society is to be an agonistic arena of organized rivalry, competition, and struggle of the partisan claims where consensus—be it reasonable, overlapping, or bipartisan—may not always be found.

Given the incommensurable value fragmentation of modern politics and society, Weber would therefore seem to embrace a civil society in which deep disagreements are reasonable, permanent, and not necessarily harmful to democracy as long as those disagreements remain peaceful.[26] The huge caveat here, though, is that violence, or the threat of violence, should pose a sharp dividing line for partisanship advocates of democracy. One step further, I believe, is that politicians involved in such power struggles must accommodate the ability to compromise without putting into question the political legitimacy of a civil society.

NOTES

1. See Fred Miller, *Nature, Justice, and Rights in Aristotle's Politics* (Oxford: Clarendon Press, 1995); also see John Gray, *Liberalism* (Minneapolis: University of Minnesota Press, 1985).
2. Thomas Hobbes, *Leviathan*, ed. and intro. Christopher Brooke (London: Penguin Classics, 2017), 47.
3. Ibid., 1–2.
4. See *Three-Text Edition of Thomas Hobbes's Political Theory,* ed. Deborah Baumgold (Cambridge: Cambridge University Press, 2017).
5. John Locke, *Second Treatise of Government,* ed. and intro. C. B. Macpherson (Indianapolis: Hackett Publishing Company, Inc., 1980), § 6.
6. Robert Nozick, *Anarchy, State, and Utopia* (New York: Basic Books, 1974), ix.
7. For Locke, justice is inconceivable without personal property—where there is no property, there is no justice. The essence of Lockean justice is the security of each individual's personal possessions as a right based in law. See, Locke 1980.
8. Nozick 1974: 12.
9. Nozick's concept of self-ownership even extends to voluntary non-coercive enslavement contracts between adults.
10. See Locke 1980.
11. See Immanuel Kant, *Groundwork of the Metaphysic or Morals*, trans. H. J. Paton (New York: HarperCollins, 2009), 96, where he states his Formula of the End (one version of his Supreme Principle of Morality or Categorical Imperative): "Act in such a way that you always treat humanity, whether in your own person or in the person of any other, never simply as a means but always at the same time as an end."
12. See G. A. Cohen, ed., *Self-Ownership, Freedom, and Equality* (Cambridge: Cambridge University Press, 1995).
13. See T. M. Scanlon, "Nozick on Rights, Liberty, and Property," in ed. Jeffrey Paul, *Reading Nozick* (Totowa: Rowman and Littlefield, 1991), 107–129.
14. See Hobbes 2017.
15. See Locke 1980.
16. See Wesley Hohfeld, *Fundamental Legal Conceptions as Applied in Judicial Reasoning,* ed. Walter Cook (New Haven: Yale University Press, 1964).

17. See H.L.A. Hart, *The Concept of Law* (Oxford: Clarendon Press, 1961).

18. H.L.A. Hart, "Legal Duty and Obligation," in *Essays on Bentham* (Oxford: Clarendon Press, 1982), 183.

19. Joseph Raz, *The Authority of Law* (Oxford: Oxford University Press, 1995), 30–41, 131.

20. Max Weber, *The Theory of Social and Economic Organization*, eds. and trans. Alexander Henderson and Talcott Parsons (New York: Free Press, 1997), 324–406.

21. Ibid., 19.

22. Ibid., 310.

23.Max Weber, *Economy and Society* (Oakland: University of California Press, 1978), 946, emphasis in the original..

24. See Max Weber, *Political Writings*, eds. Peter Lassman and Ronald Speirs (Cambridge: Cambridge University Press, 1994).

25. Bernard Williams, *In the Beginning Was the Deed* (Princeton: Princeton University Press, 2007), 1–17.

26. In *Law and Disagreement* (Oxford: Clarendon Press, 1999), Jeremy Waldron queries whether violence or threat of violence may be an appropriate dividing line for partisanship advocates.

Chapter 8

Liberalism

In political theory, liberalism is typically seen to include the concepts of liberty or freedom and equality. Of course, differing and complex views of these concepts have emerged, according, for example, to the emphasis given one concept over another and additional concepts that may be included in different versions of liberalism.[1]

Classic political liberalism is based on the individual as the bearer of rights. In recent times, however, the equality component of liberalism may be said to be the more dominant element, thus implying the concept of obligations as well as the concept of rights. John Rawls, for example, links the concept of equality to his distributive theory of justice as fairness. Moreover, for Ronald Dworkin, equality is positioned as the political sovereign virtue, and serves as the linchpin of his theory of resource equality.

My view of political liberalism includes consideration of equality as well, but does so in a conceptual framework that promotes the concepts of negative liberty, equality of concern and respect, tolerance, and diversity.

NEGATIVE LIBERTY

Isaiah Berlin identifies positive and negative liberty in "Two Concepts of Liberty," subscribing to a view of negative liberty in the form of freedom from governmental interference.[2] In doing so, Berlin looks to John Stuart Mill as articulating a political view of negative liberty in his harm principle. This view may be seen as an example of classic political liberalism with the emphasis on the liberty component of liberalism.

Thus, Mill believes that "the only purpose for which power can be rightfully exercised over any member of a civilized community, against his will, is to prevent harm to others."[3] Moreover, Mill's widely known harm principle provides that,

> the sole end for which mankind are warranted, individually or collectively, in interfering with the liberty of action of any of their number, is self-protection.[4]

Theoretically, his "one simple principle," the harm principle, operates in two steps, as follows: (1) the inquiry is made as to whether liberty is restricted, and if so, (2) a calculus of harms is developed. Standing alone, the principle's restrictions on liberty resemble the kind of deontological rule proposed by Aristotle rather than forming part of a utilitarian happiness calculus, in spite of the fact that Mill always claimed to be a utilitarian.

In this regard, Mill's utilitarian account becomes problematic and complex, due mainly to three concepts. Perhaps most obviously complicating utilitarianism's foundational question of what an individual ought to do is his idea of higher and lesser pleasures (no City of Pigs for Mill). Likewise, Mill furthers a notion of progress that adds another layer to utilitarian notions of intrinsic value by considering how decisions involve incommensurable moral values, whereby progress serves as a measure of cumulative improvement in ethics and politics. Finally, complicating utilitarian beliefs in the intrinsic value of knowledge is Mill's tendency toward fallibilism, in the Enlightenment sense, believing that all knowledge is reversible and that there are consequently no foundations of knowledge.

In addition, the harm principle seems very much like a statement proposing liberty as an intrinsic good, reminiscent of Plato, rather than posing a simpler instrumental justification. If this is the case, again, the problem indeed emerges of whether this principle may subsist in a value monist view of utilitarianism, since utilitarianism is seen as a consequentialist moral theory which promotes the single value of happiness or pleasure as its defining goal.

Although Mill intends the harm principle not to be morally dependent (and in this sense, anti-perfectionist), many judgments concerning harm depend on a rich, context-dependent concept of the good. That is, what constitutes harm is seen as socially contingent and not, importantly, a morally neutral idea, making the harm principle much more complex than it at first appears. Indeed, John Gray underscores the point: "determining when restraint of liberty is justified turns out to be an intractably difficult business, since it hinges on assessments of the relative severity of harms that, in their dependency on disputed conceptions of the good life, are inherently controversial."[5]

Mill's harm principle has thus been criticized not only for indeterminacy in what constitutes harm and its underlying concept of human interests, but also for the application of the subsumed utility principle. The traditional criticisms and received opinion of Mill's liberalism focus on his attempt to derive a liberal political theory from utilitarian moral principles, an attempt to square the circle whereby the principle of utility, which is concerned with collective well-being, is used to ground a strong principle of liberty, which is concerned with protecting the individual.

Berlin, for one, regards Mill's account as incoherent, since Mill defended liberty as having intrinsic value while also claiming to ground his argument in utilitarianism.[6] Gray's view of Mill's attempt is that "such a principle [the principle of utility] can supply only a necessary, and not sufficient, condition for the just restraint of liberty."[7] Gray's particular criticism of Mill's moral and political philosophy has to do with Mill's notion of progress, which Gray relates to an indictment of the liberal project itself, whether grounded in a view of the priority of the good, as appear in Mill's and Joseph Raz's accounts, or in a view of the priority of the right, as with the accounts of John Rawls, Ronald Dworkin, and Brian Barry, among others.

While some see these diverse vagaries as ruinous to Mill's enterprise, the harm principle has nonetheless proven to be a durable concept, one that may be effectively deployed in moral decision-making between conflicting values, including issues concerning diversity. While Mill attempted to orchestrate plural values into his account, he also articulated moral decision-making resources, enabling him to overcome the classic strong value pluralist problem of incommensurability.

VALUE PLURALISM

Situated in a classical liberal view, Berlin states that he is a value pluralist, who maintains that negative liberty derives from value pluralism. Thus, he argues that value pluralism involves making choices "between absolute claims" and that the making of choices is an "inescapable characteristic" of the human condition. From this platform, Berlin infers that individuals place "immense value on the freedom to choose."[8] In other words, Berlin reasons that because individuals must choose, consequently, the freedom to choose is valued, and a political order that protects this freedom is cherished as well. For Berlin, then, a liberal political order, based upon providing negative liberty, yields the most legitimate kind of state, and value pluralism must consequently entail liberalism.

Among criticisms of this view is the observation that Berlin's argument suffers from a classic Humean "is-ought" error. Even granting that the inevitability of choice leads individuals to strongly value the freedom to choose, it does not follow that the state ought to provide or protect such freedom. Paradoxically, to do so would lead the state to recognizing an overriding value (free choice), thereby violating value pluralism. John Gray, who makes this point, further argues that value pluralism is consistent with a range of non-liberal political orders.[9]

Although Berlin's argument has been much criticized, several contemporary thinkers, including William Galston, have attempted to revive Berlin's project. The appeal in doing so is clear. A value pluralist liberalism, Galston avers, would have the potential to "connect what one believes to be the best account of public life with comparably persuasive accounts of morality, human psychology, and the natural world."[10] Moreover, at least superficially, the inference from value pluralism to liberalism seems simple and natural.

That is, value pluralism may be viewed as a theory of the moral universe that provides for many kinds of goods and a plurality of valuable ways of life. In this particular respect, value pluralism accords well with liberalism, which, according to Mill, is a political order that attempts to provide the greatest possible freedom for individuals to "pursue [their] own good in [their] own way."[11] Moreover, Galston accepts the view that not all values are commensurable—they may neither be reduced to a single over-arching value nor completely rank-ordered. Galston's basic view of value pluralism may nonetheless prove problematic, with respect to those many forms of liberalism in which justice is viewed as a "first virtue of social institutions."[12] Likewise, his view can prove difficult for those liberals who favor a lexical ordering among goods. In Brian Barry's liberal theory, for example, equality has a prime role, and for Robert Nozick, liberty represents an overarching value.

Some classic liberals believe that individuals are ontologically superior to social groups and relations and that persons and their identities are distinct. Further, they believe that central to the concept of personhood is a capacity to choose among alternate ways of living. In such regard, they may be susceptible to the "communitarian critique of liberalism," since, by according the self as in some ways prior to the ends and substantive attachments of the person, they have "disembodied" themselves (implausibly so, say some communitarians) from their ends and values. Consequently, the attempt to instantiate even classic liberalism meets with conceptual difficulties, difficulties that reside in the tension between defining what an individual is and what defines her or his purpose or end.

EQUALITY

Many contemporary political theorists have focused on the question of equality in the distribution of benefits and burdens in society, as do the works of John Rawls and Ronald Dworkin, discussed in more detail below. These distribution schemes derive from Aristotle's concept of equality underlying his delineation of particular justice. As previously discussed, however, Aristotle's distributive scheme is based on merit.

Focusing for now on the concept of equality that drives Rawls' distributive scheme of social goods, in his approach, Rawls uses the concept of equality to mediate between individuals' needs and desires and to divide the benefits and burdens of social cooperation, since "[a]ll social primary goods—liberty and opportunity, income, wealth, and the bases of self-respect—are to be distributed equally unless an unequal distribution of any or all of these goods is to the advantage of the least favored."[13]

Thus, Rawls attempts to proffer a disinterested liberal neutrality, arguing for a premise which proposes that each member of society has an equal claim to society's goods and that an individual's natural abilities should not affect this claim. Any inequalities in the distribution of a society's material wealth may only be justified under his second principle of justice as fairness, the difference principle, if such inequalities benefit the least advantaged in society. In considering just distributions, for example, there is no reason to consider income and other primary goods produced by individuals. Instead, what should be considered are the unproduced primary goods. Thus, in partaking in an equitable sharing of primary goods, as well as their free exchange, an individual is involved in the process of freedom rather than the substance of exchanges.

Ronald Dworkin, however, promotes equality as the sovereign political virtue, as he interprets the concept of equality as equality of resources. Criticizing Rawls' difference principle as being insufficiently endowment insensitive, he argues that Rawls' difference principle is conceived to distribute only social primary goods (liberty and opportunity, income and wealth, and the bases of self-respect). In doing so, Dworkin continues, the difference principle overlooks the claims of those who are unequally endowed with natural primary goods, especially the disabled, whose actual needs would require more resources to compensate for unequal natural endowment.

In addition to being endowment insensitive, Dworkin argues, Rawls' difference principle is insufficiently ambition sensitive. If the Rawlsian difference principle cannot distinguish between inequalities that result from unequal natural endowments or from different consumption ambitions or decisions, then it runs up against the basic intuition concerning fairness residing at the heart of social justice. In his general argument against the distributive approaches suggested by a concept proposing equality of welfare, Dworkin notes that the concept seems vulnerable to the problem of expensive tastes and varying ambitions.

In objecting to supposed objective theories of welfare and equality of welfare, including that of Rawls, Dworkin believes that any attempt to make people equal in welfare aims to make them equal in something that they value differently. In fact, he notes that "an objective ranking (of activities) would be controversial even one with a generous helping of indeterminacy, and basing distribution on such a ranking is not compatible with equal concern for all."[14]

Instead, Dworkin provides a mechanism for an equality of resources by creating a hypothetical market auction that is supplemented by a hypothetical insurance scheme.[15] Thus, in Dworkin's auction procedure, everyone receives the same initial amount of money, and then they all engage in bidding for resources that are available within the political community. These resources include both external goods and, more controversially, internal resources of individuals, such as hours of time for work. Obviously, Dworkin's auction model is intended to provide the appropriate (market) measure of value for the resources that an individual holds; in doing so, it further reveals the opportunity costs of denying resources to others.

The charge has been made, however, that such an auction leads to the "slavery of the talented,"[16] which can be illustrated as follows: imagine a person who has a great talent for singing and that her talent commands a high price in a given society. Other people at the hypothetical auction are willing to bid for many hours of this person's labor to hear her sing. Consequently, the person will have to work by singing, her most lucrative employment, to satisfy the owners (purchasers) of her time. The person's free time has become a scarce commodity, and she herself has to bid for hours of her own time at the high auction price. Now, imagine another person with no such valuable talent, who, as it turns out, finds his most lucrative employment is as a common laborer. Since few are willing to pay a high price for his services, the auction sets his labor time at a low price. Consequently, he may purchase many of his hours for his own recreational or other use, demonstrating that the common laborer has more use of his own time than does the talented singer, who is enslaved by her talent in the hypothetical equal auction.

In response to generating the condition that enslaves the talented, Dworkin articulates a proviso to the hypothetical auction, an envy test. For the envy test to function effectively, great differences in the personal abilities and talents of the persons involved cannot exist. Since such a condition cannot be guaranteed and since Dworkin believes it important that no one suffers or profits by reason of what he views as the individual's undeserved natural abilities, an additional procedure must then be introduced, one based on an insurance scheme. Thus, a portion of the initially allocated equal sums of money intended for use at the auction is collected from each individual and used to establish an insurance fund to provide support for the disabled or for insufficiently talented persons.

To Dworkin, this insurance model looks less like welfare than the Rawlsian model does, which also attempts to care for the least advantaged in society.[17] Be that as it may, the re-allocations entailed in the insurance scheme do raise the question of possible disincentive consequences along with the problem of "second-best efficient egalitarianism" as, in effect, he raises the question of whether we are under a duty to help those responsible for the fact that they need help.

Dworkin's theory of resource equality may also be seen as a form of luck egalitarianism. Thus, Jerry Cohen, among others, has challenged Dworkin's choice and chance distinctions, contending that the distinction between choice and brute luck is often not easily drawn and that an individual's ambition-sensitive drives are, indeed, often matters of luck or chance.[18] Cohen further rejects Dworkin's theory of resource equality arguing that the market outcomes that drive the theory are morally arbitrary.[19]

TOLERANCE AND DIVERSITY

In an attempt to resuscitate Berlin's project of value pluralism entailing liberalism, William Galston foregrounds social diversity and tolerance; "[p]roperly understood, liberalism is about the protection of legitimate diversity."[20] Galston's approach to resuscitating Berlin's project, then, is not to argue directly that value pluralism entails liberalism, but rather, that value pluralism defeats all non-liberal options, thereby contending that it would be unreasonable for a state to impose a single way of life on its citizens. Indirectly, however, Galston does argue that value pluralism entails liberalism.

Similar to Berlin, that is, for Galston, the inevitability of choice creates a presumption in favor of expressive liberty, by which term Galston means the liberty "of individuals and groups leading their lives as they see fit."[21] Accordingly, Galston assumes that it is the mark of an illiberal regime to restrict or reject expressive liberty, and if value pluralism holds true, there could be no legitimate reason for such a restriction. Consequently, he concludes that negative liberty derives from value pluralism in the absence of any legitimate reasons for restricting it.

Regardless of its merits, Galston's argument assumes that if value pluralism defeats all non-liberal views, it must support liberalism, an argument which proceeds by way of elimination. To be successful—even if he is only indirectly arguing that value pluralism entails liberalism—for his argument to hold, Galston must exhaustively cover the terrain of illiberal regimes that do not restrict negative liberty. For example, one form of liberalism, that of libertarianism, provides a counter-example, since it functions as just such an illiberal regime which, in Galston's construct, would be clearly inconsistent with value pluralism. That is, while asserting the rights of individuals, libertarianism at the same time restricts them insofar as it denies government the power to protect multiple choices. In this fashion, Galston's argument fails to develop an effective conceptual link between value pluralism and liberalism. Indeed, in his approach, even Plato's *Republic* may be seen as consistent with value pluralism.

Berlin's and Galston's attention to what Galston terms expressive liberty, under the aegis of classic liberalism, then, has still not settled the relationship of value pluralism to liberty or other political values. Focusing specifically on the argument of whether value pluralism entails liberalism, for example, John Gray reasons that Berlin's value pluralism undermines liberalism's traditional claims to universal authority. As a result, liberalism is seen to have no more pride of place in Berlin's scheme than other legitimate political forms, and negative liberty does indeed form only one incommensurable good among others. Thus, for Gray, value pluralism asserts that illiberal societies are not necessarily inferior to liberal ones, whereby his argument moves into a Hobbesian space in which *modus vivendi* is the appropriate political order of the day and where value pluralism and liberalism are viewed as rival doctrines.[22]

In sum, while I do not agree with Galston's argument that value pluralism necessarily leads to a liberal political order, I do see the concepts of tolerance and social diversity as a natural fit to a theory of political liberalism. Thus, while Galston's ontological argument portraying the derivation of such concepts into a liberal political formulation may be flawed, I integrate their presence into the formulation of liberalism as the proper political context for the theory of law presented here, and as embracing the plural values that comprise one of the concepts of good underlying my approach.

NOTES

1. E.g., see Paul Kelly, *Liberalism* (Cambridge: Polity Press, 2004).
2. Isaiah Berlin, "Two Concepts of Liberty," in *Four Essays on Liberty* (Oxford: Oxford University Press, 1969), 118–172; here, Berlin points to Plato's ideal society as based on the concept of positive liberty, the freedom to do what one is supposed to do, thus leading to a well-ordered and stable society. Negative liberty, which Berlin sees as at the heart of John Stuart Mill's harm principle, represents freedom from governmental interference.
3. John Stuart Mill, "On Liberty," in ed. John Gray, *John Stuart Mill on Liberty and Other Essays* (Oxford: Oxford University Press, 1998), 15.
4. Ibid., 18.
5. John Gray, *Mill on Liberty* (Oxford: Routledge, 1996), 140.
6. Berlin 1996: 139, 161.
7. Gray 1996: 136.
8. Berlin1969: 48, 52.
9. See John Gray, *Two Faces of Liberalism* (Cambridge: Polity Press, 2000).

10. William Galston, *Liberal Pluralism* (Cambridge: Cambridge University Press, 2002), 47.

11. Mill 1998: 17.

12. John Rawls, *A Theory of Justice* (Cambridge: Harvard University Press, 1971), 2.

13. Ibid., 303.

14. Ronald Dworkin, *Sovereign Virtue* (Cambridge: Harvard University Press, 2000), 300.

15. Ibid., 303.

16. See John Roemer, "Equality of Resources Implies Equality of Welfare," *Quarterly Journal of Economics* 101 (1986): 751–784.

17. However, in implementing Dworkin's theory of equal resource allocation (market auction plus insurance scheme), many of the complexities of tax and money-transfer systems found in a welfare state must be taken into account.

18. See G. A. Cohen, "Expensive Taste Rides Again," in ed. Justine Burley, *Dworkin and His Critics* (Oxford: Blackwell Publishing, 2004).

19. See G. A. Cohen, *Self-Ownership, Freedom and Equality* (Cambridge: Cambridge University Press, 1995), 19–37.

20. William Galston, *Liberal Pluralism* (Cambridge: Cambridge University Press, 2002), 47.

21. William Galston, *The Practice of Liberal Pluralism* (Cambridge: Cambridge University Press, 2005), 2.

22. See Gray 2000.

Chapter 9

Group Rights

While still exploring the political foundations of law in this chapter on group rights, some of the following discussions of group rights do so in the framework of a just or unjust society. This accords with my view, stated at the outset of this study, that law should be viewed in the service of justice.

Plato recognizes groups in his vision of an ideal society, identifying three classes of persons organized in a hierarchal, orderly social structure to ensure the stability of political society, with each individual doing work appropriate to his or her class. In more limited fashion, Aristotle also recognizes groups, via his ethical theory of *eudaimonia* as applied to political constitutions. Thus, he identifies the *aristoi*, the best group of persons, as the most appropriate to rule in society. Neither classical thinker promotes group rights as such, since they both regard groups from a top-down view with regard to the governing class in society.

In this chapter, I examine various contemporary group rights theories, including approaches based on oppression and domination, communal life, gender, race, and culture. As just mentioned, these group rights accounts are often framed in the context of just and unjust societies.

OPPRESSION AND DOMINATION

In contemporary times, in response to the focus on the individual in classic political liberalism, Iris Marion Young develops a theory of group rights concerned with those minority groups in society that suffer oppression and domination. Politically, she takes a relational approach to questions of justice rather than a distributive one, while advocating a politics of difference.[1]

In this framework, Young views justice as the most important political issue, stating that, "the ideal of the just society as eliminating group differences is both unrealistic and undesirable. Instead justice in a group-differentiated society demands social equality of groups, and mutual recognition and affirmation of group differences."[2]

Accordingly, Young defines injustice as oppression and domination and delineates five forms or faces of oppression: exploitation, marginalization, powerlessness, cultural imperialism (invisibility, silencing), and systematic violence.[3] She examines these five faces of oppression as a structural problem, describing them as a condition of social groups and as a comprehensive as well as irreducible set of the various aspects of oppression experienced by social groups.

At the heart of her analysis, Young insists that the rights held by a group, rather than by its individual members, should obtain—a position prompted by her views of a pluralistic human condition in which ways of life and commitments significantly differentiate one group from another. She supports, for example, affirmative action programs not to compensate for past discrimination, but rather, as an important means for undermining oppression, in particular the oppression that results from unconscious aversions and stereotypes. In supporting affirmative action, Young is not blind to its problems, such as the supposedly impartial merit distribution of positions as well as the hierarchical division of labor in the workplace between task-defining and task-executing positions. Nonetheless, Young gives primacy to group rights, recognizing and advocating rights for groups involved in debates about equality and difference in women's liberation, bilingual education, and Native American rights.

When Young refers to a social group, she means "a collective of persons differentiated from at least one other group by cultural forms, practices, or way of life."[4] With this definition in mind and in order to overcome the difficulties created by oppression and domination, Young recognizes group rights, whether organized by gender, ethnicity, race, or sexual orientation. Such a view may prove objectionable on a moral basis, however, to those who view moral agency, including the notions of responsibility and intentional actions, as properly based in the individual rather than in groups.

The power granted to groups, for example, can be wielded over its individual members, thereby diminishing their individual rights and responsibilities, as is most evident in the situation of illiberal minority groups and their practices, discussed later in this chapter. Moreover, as mentioned above, membership in a minority group may be involuntary and not a true case of free association, since individuals may not be able to exit such groups easily, as is possible with a club or association. If the group's authority is oppressive or its way of life intolerable, group members may not have the array of options available to them that other citizens in a liberal society may have.

Beyond these objections, an ontological argument against group rights concerns social groups themselves. That is, to attribute rights to groups supposes that groups have a being and integrity matching those of individuals. This cannot be the case. Groups aggregate individuals and do not themselves simply form a human-like being to whom it would be appropriate to ascribe moral agency, values, reasoning, and moral decision-making. Adjustments have to be made to account for important differences. Indeed, members of a group who are intended to benefit from specific measures may actually criticize or oppose them.

This last observation suggests another essential point. While an individual's proclivity for ethical thought and action can and is also attributed to governments per se, the basic difference between Young's group model and a government is that these groups do not act, even in theory, for the common good, as liberal governments are intended to do.

While social diversity and pluralism reside easily within a liberal societal construct, the claim of equal recognition for groups proves problematic, since the two linchpins of the liberal account, liberty and equality, focus on the autonomous individual as the relevant moral agent. While cultural or religious groups may be allowed special exemption from a duty to obey, the reasons for such exemptions, as some liberal theorists claim, should be based on political prudence or on an estimate of the balance of advantages, and not on the diminishing of individual rights.

Group rights prove fundamentally problematic to a liberal view, then, because when moral standing is accorded to groups, individuals within the group tend to disappear from view. Indeed, social groups are not static, since the individuals comprising them all but guarantee constantly changing and unclear boundaries. Moreover, any social group that may be demarcated may be further subdivided into smaller groupings. Thus, the indeterminacy inherent to social groups and their membership not only creates a problem at the margins, but it also challenges the usefulness of the group concept itself. In other words, an indeterminacy challenge can be directed at the core concept of Young's group rights approach.

For these reasons, the disconcerting arbitrariness characterizing the defining of groups and their membership makes them difficult theoretical units to work with. Young herself acknowledges the analytical porosity in her approach, but insists nonetheless that social groups are real, preferring the position that group rights attempt to achieve equality of opportunity.[5]

COMMUNITIES

Historically, classic liberalism, with its focus on the individual, has been termed a product of the Enlightenment. Communitarianism, with its emphasis on groups or communities, has been seen as an outgrowth of the Reformation.

In contrast to the atomic individualism characteristic of both libertarian and welfare liberal strands of political liberalism, communitarians emphasize our social nature, underscoring the observation that individuals belong to groups or communities.

As part of the contemporary liberal-communitarian debate, I examine here the distributive account of Michael Walzer, a strong value pluralist who constructs a communitarian theory of justice. In *Spheres of Justice,* Walzer engages in a moral inquiry focusing on the concept of equality for purposes of determining what makes a just society.[6] The answers Walzer articulates are grounded in an understanding that "the aim of political egalitarianism is a society free from domination" and that the nature of society and various social meanings of the good are pluralistic.[7]

As its core notion, Walzer's argument proffers complex equality which, for him, has to do with the autonomy of various spheres of justice in which diverse societies may have distributions of different social goods for different internal reasons by different agents to different people, all of which may be different at different times.[8] These spheres may also reflect social meanings within a society, and in so doing, they have a bearing on Walzer's conception of the nature and the point of political society. Fundamentally, in Walzer's view the presence or absence of complex equality within a society serves as an index of whether or not the society is just. His concept of complex equality is patently intricate; its usefulness as the centerpiece of a positive theory of distributive justice is attenuated in part by its complexity, but also due to basic theoretical problems in its formulation.

Walzer's political construct may also be seen as part of the communitarian critique of the universal claims of liberal theory, and especially of Rawls' formulation of the original position in *A Theory of Justice*. Walzer's view is that effective social criticism must derive from and resonate with the traditions and habits of actual people particularly located in time and space. His baseline thus diverges in focus from other communitarian criticisms of the devaluation of community by liberal political thinkers, criticisms that focus on ontological or metaphysical claims about the social nature of the self, as well as on normative claims about the value of community.[9] In contrast to these thinkers, Walzer's claim may be seen as a methodological one, a claim concerned with the importance of social context and human traditions in moral and political reasoning. Indeed, Walzer states that the central process in his theory of distributive justice comes from his view that "[p]eople conceive and create goods, which they then distribute among themselves."[10]

In abbreviated form, the principles of Walzer's theory may be stated, as follows:

1. All the goods with which distributive justice is concerned are social goods.
2. Men and women take on concrete identities, because of the way they conceive and create and then possess and employ social goods.
3. There is no single set of primary social goods, just and unjust, which change over time and differ across all moral and material worlds.
4. It is the meaning of goods that determine their movement.
5. Social meanings are historical in character, and thus, distributions, just and unjust, change over time.
6. When meanings are distinct, distributions must be autonomous.[11]

The political context in which Walzer's distribution of social goods operates needs to be examined too, since it seems that unlike other goods within a society which may be distributed according to some social meaning, membership in the polity appears to be a unique good for Walzer, and accordingly, not so distributable. Problematically, this membership principle seems to be a condition precedent to the operation of Walzer's distributive scheme. In contrast, in *A Theory of Justice,* Rawls solves the problem of membership by assuming a closed society as the political context for the operation of his two principles of justice as fairness. Not satisfied with Rawls' theoretical construct, however, in *Spheres of Justice,* Walzer specifically discusses issues of immigration and citizenship, thereby evaluating membership in the polity as a necessarily unique and primary good.

Walzer's main concern thus focuses on how to prevent the dominance of one particular social good—and thereby of the individuals whose power is based on their possession of this particular social good—over a wide range of other goods. In attempting to reduce such dominance, he develops a notion of complex equality, which in his view more effectively satisfies the diversity of social goods than criteria used in other distributive justice schemes that focus on free exchange, desert, and need.[12] In the course of his deliberations, Walzer's answer to the problem of dominance becomes political pluralism, suggesting at the same time that a capitalist society cannot agree that all goods are translatable into cash values. His political pluralism, however, is premised upon and exhibits an understated value pluralism. And yet, one does not necessarily entail the other.

With Walzer devoting an entire chapter in *Spheres of Justice* to the topic, Jeremy Waldron contends that Walzer's theory of justice is all about money, since Walzer argues that various social goods and their distribution must be viewed in terms of their exchangeability or non-exchangeability for cash. Waldron attributes this preoccupation with wealth to Walzer's concern that currency may become a dominant good, a good whose possession enables individuals to command a wide range of other goods.[13]

Waldron is correct in highlighting Walzer's preoccupation with one social good dominating others in order to guard against an individual or group who may, by controlling or monopolizing that good, control political society. Waldron is further correct in identifying money as a social good that has been a primary object of various theories of distributive justice. Nonetheless, Waldron's reading of Walzer may be extreme. A more charitable reading would interpret Walzer's project as integrating a theory of distributive justice—and such theories are often concerned with the distribution and redistribution of money and wealth and concomitant opportunities—into notions of social equality.

Still, in his critique of the concept of "blocked exchanges" (Walzer's term for those social goods that are not exchangeable for money), Waldron does correctly demonstrate the category confusion that Walzer perpetrates in his development of a list of fourteen goods, many of which are better seen as rights rather than goods. Included in Walzer's list of goods, for example, are the basic liberties of the freedoms of speech, press, religion, and assembly.[14] Waldron underscores his point with the analogy that although Walzer describes the American Bill of Rights as a "series of blocked exchanges," the Founding Fathers did not word the First Amendment thus, "Congress shall not *accept money as an inducement for* abridging the freedom of speech."[15] Consequently, the goods/rights confusion in Walzer's account raises further questions concerning whether political pluralism can exist without value pluralism and what motivation impels his theory of goods.

Regarding Walzer's concept of complex equality, Richard Arneson claims (as Walzer himself acknowledges[16]) that Walzer sets up a concept of simple or literal equality as a foil to identify a society "in which everything is up for sale and every citizen has as much money as any other."[17] In the course of his argument, Walzer objects to the equality of money in particular, because attempting to maintain it leads to state tyranny. After an initial equal distribution of money, individuals within a society—because of their different desires, plans, talent, luck, and ambition—would increasingly develop inequalities in their wealth and incomes. In order to maintain equality of wealth, a large and powerful state that frequently redistributes resources would prove necessary. For Robert Nozick, this would constitute an unjustifiable constraint on personal liberty. This is where Walzer parts company with Nozick—that is, Walzer gives less credence to the inviolability of an individual's rights.

For Walzer, goods in a society are socially constituted, and these distinct social goods are each associated with distinct social practices and a shared understanding of the goods as well as of the proper criteria for their distributions. Contrary to Nozick, then, Walzer believes that a liberal state may intervene to make practices conform to a communal understanding of the goods circulated in various spheres. Thus, it would appear that Walzer would subscribe to the rejoinder made to Nozick that if people care about equality and conceived of it as a public good, they should be allowed to assume restrictions to their liberty in order to maintain that egalitarian condition.

Anchored in an implicit assumption that everyone recognizes the same goods and the same sense of communal life, for Walzer, the proper, just distribution of a good constitutes part of that particular good's social meaning. Complex equality obtains then, when distribution in all spheres in a society is autonomous, and further, distribution is autonomous when goods are distributed according to their social meanings. Asserting that a just society prevails when complex equality exists, however, Walzer's basic formulation of the concept of complex equality and its core place in his positive theory of distributive justice is problematic, generating questions stemming from the defects of his theory, such as: What spheres exist within a society? Who are its members? Who and by what authority are "shared understandings" of goods and their proper distribution developed within a given sphere? How is the product of such autonomous distributions within autonomous spheres determined? Such questions should be important in his approach, because distributions like these function as markers that indicate whether a society is just or unjust. How useful is a concept of equality in formulating the complex equality calculus? In the final analysis, does a just society result from a hitherto questionable complex equality distributive calculus?

As presented here, Walzer's positive theory of distributive justice based on the notion of complex equality, suffers from defects in its conceptual construction and formulation. As he himself suggests in his "Response," written a dozen years after *Spheres of Justice* to address various criticisms of his account, perhaps complex equality may best be viewed as a metaphor and his negative argument in *Spheres of Justice* taken most appropriately as interpretative social criticism. We are left with the problem of evaluating how useful his social critique may be.

GENDER

Contemporary discussions of gender have moved beyond feminism in the narrow sense to include issues of gender identity and sexual orientation, some of which have been associated with gender fluidity and human rights arguments.

In her group rights theory, Iris Marion Young presents the traditional argument for feminism when examining how gender defines women as oppressed and dominated, thereby necessitating special representation and rights, including the appropriate institutional mechanisms and public resources to exercise these group rights. In contrast to Young, Susan Okin develops a liberal feminist account grounded in the autonomous individual. While Young seeks to replace the liberal-communitarian debate with the politics of difference, Okin examines different cultural groups mainly to ensure that no gender discrimination persists.[18] While contrasting in approach, both feminist thinkers point to the challenges of maintaining group rights without reducing the agency of the individual and to the problems resulting from theorizing on the basis of a homogenous society, such as presented in Plato and Aristotle, which marginalizes the complexities attendant to diverse or pluralistic societies.

With respect to feminist concerns, Susan Okin recognizes clashes with multicultural concerns and argues that cultures are suffused with practices of gender, with some cultures endorsing the control of men over women in various ways, often informally in the private sphere of domestic life. If, for example, more powerful male members of a culture determine or articulate the group's beliefs, practices, and interests for the good of the group, the group rights are anti-feminist. Critically, a multicultural approach, Okin contends, does not take cognizance of this problem because it treats culture as monolithic, without taking into account the broad differences within particular minority cultures and because multicultural concerns play out in the public rather than the private sphere.

For Okin, problems multiply as the question of how to assess patriarchy in different cultural contexts is played against defining what constitutes harm. In balancing between cultural accommodation and other social costs, the role of intention becomes critical. In such situations, Okin explores the dilemma of what should be done when the claims of minority cultures or religious groups clash with the norm of gender equality, conceding that the claims of feminism and multiculturalism are not often easily reconciled. Nonetheless, while Okin argues that the state should support the liberal priority with respect to the feminist charge that women should not be disadvantaged because of their gender and that they should have the opportunity to have lives as fulfilling and freely chosen as men's lives, she also argues for the multicultural claim made in liberal democracies as ensuring the individual rights of members in minority cultural groups, and that these rights should be protected by special group rights or privileges.

This lack of attention to the private sphere, however, proves to be a significant concern since personal, sexual, and reproductive life functions frequently constitute the dominant theme and central point of contention. Indeed, many cultural and religious groups demonstrate a great deal of concern with personal law, such as is the case with Islamic Sharia laws, pertaining to such matters as marriage, divorce, child custody, gender propriety, as well as the division and control of family property. Consequently, with respect to power, cultural practices have a much greater negative impact on women than on men.

In her feminist framework, then, Okin argues that one of the principal aims of culture is to control women. The drive to control women remains particularly strong in various fundamentalist versions of many religions. Citing examples, she contends that sometimes culture and tradition are so closely linked to the control of women that they are equated. Okin recognizes that Western liberal democracies depart more from patriarchal models than is the case with many other nations. However, pointing to Will Kymlicka (whose multicultural account is treated later in this chapter as a representative multiculturalist), Okin contends that multiculturalism still does not examine the relation between gender and culture or the tensions between feminism and multiculturalism.

Okin recognizes that Kymlicka accords various group rights based on individual rights, but confines such privileges and protections to cultural groups that are internally liberal. Consequently, he would not allow such rights to oppressive groups. However, as Okin further argues, Kymlicka fails to acknowledge that the subordination of women is often informal and private and that, critically, his public sex discrimination test, if applied to the private spheres of the world's cultures, would pass in few cultures. She concludes that minority group rights are not part of the solution of the endemic problem of gender discrimination and may, in fact, exacerbate the problem.

CRITICAL RACE THEORY

Critical race theory, or CRT, centers on societal dynamics in the United States and denotes a broad conceptual framework built to examine racial bias in laws, social institutions, and structures, as well as to consider political and economic inequalities. More specifically, critical race theorists hold that racism is inherent in the law and legal institutions of the United States insofar as they function to create and maintain social, economic, and political inequalities between whites and nonwhites, especially African Americans. Further, CRT theorists are generally dedicated to applying their understanding of the institutional or structural nature of racism to the concrete (if distant) goal of eliminating all race-based and other unjust hierarchies.

Scholars of CRT view race as a social construct with no biological basis. Rather, racism and disparate racial outcomes are the result of complex, changing, and often subtle social and institutional dynamics. CRT theorists further argue that the social and legal construction of race advances the interests of white people at the expense of people of color, and that the liberal notion of American law as "neutral" plays a significant role in maintaining a racially unjust social order, where formally color-blind laws continue to inscribe racially discriminatory outcomes.[19]

Critical Race Theory had its beginnings in the mid-1970s in the writings of several American legal scholars, including Derrick Bell, Alan Freeman, Kimberlé Crenshaw, Richard Delgado, Cheryl Harris, Charles R. Lawrence III, Mari Matsuda, and Patricia J. Williams. CRT also draws from the work of thinkers such as Antonio Gramsci, Sojourner Truth, Frederick Douglass, and W. E. B. Du Bois, as well as from the Black Power, Chicano, and radical feminist movements from the 1960s and 1970s.

Academic critics argue that Critical Race Theory is based on storytelling instead of evidence and reason, rejects truth and merit, and is positioned against liberalism. Other recent critics of this school of thought include politically conservative U.S. lawmakers who have sought to ban or restrict the instruction of CRT education in primary and secondary schools, in public universities and colleges, as well as to eliminate CRT findings in relevant training practices of federal agencies. Advocates of such bans argue that CRT is false, anti-American, villainizes white people, promotes radical leftism, and indoctrinates children. Some have made CRT a catchall target for opposition to equity efforts, affirmative action and what some identify as "wokeness."

Currently, CRT is certainly politically controversial. While CRT theorists have criticized liberalism as the hegemonic ideology of the West, its opponents often argue that any form of "race consciousness" is in itself racist, thereby claiming that anti-racist reforms, like affirmative action or housing subsidies, provide temporary deviations from the normative ideals of neutrality. Ontologically, however, liberal ideals that imagine individuals abstractly outside of their historical and social contexts thwart efforts to address the effects of historical legacies on current social relations, property distributions, group welfare and security, and the determination of merit.

In 1984, Richard Delgado attempted to show that the academic scholarship that pursues anti-racist ends is hobbled by an incapacity of effective self-reflection. He set out to find the top twenty law review articles on civil rights—those most often cited and those published in the most well-established journals—and found that all were written by white men. Moreover, this "elaborate minuet" of exclusively internal engagement regarding the best means to move forward on racial justice, albeit strong, revealed a considerable lack. How could it be, Delgado wondered, that even an idea such as having a "withered self-concept" would be best represented in the work of white authors citing other white authors rather than the important work by people of color on the phenomenal effect of racist societies?

Anecdotally, when he asked the author of one article on this topic why theorists such as W. E. B. Du Bois, Kenneth Clark, Frantz Fanon or others were not cited, the author explained that he preferred the source he cited, because it was "so elegant." Thus, for Delgado, such criticism appears as a suspect species of *ad hominem* argument, creating concerns about the politics of citation. Moreover, from Delgado's perspective, ruling out considerations of social identity in the development of intellectual work diminishes the quality of that intellectual work, but in a manner that liberal premises could never reveal. Judging which are the top articles by the number of their citations may appear to be a neutral standard, but in fact, doing so perpetuates injustice while concealing that injustice.

Connected to this issue has been the ongoing problem of how merit is conceptualized. If conventional hiring processes, for example, do not consider the social identity of the candidate, then preferential hiring is defined a deviation from the norm and candidates must meet a higher bar to establish even temporary legitimacy. With examples like these Critical Race theorists have endeavored to show that merit-based decisions often promulgate implicit racism.

CULTURE

In *Multicultural Citizenship, Will Kymlicka observes* that most countries today are culturally diverse: there exist about 200 independent states containing over 600 living languages and 5,000 ethnic groups. Such cultural diversity gives rise to important and potentially divisive questions involving regional autonomy, political representation, land claims, education curriculum, language rights, integration, and immigration and naturalization policies.[20]

In his work, Kymlicka defines *culture* as a nation or a people, conceived of as "an intergenerational community, more or less institutionally complete, occupying a given territory or homeland, sharing a distinct language and history."[21] As an empirical observation, Kymlicka notes that in the modern world, just as societal cultures are almost invariably national cultures, so too nations are almost invariably social cultures. Further, with the term *multicultural*, Kymlicka designates a state in which the "members either belong to different nations (a multination state), or have emigrated from different nations (a polyethnic state), and . . . this fact is an important aspect of personal identity and political life."[22]

In isolating common threads found in both Kymlicka's multicultural thesis and other proponents of multiculturalism, Paul Kelly identifies two roles of culture:

1. In terms of a methodological argument, similar to the arguments of communitarians regarding liberalism and social atomism, multiculturalists view culture as the context that shapes an individual's identity and is inseparable from who we are as persons.

2. In terms of a social thesis, multiculturalists view culture as providing a moral resource, in addition to providing a context for personal and moral identity.[23]

Indeed, for Kymlicka, culture provides the moral resources (values, beliefs, and obligations) from which an individual may construct an autonomous and valuable life. By providing the moral resources to make choices and thus promote an individual's autonomy, Kymlicka argues that culture constitutes part of a liberal platform from which an individual may engage the world. From identifying the problem set, Kymlicka moves on to setting himself the task of "finding morally defensible and politically viable answers to these issues [which pose] . . . the greatest challenge facing democracies today."[24] The political solution he devises in his account of justice is to supplement traditional human rights with minority cultural rights.

Perhaps overstating his disagreement, Brian Barry avers that, on the contrary, with regard to modern liberal societies, "the notion that membership in some community is a constitutive element in anybody's identity is vastly implausible."[25] In addition to contesting the ontological question of whether culture is constituent or not of the self, also at the conceptual level of minority cultural rights, Kymlicka and Barry part ways as well in their broader liberal frameworks.

Thus, Barry advocates a difference-blind approach to culture in the political realm, and more generally, he rejects group-based rights as antithetical to the universalist liberal project, which he views as based on the individual. Consequently, he claims that Kymlicka's views are not liberal at all, since they are not universalist in nature and allow for cultural relativism. More narrowly, Barry believes that the task of a just society is to provide for a fair and equal distribution of social goods.

In contrast, Kymlicka ascribes to a rights-based, distributive account of justice whereby rights are distributed equally to citizens within a multicultural political order, unless one is a member of a qualified minority culture, in which case additional rights obtain. In a classic liberal response, in which the concept of negative liberty occupies much of the political terrain, Barry accuses Kymlicka here of posing a false choice between liberalism as autonomy and liberalism as tolerance, asserting that claims for cultural rights and for equality of treatment are incompatible. Further along these lines, Kymlicka and Iris Marion Young share the view that, psychologically, individuals develop in an influence-generating social context. In response, Barry argues against politically transferring identity development into group rights; rights should be defined as situated in the individual, rather than groups.

To bolster his approach, Kymlicka develops a taxonomy of minority cultural groups, so that a national minority or minority nation comprises a people present at the establishment of a new nation, who had a prior history of self-government, as effected through institutions, and who were bound together by a common culture and language.[26] He proffers the nation of Canada as an example to illustrate his criteria, in which two such minority nations exist.

Without going into detail regarding Kymlicka's view of Canada, Young criticizes the dichotomy that Kymlicka creates between nation and ethnicity as "creat[ing] too rigid and even contradictory an account of multicultural citizenship. Loosening this distinction and creating a continuum would better serve Kymlicka's purposes."[27] By way of example, she points to the case of African Americans, who are neither an incorporated national group nor an immigrant group, but descendants of slaves, who had been "transported to a new land by the most brutal force, violently deprived of their original cultures, but also forced to remain segregated from the new culture."[28] Young's point is that a rigid choice vs. chance principle used to generate the category of a minority nation confuses the notion of multiculturalism. Cultural minorities vary along a continuum including their participation in the national culture.

While Young articulates reservations regarding Kymlicka's characterization of multiculturalism, Barry attacks Kymlicka's account along the lines of category confusion. That is, he accuses Kymlicka of equating nationhood with cultural distinctiveness by definitional fiat, and he takes Kymlicka to task for his multination concept and for using Canada as an example. Further, with regard to Kymlicka's concept of polyethnicity, whereby members of a polyethnic state emigrated from different nations (United States, Canada, and Australia), Barry remains uneasy. He characterizes Kymlicka's cultural conception as inapposite, and perhaps more damning, as lacking explanatory power in the case of the United States, where discrimination against African Americans has not occurred along cultural lines at all. In addition, with regard to the taxonomy of Kymlicka's cultural communities, Barry points to the slipperiness and arbitrariness of the immigrant-national communities typology in three of Kymlicka's examples involving Spanish-speaking immigrants and national minorities in the United States.[29]

As discussed earlier, while some commentators continue to view liberty as the key concept fueling liberalism, others claim that the core value of liberalism is articulated in equality rather than liberty. Further, among liberal egalitarians, some emphasize the substantive moral value of the concept (equality of concern and respect), while others concentrate on the political nature of the concept, focusing on the fair distribution of rights and the economic resources necessary to protect individuals.

Kymlicka is an egalitarian in the Dworkian sense, since he accepts the idea of equality of concern and respect as the basis of any viable moral and political theory. For a multicultural society, the problem of a distributive approach to justice remains in determining what should be distributed in order for a just society to provide each person equal concern and respect. Here, cultural rights provide Kymlicka with the theoretical underpinning for opportunity egalitarianism. For Kymlicka, that is, respect for an individual's culture provides a significant platform allowing for the requisite equal concern and respect for the individual. In this context, Kymlicka defines culture as a building block integral to how he views equality of concern and respect for the individual, thereby providing the basis for his positing of cultural rights in a liberal political framework.

Ultimately, multiculturalists regard Barry's faith in the robust enforcement of classic difference-blind liberal principles as wanting. In developing his thesis, Barry does minimize the problematic nature of multicultural concerns, especially with respect to questions of customs practiced by illiberal religions in liberal societies, thereby evoking a situation reminiscent of the difficulties encountered when trying to apply Mill's liberty principle to determine what distinguishes harm from mere offense. Indeed, Barry appears to be somewhat oblivious to the depth of multicultural issues.

As may be derived from this discussion, the complexities involved in any group approach stem in large part from its intermediate positioning between individuals and states. Like a state, a group can exercise some sort of control over individuals, and like individuals, a group can act to effect ethos-based guidance. However, unlike a state, a group is neither geopolitically circumscribed nor acting in the best interests of its members based on law within that territory, and unlike individuals, a group does not have the flexibility to make moral decisions.

Such views provide support for the designation of the individual as the proper bearer of rights in political society, and not groups. As lodged in the individual, the question of just or unjust actions can be most effectively determined along moral lines, with cultural contexts and traditions including those of both groups and states, functioning as critical touchstones. Issues regarding the oppression of groups—whether by race, religion, gender, or culture—may be addressed by integrating the concepts of tolerance and social diversity in the formulation of the politically liberal platform presented here, shoring up the elements of negative liberty and equality of concern and respect, as the political context for the theory of law presented in this study.

NOTES

1. See Iris Marion Young, *Justice and the Politics of Difference* (Oxford: Oxford University Press, 1990).
2. Young 1990: ch. 2.

3. Ibid., 190.
4. Ibid., 173.
5. Ibid., ch. 2.
6. Michael Walzer, *Spheres of Justice* (New York: Basic Books, 1983).
7. Ibid., xiii.
8. See Michael Walzer, "Response," in eds. David Miller and Michael Walzer, *Pluralism, Justice and Equality* (Oxford: Oxford University Press, 1995), 283.
9. See Michael Sandel, *Liberalism and the Limits of Justice* (Cambridge: Cambridge University Press, 1998); also see Stephen Mulhall and Adam Swift, *Liberals and Communitarians* (Oxford: Blackwell, 1996).
10. Walzer 1983: 4.
11. Ibid., 5–8.
12. Ibid., 21–26.
13. See Jeremy Waldron, "Money and Complex Equality," in eds. David Miller and Michael Walzer, *Pluralism, Justice and Equality* (Oxford: Oxford University Press, 1995), 144–170.
14. Walzer 1983: 100–103.
15. Waldron 1995: 156, emphasis in the original.
16. Ibid., 283.
17. Richard Arneson, "Against Complex Equality," in eds. David Miller and Michael Walzer 1995: 227–228.
18. See Susan Okin, *Is Multicultualism Bad for Women?* (Princeton: Princeton University Press, 1999).
19. See Richard Delgado and Jean Stephancic, *Critical Race Theory* (New York: New York University Press, 2012).
20. Will Kymlicka, *Multicultural Citizenship* (Oxford: Oxford University Press, 1995).
21. Ibid., 18.
22. Ibid.
23. Paul Kelly, "Introduction," in ed. Paul Kelly, *Multiculturalism Reconsidered* (Cambridge: Polity Press, 2002), 5–9.
24. Kymlicka 1995: 1.
25. Brian Barry, "Second Thoughts," in Kelly 2002: 223.
26. See Kymlicka 1995: chap. 2.
27. Iris Marion Young, "A Multicultural Continuum," *Constellation* 4;1 (1997): 49.
28. Ibid., 50.
29. See Brian Barry, *Culture and Equality* (Cambridge: Polity Press, 2001).

Chapter 10

International Relations

There are about 200 separate nation-states. How may relations between and among these states be guided or regulated? What mechanisms and institutions may be positioned or promoted to secure a peaceful, stable world order?

Thoughts on what we now call international relations have been articulated since at least the fifth century B.C.E. Thucydides' *History of the Peloponnesian War*, Book I, for example, describes human nature's priority of self-interest over morality as a foundational issue, associating the absence of government with anarchy, and expressing security as an especial concern. Further, in expressing skepticism about the relevance of morality in international affairs, Thucydides relates the Melian Dialogue, the classic debate between idealist and realist views, to explore whether international politics should be based in a moral order derived from principles of justice, or whether such matters merely provide the arena for conflicting interests and power.[1]

In their roughly contemporary accounts of justice, both Plato and Aristotle occupy the position of political idealists, in that they believe that there are universal moral values in which political life can be based. While idealism in international politics has no commonly accepted meaning, generally, such idealism seeks to advance certain ideals or moral goals such as peace and stability, to make the world a more just place to live. Ontologically, the concept may be interpreted to promote a cosmopolitan and harmonious world order. In contrast, the realist approach to international relations emphasizes the role of power in the development of norms of justice. Its theoretical arguments are found in the widely known tradition including Machiavelli and extending at least as far back as Glaucon's challenge to Socrates.[2]

REALISM AND COSMOPOLITANISM

The two main accounts of international relations are known as realism and idealism or cosmopolitanism. Both accounts attempt to address the question of what political order among nations may obtain. Put another way, assuming that a Hobbesian state of nature does not adequately define international relationships, the task is to identify the appropriate political conditions and institutions for global order and security. Outside of the United Nations, which has significant limitations with respect to meting out such global demands, there is no single existing supranational cooperative scheme that regulates relations among nations, including questions of war and peace.

Suggested by the United Nations' limits, neither a realist nor a cosmopolitan view can suffice. Instead, I argue that the concept of due concern and respect may help guide just international relations. Further, communications in the substantive sense of a method of resolving disputes, as well as an instrumental sense of conveying values of international institutions through time, may play a key role in establishing and maintaining a peaceful, stable world order. Thus, a liberal political order with components of liberty and equality, as defined through tolerance and diversity, may be mapped onto an international format in questions of justice among nations, perhaps even onto existing institutions, such as the U.N.'s International Court of Justice, as well as more limited international governance structures.

In contemporary times, Charles Beitz sets up a Hobbesian framework as the basis for the realist view in international relations: international relations between states exist in a Hobbesian state of nature, a state of anarchic war where might makes right.[3] Such a view of international relations is realist in the sense that it advocates viewing states as they "really are," rather than portraying them in idealistic circumstances or according to their purported ideals. States are given, in effect, an exemption from the moral constraints that apply to individuals. As a result, the rulers of states are guided by and morally bound to only the interests of their own nations without regard to the rights and interests of other nations. In other words, states defend and promote domestic national interests in an anarchic international arena, thereby echoing a Hobbesian view.[4]

Arguing against such Hobbesian anarchy, Beitz develops a contrasting and normative view in order to provide a moral basis for guiding international relations. He begins his project by postulating that for the Hobbesian state of nature analogy to work at the level of international relations, four propositions must obtain, as follows:[5]

1. The actors in international relations are states.
2. States have relatively equal power (the weakest can defeat the strongest).
3. States are independent of each other in the sense that they can order their internal (i.e., non-security matters) affairs independently of the internal policies of other actors.

4. In the absence of a superior power capable of enforcing rules of cooperation, states cannot count on reciprocal compliance to such rules.

Beitz then makes the case that none of these Hobbesian conditions obtain in contemporary international relations.[6] By successfully making the point, Beitz believes he defeats the basis of realist claims and its pervasive view that international relations should be treated as in a constant state of war. To support his position with regard to negating the third Hobbesian condition, Beitz shifts his ground from interdependence and cooperation (a contingent platform) to rely more upon the Kantian notion detailing the capacities of individuals to act as moral agents in order to provide a moral grounding for his cosmopolitan theory of international relations.[7]

He acknowledges, however, that rejecting a Hobbesian state of nature approach to international relations does not mean that the international realm should be analogous to a domestic society for all purposes. Rather, he contends that it would be better to understand international relations as "occupying a middle ground . . . there are, in international relations, both shared and opposed interests, providing a basis both for cooperation and competition. But effective institutions for exploring bases of cooperation are insufficiently developed."[8]

Rather than accepting a Hobbesian state of nature framework, that is, Beitz looks to the natural law tradition of John Locke and Samuel Pufendorf, for whom moral obligations exist even within a state of nature,[9] as he seeks to articulate a normative basis for international politics. If nations do have moral obligations to other nations, then what type of political order allows nations to fulfill such moral obligations?

By advocating the extension of the difference principle of justice as fairness to an international context, at times Beitz seems more Rawlsian than Rawls. That is, Beitz ignores that the basic liberty principle in Rawls' formulation of justice as fairness obtains domestically only under special conditions. Even Rawls himself does not advocate the exporting of the difference principle globally.

Beitz nonetheless contends that the existing resource endowment of states is, to use a Rawlsian phrase, "morally arbitrary," and therefore not an issue to which states would willingly wish to devote their energies. Further, Beitz argues that the interdependence among nations actually means that the idea of a self-contained, insular society must be abandoned. This leads Beitz to conclude that distributive justice must apply among nations, and the Rawlsian difference principle should privilege the least advantaged globally, culminating in a radical redistribution of resources. As also indicated above, at this point, Beitz grounds his reasoning less on the contingent notion of the interdependence of peoples and more along Kantian lines.

That is, Beitz attempts to develop a normative approach to international relations that results in a moral cosmopolitan theory that reaches back to a Lockean natural law tradition in which moral obligations exist even in a state of nature. By linking the moral basis of his cosmopolitan doctrine to a universal feature of political liberalism—equal concern and respect for the individual—Beitz nuances the approach to develop a brand of cosmopolitan liberalism. In addressing the question of global obligations of justice, however, Beitz seems primarily focused upon the redistribution of natural resources from wealthier nations to the least advantaged nations. His distributive concern seeks to eliminate the political (states and institutions) from the resultant scheme, creating problems, especially with respect to his theory's efficacy in regard to the subject of distributions (natural resources) as well as with respect to the mechanisms deployed to effect such distributions. Related to these pragmatic infelicities, problems emerge on the theoretical level as well, with his attempted extraction and deployment of the Rawlsian difference principle out of its original domestic political context and with the moral universality of his claims.

Interestingly, as Beitz's initial attempt to fit international distributive justice into a Rawlsian formulation suggests, a weakness in Rawls' theory resides in the attempt to base the requirements of justice, in the special conditions where justice as fairness would obtain, on contractual foundations of mutual advantage, since such conditions are morally contingent. For Rawls, the difference principle articulated in *A Theory of Justice* expresses a relatively egalitarian concept of distributive justice characteristic of liberal political theory, one that has no international analogue. Rawls does, however, provide for a duty of assistance in *The Law of Peoples*, which would require a greater level of international transfers than currently exist, but importantly, he sees the global extension of the difference principle as incorrect. Instead, in *The Law of Peoples*, Rawls develops principles to guide a liberal society in the conduct of its foreign policy, including relations with other states, its contributions to forming and interpreting international law, and its views about the structure and policies of international organizations. These principles are intended to direct and limit a liberal society's concept of its own national interest.

LAWS AND CUSTOMS OF PEOPLES

In *The Law of Peoples*, Rawls takes a position on global justice somewhere between the realist and cosmopolitan approaches to international relations. While domestically, his concern is indeed to develop a theory of justice, internationally, Rawls' arguments revolve about concepts such as legitimacy and the laws of peoples.[10]

As suggested, Beitz's initial attempt to fit international distributive justice into a Rawlsian formulation reveals a weakness in Rawls' theory. That is, Rawls attempts to base the requirements of justice in the special conditions where justice as fairness would obtain, on contractual foundations of mutual advantage, since such conditions are morally contingent. For Rawls, the difference principle articulated in *A Theory of Justice* expresses a relatively egalitarian concept of distributive justice characteristic of liberal political theory, one that has no international analogue.

Rawls does, however, provide for a duty of assistance in *The Law of Peoples,* which would require a greater level of international transfers than currently exist, but importantly, he sees the global extension of the difference principle as incorrect. Instead, in *The Law of Peoples*, Rawls develops principles to guide a liberal society in its conduct of foreign policy, including relations with other states, the policy's contributions to forming and interpreting international law, and its views on the structure and policies of international organizations. These principles are intended to direct and limit a liberal society's concept of its own national interest.

The Law of Peoples, then, may be seen as an extension of Rawls' *Political Liberalism,* with the same emphasis on politics and institutions transferred to the international realm.[11] In effect, his law of peoples presents an analogue in foreign affairs to his concept of social justice in a society's domestic affairs. Indeed, by *"the law of peoples,"* Rawls seems to mean a society with a common political culture organized as a state by means of a social contract doctrine, with "peoples" replacing the "persons" in his earlier formulation. Principles of *The Law of Peoples* thus result from a hypothetical agreement among representatives of various peoples meeting in what Rawls postulated as an original position. In the international original position, Rawls includes representatives of both liberal and hierarchal societies, provided that in both cases, the societies are well ordered.

Centrally, the problem that Rawls addresses in *The Law of Peoples* is the fact of pluralism, specifically the pluralism of cultural and religious conceptions of the good society as found internationally. Rawls further delimits global pluralism to reasonable pluralism, whereby a peaceful international life is one in which liberal societies may flourish. Given the fact of pluralism, he argues there must be a basis upon which reasonable and decent peoples can cooperate willingly. He thus articulates eight principles to provide a solution to the problem, and he contends that representatives in an international original position would agree to a similar list of principles, as pertaining to nations:[12]

1. Peoples are free and independent, and their freedom and independence are respected by other peoples.

2. Peoples are to observe treaties and undertakings.
3. Peoples are equal and are parties to the agreements that bind them.
4. Peoples are to observe a duty of nonintervention.
5. 5. Peoples have the right of self-defense but no right to instigate war for reasons other than self-defense.
6. Peoples are to honor human rights.
7. Peoples are to observe certain specified restrictions in the conduct of war.
8. Peoples have a duty to assist other peoples living under unfavorable conditions that prevent their experiencing just or decent political and social governance.

As such, Rawls' law of peoples essentially divides into ideal and nonideal theory. Consisting of principles that apply in an idealized political society of well-ordered domestic societies in which the principles are fully complied with, ideal theories (also like those of Plato and Aristotle) depict societies that operate in conditions that favor just (or decent, hierarchically structured) institutions. Nonetheless, the principles of ideal theory, Rawls contends, also apply to conduct in the nonideal world in two ways: (a) by regulating relations among well-ordered, liberal, and hierarchical societies; and (b) by establishing goals for such well-ordered, liberal, and hierarchical societies to pursue with societies that are not well ordered. The most general such goal is to "bring all societies eventually to honor [the law of peoples] and to be full and self-standing members of the society of well-ordered peoples, and so secure human rights everywhere." This goal also serves as the foundation for international distributive obligations of well-to-do societies, as such actions fall under Rawls' principle to provide assistance, specifically to those societies facing unfavorable conditions, for developing institutions capable of satisfying their own peoples' needs and human rights.

WAR

In developing his theory of global political justice, Beitz explains that he does not focus on questions of war and peace, one of the central concerns of international relations. He accounts for this omission on two grounds: first, scholarship on just war theory has received considerable philosophical attention in recent years. Second, any just war theory must rest upon a more general theory of international right, which is what he prefers to discuss.

Yet, to reiterate, war is central to international relations. In approaches to international relations, war is widely understood as an actual, intentional, and widespread armed conflict between nations, states, or groups within a nation or state. Further, looking beyond Carl von Clausewitz's dictum defining war as constituting an extension of policy, it can be argued that war concerns the creation of policy; in other words, war entails governance. Just war theory (*ius ad bellum*), which has Greco-Roman roots and has been developed especially in the framework of a Christian theological tradition, accepts the notion that while war is evil, it may represent the lesser of two evils.

The goal of just war theory is to develop criteria to determine whether a war is morally justifiable, including whether there is a right to go to war (*ius ad bellum*), the right conduct in war (*ius in bello*), and more recently, the morality of post-war settlement and reconstruction (*ius post bellum*). Consideration of whether a war constitutes a just war (*ius ad bellum*) includes a variety of moral, political, and pragmatic considerations, such as: Will the war be fought for a good cause or out of good intentions? Will the war be declared by a lawful authority? Have all other ways of resolving the conflict been explored? Is there a reasonable chance of success in conducting the war? Are the means of the conduct of war commensurate with its goals?

As self-professed Kantians, John Rawls and Michael Walzer support the concept of a just war.[13] In reviewing Kant's own views on the topic, however, debate ensues, with some commentators believing that he embraced the concept, referring to "The Doctrine of Right," in Part One of the *Metaphysics of Morals*, while others point to Kant's Perpetual Peace as evidence that he rejected the notion, disclaiming the views of just war proponents Grotius, Vattel, and Pufendorf as "sorry comforters."[14]

INTERNATIONAL LAW

What role should international law play in relations among nations? What are the proper goals of international law? What are its proper domains—international human rights law, international environmental law, international criminal law?

First, the criteria for determining the existence of statehood are well-established in customary international law: a defined territory, a permanent population, an effective government, the capacity to enter into relations with other states, and independence.[15] This definition of statehood may be seen to set the baseline for the idea of sovereignty, which may also include the notion of self-determination. Yet recently, a legal challenge to the concept of sovereignty emerges in the phenomenon of international organizations. What are the boundaries between domestic and international legal spheres, for example, in the case of basic human rights, as articulated by the United Nations?[16]

It is understood that international law lacks a centralized enforcement mechanism for the agreements made and customs acknowledged by and among nation-states. In recent times, however, there has been more enforcement through the United Nations and its Security Council for collective peace and security, and through the International Court of Justice and other courts and tribunals for dispute resolution over matters such as human rights, trade, investments, and international crimes.

Assessing various aspects of international law raises the question of legitimacy. This assessment may be descriptive, in the sense of an international legal norm enjoying legitimacy to the extent that it exerts a high level of "compliance pull" among international actors,[17] or such an assessment may be normative, in the sense of international law generating reasons for action, or at an extreme, justifying a "right to rule."[18]

Thus, one prominent approach traces legitimacy of international law to the actual consent (explicit or implicit) of its subjects. Certainly, consent plays a prominent role in the formation of international treaties.[19] As to customary international law, however, consent as a basis becomes more problematic.[20] For instance, why are newly-formed states bound by rules for which they had neither the opportunity to consent, nor the time to form beliefs or positions? Critics of customary international law state that the existence and content of such international legal norms are indeterminate and violate notions of notice and clarity.

H.L.A. Hart makes the case that international law should be seen as "primitive law," in that it does not have secondary rules—that is, for Hart, law has primary rules which impose obligations, and secondary rules which are rules about rules, pertaining to the ways in which primary rules may be identified (under his well-known rule of recognition), changed, and adjudicated.[21] Interestingly, since Hart wrote *The Concept of Law*, the Vienna Convention on the Law of Treaties has been adopted by member nations, and it is generally seen to reflect customary international law. Moreover, it contains both Hartian primary and secondary rules, as it itself is a treaty about treaties, their adoption, amendment and interpretation.

One alternative to consent or voluntarist theories has been posed by Joseph Raz in his "service conception of authority," in which Raz states that "A has legitimate authority over B if the latter would better conform with reasons that apply to him if he intends to be guided by A's directives that if he does not."[22] How do you integrate this theory with proper respect for sovereignty? Can any domain of international law achieve legitimacy in these terms, especially given the absence of reliable enforcement mechanisms at the global level?

Yet another way to deal with legitimacy in international law without consent as a basis is expressed by Ronald Dworkin, who claims that we can discern binding requirements of international law by asking what tests or arguments should a hypothetical court adopt to determine the rights and obligations of states and other actors such that it would be appropriate for it to enforce coercively.[23] Dworkin's hypothetical court, however, suffers from significant indeterminacy, with the legitimacy question centered on the judicial enforcement of law.

Finally, some believe there is a close link between democracy and legitimacy, at least in the domestic arena. In the international context, however, significant problems in this framework emerge, such as whether non-democratic states should have full sovereign rights and whether international law should encourage the spread of democracy globally, for instance, by promoting and upholding a human right to democracy.[24]

THE RULE OF LAW

The term "rule of law" may be seen as an ideal of political morality and refers to the primacy of laws and institutions of the legal system in the structure of governance. The term has been used with a variety of meanings. One question that arises is whether the rule of law extends to the evaluation of international law, and if so, under what interpretation and with what particular implications.

Legal theorists who explore what the rule of law means can be arranged along a line from thin (formal procedural) to thick (substantive) versions. Thin accounts of the rule of law, for example, emphasize formal-procedural accounts of the rule of law. At the opposite end, thick accounts favor substantive accounts of the rule of law, sometimes concluding that the rule of law does not apply to international law, since it imposes demands that cannot conceivably be made of international, as opposed to domestic, law.

One such advocate of a thick account of the rule of law identifies five requirements imposed by the rule of law:[25]

> First, that no one is outside the law, still less above it; second, that it is by some means or in some sense democratic, at least in the sense of being accountable to others; third, that its instituted authorities—notably the Security Council—are in principle subject to legal constraint; fourth, that there is something like a constitution of international society; and fifth, that society is not irremediably unjust.

In sum, as to the rule of law, for Plato the true constitution of a city-state is under the rule of a philosopher-king. One can infer that he does not believe in the rule of law as providing the best method of obtaining justice even among law-abiding societies (kingship, aristocracy, and tyranny).[26] For Aristotle, the rule of *aristoi*, the best persons, represents the ideal constitution, one in which citizens are fully virtuous; rejected are the rival claims of the rule of law, as well as a supremely virtuous king.[27] Although John Locke may be seen as a supporter of the rule of law, he makes his views more complicated by his account of pre-political property rights.[28]

In contemporary times, many view the rule of law as an analogue for law and order, in effect positioning legislators, judges, and the coercive powers of government as supreme.[29] Some break down the term as principles that address the formal aspects of governance by law, while others emphasize principles that address procedural aspects of the legal system, and still others call for principles that embrace certain substantive values.[30] To the extent to which the term implies the supremacy of law and legal systems in political rule, I disagree. Instead of the rule of law conceived in one of the foregoing manners, I believe that law should serve the demands of justice, as argued in Part V of this study *infra*.

NOTES

1. Thucydides, *History of the Peloponnesian War*, trans. Martin Hammond (Oxford: Oxford University Press, 2009).
2. See Niccolò Machiavelli, *The Prince*, trans. W. K. Marriot (London: Penguin Books, 2004)); also see Plato, *The Republic*, trans. Desmond Lee (London: Penguin Books, 2003).
3. See Charles Beitz, *Political Theory and International Relations* (Princeton: Princeton University Press, 1999).
4. See Hobbes, *Leviathan*, ed. J. C. A. Gaskin (Oxford: Oxford University Press, 1998).
5. Beitz 1999: 36.
6. Contradicting these four propositions, e.g., are: (1) international alliances and coalitions; (2) vast disparities of national power; (3) United Nations, World Bank, International Fund, et al.; (4) international postal service, World Health Organization, European Union, et al.
7. See Charles Beitz, "International Liberalism and Distributive Justice," *World Politics* 51;2 (1999): 269–296.
8. Beitz 1999: 50.
9. See John Locke, *Second Treatise of Government*, ed. Crawford Macpherson (Indianapolis: Hackett Publishing, 1980); also see Samuel Pufendorf, *On the Duty of Man and Citizen According to Natural Law,* ed. James Tully, trans. Michael Silverthorne (Cambridge: Cambridge University Press, 1991).
10. See John Rawls, *The Law of Peoples* (Cambridge: Harvard University Press, 1997).

11. See John Rawls, *Political Liberalism* (New York: Columbia University Press, 1993).

12. Rawls 1997: 37.

13. Ibid.; also see Michael Walzer, *Just and Unjust Wars* (New York: Basic Books, 2015).

14. See Howard Williams, *Kant and the End of War* (New York: Palgrave Macmillan, 2012); also see Pauline Kleingeld, *Kant and Cosmopolitanism* (New York: Cambridge University Press, 2012).

15. See James Crawford, *The Creation of States in International Law* (Oxford: Clarendon Press, 2006).

16. See the Universal Declaration of Human Rights of the United Nations consisting of 30 Articles passed by the United Nations General Assembly in 1948: https://www.un.org/en/about-us/universal-declaration-of-human-rights: General Assembly Resolution 217A.

17. See Thomas M. Franck, "The Emerging Right to Democratic Governance," *American Journal of International Law* 86;1 (2017): 46–91.

18. See Joseph Raz, "The Problem of Authority," *Minnesota Law Review* 90 (2006): 1003–1044; also see Leslie Green, "Legal Obligation and Authority," *The Stanford Encyclopedia of Philosophy* (Winter 2012).

19. But see the Charter of the United Nations, as amended (www.un.org/en/about-us/un-charter), whereby a member nation, in effect, gives its irrevocable consent upon becoming a member—a member nation may be expelled, but may not leave voluntarily.

20. The Statute of the International Court of Justice Article 38(1) defines *custom* as "general practice accepted as law," www.icj-cij.org/statute.

21. See H.L.A. Hart, *The Concept of Law*, ed. Leslie Green (Oxford: Oxford University Press, 2012), 94.

22. Joseph Raz, *Reason and Value*, eds. R. Jay Wallace, Phillip Pettit, Samuel Scheffler, and Michael Smith (Oxford: Clarendon Press, 2004), 1014.

23. See Ronald Dworkin, "A New Philosophy for International Law," *Philosophy & Public Affairs* 41;1 (2013): 2–30.

24. See Thomas M. Franck, "The Emerging Right to Democratic Governance," *American Journal of International Law* 86;1 (2017): 46–91; also see his *Fairness in International Law and Institutions* (Oxford: Clarendon Press, 1998): ch. 4; further, see Dworkin 2013.

25. See James Crawford, *Chance, Order, Change* (Boston: Martinus Nijhoff, 2014), 343.

26. Plato, *The Statesman*, trans. J. B. Skemp (London: Bristol Classical Press, 2002), 291d–e and 301b–c.

27. See Aristotle, *Politics*, trans. T. A. Sinclair, rev. Trevor Saunders (London: Penguin Books, 1992), III.

28. See John Locke, *Second Treatise of Government*, ed. Crawford Macpherson (Indianapolis: Hackett Publishing, 1980), ch. 5.

29. This analogue easily leads to questions beyond the scope of this study concerning autocratic forms of government and political rule vs. democratic versions of government and political rule.

30. E.g., see Lon L. Fuller, *The Morality of Law* (New Haven: Yale University Press, 1964); also see Joseph Raz, *The Authority of Law* (Oxford: Oxford University Press, 1995); and Tom Bingham, *The Rule of Law* (London: Allen Lane, 2010).

PART IV

Contemporary Theories of Law

Chapter 11

Natural Law

In this part of the study, I examine salient features of the legal theories of prominent contemporary legal theorists. Underlying these theories are different conceptions of law, morality and politics, as well as complex interplays between various aspects of such concepts. Mostly, these contemporary theories can be categorized as coming from the natural law tradition or from legal positivism.

The term natural law as used in reference to legal theory may be seen as misleading, since it does not refer to laws of nature in a scientific sense. On the contrary, in legal theory, the term can refer to natural law moral theory, including those moral standards that govern human behavior as derived from the nature of human beings and the world. The term can also refer to natural law legal theory which may, in part, intersect with concerns of natural law moral theory. For instance, the classical natural law theory of Thomas Aquinas focuses on the overlap between natural law moral and natural law legal theories.

Following in the natural law tradition of Aquinas among contemporary legal theorists are John Finnis and Lon L. Fuller. While Finnis pursues the question of what is truly good for individuals, Fuller foregrounds the goal orientation characterizing individual behavior to natural law issues. Fuller also engaged in a well-known debate with the legal positivist H.L.A. Hart (treated later in this chapter). While the debate has focused on Fuller's eight principles of law, the underlying dispute has to do with the conceptual connection between law and morality.

SUBSTANTIVE NATURALISM

In contemporary times, the prominent natural law theorist John Finnis may be viewed as developing classical natural law theory further. Thus, to articulate his thoughts on natural law, he adopts two key features of the natural law theory of Thomas Aquinas: (1) God's role as the giver of natural law, and (2) human beings as the recipients of natural law, with natural law comprising principles of practical rationality by which human action may be judged as reasonable or unreasonable.[1] Finnis argues that the purpose of law is to establish "what is really good for human beings," thereby evoking an Aristotelian version of what constitutes a worthwhile, valuable life (*eudaimonia*): the good over the right.

The question that Finnis pursues in his early work is: How does law fit within the moral requirement to seek the common good? In attempting to resolve this question, he argues that Aquinas employed a prime rule approach which bears on basic goods, and that Aquinas' prime rule is the rule of universal love: one should love one's neighbor as oneself.[2] This prime rule does not explain, however, how we grasp this first principle of morality as correct. Ontologically put, what is the relationship between our knowledge of basic goods (which Finnis defines) and our knowledge of the prime rule? Further, in terms of method, is there a test whereby a natural law theorist may distinguish between correct moral rules and incorrect ones? Finnis denies that any such test exists.

Thus, in *Natural Law and Natural Rights*, Finnis sums up his theory of law, as follows:

> [T]he term "law" . . . refer[s] primarily to rules made, in accordance with regulative legal rules, by a determinate and effective authority (itself identified and, standardly, constituted as an institution by legal rules) for a "complete" community, and buttressed by sanctions in accordance with the rule-guided stipulations of adjudicative institutions, this ensemble of rules and institutions being directed to reasonably resolving any of the community's co-ordination problems (and to ratifying, tolerating, or overriding co-ordination solutions from any other institutions or sources of norms) for the common good of that community.[3]

With regard to legal validity, an especial concern among contemporary legal theorists, Finnis states that classical natural law theorists were not concerned with providing a conceptual account, but rather, they were interested in explaining the moral force of law: "the principles of natural law explain the obligatory force (in the fullest sense of 'obligation') of positive laws, even when those laws cannot be deduced from those principles."[4]

BASIC GOODS

Finnis also defends various principles of practical reasonableness in his natural law theory without reference to a prime rule, "[T]hese requirements are requirements not only of reason but also of nature." Finnis continues to assert that there are seven basic goods, all of which are not derivative, self-evident, and fundamentally equal: (1) life, (2) knowledge, (3) play, (4) aesthetic experience, (5) sociability (friendship) (6) practical reasonableness, and (7) religion.[5]

The seven basic goods provide a platform for Finnis' development of natural law theory insofar as he argues that it is always wrong to intend the destruction of a basic good.[6] For instance, if a person never tells lies, because s/he understands that to tell lies would be to respond in a manner that is destructive to the good, then lying is always wrong. If it is always wrong to tell lies, moreover, our grasp of moral truth depends on our possessing, or recognizing the possessor of, practical wisdom.

Finnis also expands on the nature of these basic goods:[7]

1. Life: the drive for self-preservation includes every aspect of life which puts a human being in good shape for self-determination. It includes bodily health, freedom from pain, and the transmission of life by procreation. In a 2011 postscript, Finnis added the institution of marriage (a man and a woman) to this category.
2. Knowledge: This basic good is desirable for its own sake for it's preferred to be well-informed rather than ignorant.
3. Play: Listing recreation, enjoyment, fun, Finnis provides the example of engaging in a performance for no other reason than the performance itself.
4. Aesthetic experience: For Finnis, this basic good bespeaks an appreciation of beauty in art or nature.
5. Sociability (friendship): At its minimum, sociability foregrounds peace and harmony, while in its strongest form it allows for the flowering of full friendship and may be witnessed when acting in the interests of one's friends or for the sake of a friend.
6. Practical reasonableness: Finnis defines this basic good as using one's intelligence to solve problems of deciding what to do, how to live, and shaping one's character.
7. Religion: Finnis does not mean a religion per se, but rather concern about an order of things that transcends individual interests.

Further as to his Aristotelian concept of "practical reasonableness," Finnis states that: "The principal concern of a theory of natural law is to explore the requirements of practical reasonableness in relation to the good of human beings who, because they live in community with one another, are confronted with problems of justice and rights, of authority, law, and obligation."[8] Emphasizing the importance of practical reasonableness, Finnis lists nine basic requirements of practical reasonableness:[9] (1) The good of practical reasonableness structures the pursuit of goods generally. That is, it shapes our participation in other goods, while it also helps us choose what to do, what projects to commit our time to; (2) a coherent plan of life; (3) no arbitrary preference among values; (4) no arbitrary preference amongst persons; (5) open-minded dedication to one's projects; (6) the relevance of consequences, ensuring that actions should be reasonably efficient; (7) respect for every basic value in every act; (8) the requirements of the common good which motivate an individual to advance the interests of the community; (9) remaining true to one's inner conscience.

With his lists of basic goods and practical reasonableness as derived from natural law, Finnis maps concepts onto actions and argues for the intrinsic moral authority of natural law and underscores that basic morality is derived from "the principles that the common good is to be advanced, that authoritative determination of co-ordination problems is for the common good, and that legal regulation is (presumptively) a good method of authoritative determination."[10] Arguing that legal positivism is opposed to and distinct from natural law theory, he asserts that positive law fails in its normative purpose; i.e., to promote the common good. Accordingly, positive law cannot be considered law in the best and fullest sense of the term and is legally as well as morally defective.

In terms of the relation between natural law theorists and positivism, Finnis emphasizes that natural law theorists do not conceive their theories in opposition to legal positive theories. Indeed, he refers to many instances of overlap between the two approaches.[11] And it does indeed appear that the traditional debate between natural law theorists and legal positivists over the relationship between law and morality has become more complex in contemporary times. Regardless, many contemporary self-described legal positivists view their legal theories in opposition to or distinct from natural law theories, including that of Finnis.

PROCEDURAL NATURALISM

Like John Finnis, Lon L. Fuller rejects the conceptual naturalist idea that there are necessary substantive moral constraints on the content of law.[12] But unlike Finnis, Fuller believes that law is necessarily subject to a procedural morality. In Fuller's view, human activity is necessarily goal-oriented or purposive in the sense that people engage in a particular activity in order to achieve some end. Insofar as human activity is essentially purposive, according to Fuller, particular human activities can be understood only in terms that make reference to their purposes and ends.

Thus, since lawmaking is essentially a purposive activity, Fuller argues it can be understood only in terms that explicitly acknowledge its essential values and purposes:

> The only formula that might be called a definition of law offered in these writings is by now thoroughly familiar: law is the enterprise of subjecting human conduct to the governance of rules. Unlike most modern theories of law, this view treats law as an activity and regards a legal system as the product of a sustained purposive effort.[13]

To the extent that a definition of law can be given, then, it must include the idea that law's essential function is to "achiev[e] [social] order through subjecting people's conduct to the guidance of general rules by which they may themselves orient their behavior."[14]

FUNCTIONAL ARGUMENT

Fuller's functionalist conception of law implies that nothing can count as law unless it is capable of performing law's essential function of guiding behavior. And to be capable of performing this function, a system of rules must satisfy the following principles; they must be: (1) expressed in general terms, (2) publicly promulgated, (3) prospective in effect, (4) expressed in understandable terms, (5) consistent with one another, (6) so formulated as not to require conduct beyond the powers of the affected parties, (7) stable enough and not changed so frequently that the subject cannot rely on them, and (8) administered in a manner consistent with their wording.[15]

In Fuller's view, no system of rules that fails minimally to satisfy these functionalist principles of legality can achieve law's essential purpose of achieving social order. His crux of his argument stems from obligation, insofar as these eight features are necessary conditions for anyone morally obliged to obey the law:

> A total failure in any one of these eight directions does not simply result in a bad system of law; it results in something that is not properly called a legal system at all. . . . Certainly there can be no rational ground for asserting that a man can have a moral obligation to obey a legal rule that does not exist, or is kept secret from him, or that came into existence only after he had acted, or was unintelligible, or was contradicted by another rule of the same system, or commanded the impossible, or changed every minute.[16]

Fuller concludes that his eight principles are "internal" to law in the sense that they are built into the conditions for law,[17] and they constitute a morality, because law necessarily has positive moral value in two respects: (a) law conduces to a state of social order, and (b) it does so by respecting human autonomy since rules guide behavior.

Since no system of rules can achieve these morally valuable objectives without minimally complying with the principles of legality, it follows, in his view, that they constitute a morality. Since these moral principles are built into the conditions for law, they are internal and hence represent a conceptual connection between law and morality, and thus deny the legal positivist tenet that law has no necessary connection with morality.

Fuller's conceptual naturalism nevertheless fundamentally differs from classical naturalism. First, Fuller rejects the classical naturalist account that there are necessary moral constraints on the content of law, holding instead that there are necessary moral constraints on the procedural mechanisms by which law is made and administered: "What I have called the internal morality of law is . . . a procedural version of natural law . . . [in the sense that it is] concerned, not with the substantive aims of legal rules, but with the ways in which a system of rules for governing human conduct must be constructed and administered if it is to be efficacious and at the same time remain what it purports to be."[18]

That is, classical naturalists view morality as providing substantive constraints on the content of individual laws; an unjust norm, in their view, is conceptually disqualified from being legally valid. In contrast, Fuller views morality as providing a constraint not on the content of individual laws, but on the existence of a legal system: "A total failure in any one of these eight directions does not simply result in a bad system of law; it results in something that is not properly called a legal system at all."[19] Fuller has been termed a conservative natural law theorist, and his claims that order, coherence, and clarity have an affinity with goodness and morality do not seem extreme.

HART-FULLER DEBATE

The Hart-Fuller debate began as a lecture by the legal positivist and anti-natural law advocate H.L.A. Hart at Harvard Law School in 1958. His lecture was subsequently published in the Harvard Law Review.[20] The editors also invited the natural law and anti-positivist theorist Lon L. Fuller to prepare a response to Hart's paper, which was also published in the same issue of the *Harvard Law Review*.[21]

Fuller's response made two main objections to the separation of law and morality views expressed by Hart. Fuller's first objection addresses the systemic nature of law, with what he termed the "external" morality of law. Thus, he argues that successful legal orders necessarily have morally acceptable purposes and aims to support the competency of the legal system. His second objection concerns what he terms the "internal" morality of law. Here, Fuller argues that for a legal order to exist legitimately and provide a system of rules for guidance of conduct, the law must contain its own implicit morality.[22] Given these objections, Fuller accordingly concludes that the separation of law and morality which legal positivists advocate cannot be maintained.

In 1961, Hart published *The Concept of Law* (examined in the next chapter) which expresses his version of a "soft" or inclusive legal positivism. Moreover, Hart treats the issue of the separability of law and morality and covers topics of legal systems including such matters as primary and secondary rules, what he terms the Rule of Recognition, internal and external views of law, custom and convention in the law, and international law—a broad and deep undertaking. In 1964, Fuller published *The Morality of Law* (as discussed earlier in this chapter), which expresses his concerns about the inner morality of law and addresses his views on procedural naturalism, as well as his functional argument for the law.

Eventually, Fuller's debate with Hart devolved into a debate about Fuller's eight principles of legality, as catalogued above.[23] Thus, in Hart's 1965 review of *The Morality of Law*, he severely criticized Fuller's work:

> [T]he crucial objection to the designation of these principles of good legal craftsmanship as morality . . . is that it perpetrates a confusion between . . . the notions of purposive activity and morality. Poisoning is no doubt a purposive activity, and reflections on its purpose may show that it has its internal principles. ("Avoid poisons however lethal if they cause the victim to vomit," or "Avoid poisons however lethal if their shape, color, or size is likely to attract notice.") But to call these principles of the poisoner's art "the morality of poisoning" would simply blur the distinction between the notion of efficiency for a purpose and those final judgments about activities and purposes with which morality in its various forms is concerned.[24]

In his 1969 revised edition of *The Morality of Law*, Fuller adds a lengthy "Reply to Critics" as a fifth chapter in the book. Here, Fuller contrasts two different approaches to the regulation of human conduct: (1) a "one-way projection of authority"; and (2) a cooperative exercise in "self-directed action" in which government and citizens are mutual participants.[25]

For Fuller, his eight specific principles of law represent the practical success conditions for our decision to engage in a reciprocal mode of regulation. And thus, the Hart-Fuller debate has pitted natural law and positivist arguments that refuse to concede ground.

NOTES

1. See John Finnis, *Natural Law and Natural Rights* (Oxford: Clarendon Press, 1980).
2. Ibid., 126.
3. Ibid., 276.
4. Ibid., 23–24.
5. Ibid., 86–90.
6. Ibid., 118–123.
7. Ibid., 86–90.
8. Ibid., 351.
9. Ibid., 100–127.
10. Ibid., 138.
11. See John Finnis, *The Collected Essays of John Finnis*, 5 vols. (Oxford: Oxford University Press, 2013).
12. See Lon L. Fuller, *The Morality of Law* (New Haven: Yale University Press, 1969).
13. Ibid., 106.
14. Lon L. Fuller, "A Reply to Professors Cohen and Dworkin," *Villanova Law Review* 10;4,5 (1965): 655–657.
15. See Fuller 1969: 46–90.
16. Ibid., 39.
17. See chapters 1 and 12 *infra* regarding the internal view of law.
18. Fuller 1969: 96–97.
19. Ibid., 39.
20. H.L.A. Hart, "Positivism and the Separation of Law and Morals," *Harvard Law Review* 71;4 (1958): 593.
21. Lon L. Fuller, "Positivism and Fidelity to Law," *Harvard Law Review* 71;4 (1958): 630.
22. On these two points, see Fuller 1969: 642, regarding Fuller's objection to Hart's "external" morality of law and his insistence on an "internal" morality of law.
23. See Fuller 1969: 46–90.
24. H.L.A. Hart, "Review of Lon L. Fuller, *The Morality of Law*," *Tennessee Law Review* 33 (1965–1966): 563.
25. Fuller 1969: ch. 5.

Chapter 12

Social Facts

A primary thesis of legal positivism extending back to the accounts of Jeremy Bentham and John Austin is that legal facts are fully grounded in social facts. Legal facts hold solely in virtue of social facts, with the exclusion of any moral facts. H.L.A. Hart's contemporary legal theory of social facts has come to be known as inclusive legal positivism, or in his own words, "soft positivism." He uses Austin's command theory of law, and his criticisms of Austin's theory, to construct a platform for his account of law as rules and to articulate an "internal" point of view of the law.

Ronald Dworkin has argued forcefully against Hart's theory of law and his "rule of recognition," as he pursues a "third-way" theorizing of law, one which is neither naturalist nor positivist. Dworkin's concerns about legal positivism not only have to do with Hart's rules of law and whether moral principles can count as authoritative legal texts, but also with the deeply conventionalist views underlying legal positivism.

The debate between Hart and Dworkin, examined later in this chapter, initially began with Dworkin disputing Hart's claim that law is a model of rules. Hart responded, however, that he never made any such claim. Their long-running debate, marked by misunderstandings of each other's positions, generated a number of disparate issues, but ultimately, their debate centers on the relation of, and separability between, legality and morality.

INCLUSIVE LEGAL POSITIVISM

John Austin is known for his assertion that "the key to the science of jurisprudence" lies in the claim that "law is the order or command backed by a threat of a sovereign properly so-called." Thus, the key concepts of Austin's account are: commands, sanctions, habits of obedience (or compliance), and the sovereign (not sovereignty). Hart, however, argues that these resources are inadequate to explain important aspects of temporal and normative dimensions of law. For instance, the existence of a habit of obedience (compliance) is inadequate to explain the concept of authority, which is central to an understanding of the law.

Specifically, Hart criticizes the concept of law that is formulated by John Austin in *The Province of Jurisprudence Determined* (1832), which proposes that all laws are commands of a legally unlimited sovereign. Here, Austin claims that all laws are coercive orders that impose duties or obligations on individuals. In effect, Hart uses Austin's command theory of law as a stepping stone to present his own internal point of view about law, and to justify his quite different form of legal positivism.[1] Thus, Hart argues that: (1) contrary to Austin's theory, law contains much greater variety than is presented by a theory that equates law with commands; (2) theories that equate law with the command of a sovereign cannot account for the legal status of custom and may also have difficulty accounting for judicial legislation; (3) many communities do not have anything that would count as "sovereign" in the sense used by Austin, a power that has no limits or constraints; and (4) Austin's theory cannot distinguish a legitimate legal system from the rule of gangsters or terrorists.

That is, in *The Concept of Law*, Hart analyzes the relations among law, coercion, and morality, while further attempting to clarify the question of whether all laws may be properly conceptualized as coercive orders or as moral commands. He concludes that there is no logically necessary connection between law and coercion or between law and morality, arguing that to classify all laws as coercive orders or as moral commands is to oversimplify the relations among law, coercion, and morality. Moreover, to conceptualize all laws as coercive orders or as moral commands is to impose a misleading appearance of uniformity on different kinds of laws and on different kinds of social functions which laws may perform. In effect, rather than analyzing a set of conceptual truths, Hart may be seen as writing about the nature of law.

LEGAL SYSTEMS

Under Hart's approach, all legal systems (or at least all sophisticated legal systems) have a rule of recognition, which sets the criteria for the most basic norm in the chain of justification and authorization within a legal system. Implied in his approach is that each legal system has only one such rule of recognition.[2]

Accordingly, Hart argues that the foundations of a legal system do not consist, as Austin claims, of habits of obedience to a legally unlimited sovereign, but instead they consist of adherence to, or acceptance of, an ultimate rule of recognition by which the validity of any primary or secondary rule may be evaluated. If a primary or secondary rule satisfies the criteria which are provided by the ultimate rule of recognition, then that rule is legally valid.

Hart further delineates two minimum requirements that must be satisfied in order for a legal system to exist: (1) private citizens must generally obey the primary rules of obligation; and (2) public officials must accept the secondary rules of recognition, change, and adjudication as standards of official conduct. If both of these requirements are not satisfied, then primary rules may only be sufficient to establish a pre-legal form of government.

If law cannot ultimately be grounded in force, or on a presupposed norm, on what does its authority rest? Hart's solution resembles Hans Kelsen's in its emphasis on the normative foundations of legal systems, although Hart rejects Kelsen's metaphysical, Kantian view of authority in favor of an empirical, Weberian one.[3] For Hart, that is, the authority of law is social. The ultimate criterion of validity in a legal system is neither a legal norm nor a presupposed norm, but a social rule that exists only because it is actually practiced and used to guide conduct.

In positing social authority, Hart continues to argue that laws may differ from the commands of a sovereign, because they may apply to those individuals who enact them as well as to other individuals. Laws may further differ from coercive orders in that they may not necessarily impose duties or obligations, but instead confer powers or privileges. Moreover, laws may require individuals to undergo punishment for injuring other individuals. Laws may also specify how contracts are to be made; how official documents are to be created; how legislatures are to be assembled and how courts are to function; and how new laws are to be enacted as well as how old laws are to be changed. Thus, not all laws may be regarded as coercive orders, since some laws may confer powers or privileges on individuals without imposing duties or obligations on them.

PRIMARY AND SECONDARY RULES

Laws that impose duties or obligations on individuals are described by Hart as "primary rules of obligation." In order for a system of primary rules to function effectively, "secondary rules" may also prove necessary in order to provide an authoritative statement of all the primary rules. Critically, primary rules impose obligations, while secondary rules confer powers. Further, secondary rules may be necessary in order to allow legislators to make changes in the primary rules if the primary rules are found to be defective or inadequate.

Secondary rules may also prove necessary in order to enable courts to resolve disputes over the interpretation and application of the primary rules. The secondary rules of a legal system may thus include: (a) rules of recognition,[4] (b) rules of change, and (c) rules of adjudication. More important than the primary rules that obligate compliance with standards of conduct, these secondary rules reside at the core of Hart's account.

In order for the primary rules of a legal system to function effectively, the rules must be sufficiently clear and intelligible to be understood by those individuals to whom they apply. If the primary rules are not sufficiently clear or intelligible, then there may be uncertainty about the obligations which are imposed on individuals. Especially if secondary rules are to serve primary rules, vagueness or ambiguity of secondary rules of may cause pragmatic uncertainties, such as: whether powers have been conferred on individuals in accordance with statutory requirements, whether legislators have the authority to change laws, or whether courts have jurisdiction over disputes concerning the interpretation and application of laws.

Recognizing the critical role of interpretation in laws, Hart thus argues that primary rules of obligation are not in themselves sufficient to establish a system of laws that can be formally recognized, changed, or adjudicated. Hart does not claim that a union between primary and secondary rules is the only valid criterion of a legal system or that a legal system must be described in these terms in order to be properly defined. He nonetheless argues that primary rules must be combined with secondary rules in order to advance from the pre-legal to the legal stage of determination. In other words, a legal system may effectively be established by means of a union between primary and secondary rules.

RULE OF RECOGNITION

The most important secondary rule for Hart is the rule of recognition, which is secondary in that concerns the validity of primary rules. It also serves as a social rule, because of social facts, that comprise its basis and informs its content and because it establishes a group-wide standard. With regard to the latter, members of the group respond to the standard as the official manner in which the law is to be determined in their community. Moreover, because the rule of recognition is a social rule, it is capable of being an ultimate rule; it does not exist by virtue of any other rule. Its existence is secured simply because of its acceptance and practice. The primary rules of the legal system, by contrast, are not ultimate because they exist by virtue of the rule of recognition.

In critiquing Hart's rule of recognition, Joseph Raz has argued that there is no reason to assume that each legal system has only one rule of recognition; indeed, legal systems could well have two or more rules of recognition.[5] Raz further offers three different objections to Hart's rule of recognition: (1)

Whether there is one rule of recognition in a given community depends not only on the facts, but also on an account of the individuation of norms and values; (2) certain standards of conduct may be binding on officials, even though the rule of recognition may not pick out the standards that judges have a duty to apply; and (3) the rule of recognition can never specify the identity conditions of a legal system, because the law is always the law of a particular group or community, and that means that the identity conditions of a legal system depend on the conditions of groups and political communities. Thus, in Raz's account of exclusive legal positivism (in contrast to Hart's inclusive version), Raz does not recognize a rule of recognition. Rather, he discusses law with respect to criteria of legality or authoritative sources of law.[6] Ronald Dworkin, on the other hand, has argued that legal systems have principles as well as rules, legal standards that cannot be correlated with the sort of content-neutral criteria associated with a Hartian rule of recognition.[7]

EXTERNAL AND INTERNAL POINTS OF VIEW

To describe or evaluate a legal system, Hart develops distinctions between external and internal points of view. For him, the external point of view is that of an observer who does not necessarily have to accept the rules of the legal system. Thus, the external observer evaluates the extent to which the rules of the legal system produce a regular pattern of conduct for individuals to whom the rules apply. The internal point of view, on the other hand, expresses a critical, reflective attitude that individuals take toward rules of a legal system, and the behavior that such rules require.

Accordingly, the internal aspect of rules distinguishes rules from habits, in that habits may be viewed as regular patterns of conduct but are not usually viewed as standards of conduct. While the external aspect of rules may in some cases enable observers to predict the conduct of individuals, they may have to consider the internal aspect of rules in order to interpret or explain the conduct of individuals.

CUSTOM AND CONVENTION

Custom refers to habit or to regular patterns of behavior. For Hart, law ultimately rests on custom insofar as customs dictate who shall have the authority to decide disputes, what they shall refer to as binding reasons for decisions (i.e., as sources of law), and how laws may be changed. Convention, on the other hand, is about agreement that may be accepted formally or informally. Since legal positivists are basically conventionalists, not surprisingly, Hart's legal system depends on convention and the acceptance of its precepts. He believes that there must be agreement about the criteria of legality in order for there to be law.[8]

Consequently, in Hart's view, the legal system is rule-based all the way down, and at its root is a social norm that has the kind of normative force of customs. Thus, officials take the internal point of view when they depend on the regularity of behavior as a standard for guiding and evaluating their own and others' behavior. This becomes apparent in their conduct and their speech and includes their resorting to various forms of social pressure to support the rule and the ready application of normative terms such as "duty" and "obligation" when invoking it.

INTERNATIONAL LAW

While I discussed international law in chapter 10, Hart's approach presents its limits, and accordingly, his account gives international law short shrift, since he claims that international law may not have all of the elements of a fully-developed legal system. Thus, international law may lack secondary rules of recognition, change, and adjudication. International legislatures may not always have the power to enforce sanctions against nations, who transgress against international law. International courts may not always have jurisdiction over legal disputes between nations. International law may also be disregarded by some nations who do not face any significant pressure to comply. Moreover, nations that do comply with international law must still be able to exercise their sovereignty. Hart's views on international law, then, are based on a closed or static model of society, one that runs *contra* to cosmopolitan views of international relations and even John Rawls' view of the law of peoples.[9]

LAW AND MORALITY

Hart defines legal positivism as a theory that recognizes no logically necessary connection between the content of law and morality, leading to the assertion the existence of legal rights and duties may be devoid of any moral justification.[10] Nonetheless, he describes his own legal theory as a "soft positivism," in that he admits that rules of recognition, as discussed above, may consider the compatibility or incompatibility of a rule with moral values as a criterion of the rule's legal validity. For Hart, then, moral and legal rules may overlap, because moral and legal obligation may be similar in some situations, and they may also differ in other situations. Moreover, moral and legal rules may apply to similar aspects of conduct, such as the obligation to be honest and truthful or the obligation to respect the rights of other individuals, although moral rules cannot always be changed in the same way that legal rules can be changed.

NOT NATURAL LAW AND NOT LEGAL POSITIVISM

Hart's interpretation of the relation between law and morality thereby differs dramatically from that of Ronald Dworkin, who in *Law's Empire* suggests that every legal action has a moral dimension.[11] Dworkin further rejects Hart's concept of law as acceptance of conventional patterns of recognition and describes law not merely as a descriptive concept, but as an interpretive concept which combines jurisprudence and adjudication.

In this context, Dworkin's "semantic sting" argument addresses the conditions of legal validity, as follows:

> A legal system is a system of norms. Validity is a logical property of norms in a way akin to that in which truth is a logical property of propositions. A statement about the law is true if and only if the norm it purports to describe is a valid legal norm. . . . It follows that there must be certain conditions which render certain norms, but not others, legally valid. Hence it also follows that there can be two types of disagreement over the truth or falsehood of propositions about the law. People can disagree over the question "What are the conditions of legal validity?," in which case their disagreement is a theoretical one. Or they can agree on the conditions of validity, and disagree as to whether or not those conditions actually obtain in a given case or not.[12]

Perhaps the best way to interpret Dworkin's semantic sting argument is as a general argument against conventionalism in legal positivism, since he presents a new conception of jurisprudence aiming to present itself as a rival to conventionalism.

LAW AS INTERPRETATION

As mentioned above, Ronald Dworkin has argued forcefully against Hart's theory of law, asserting that legal systems have principles as well as rules and legal standards that cannot be correlated with the content-neutral approach associated with Hart's rule of recognition.[13] However, it seems that Dworkin's legal principles represent moral reasons for changing the law, rather than describing aspects of the law as it currently is.[14]

Dworkin entered the legal positivist fray through his concept of constructive interpretation. According to Dworkin, an interpretation (including of a social practice) must meet some minimal level of fit with the practice being interpreted; otherwise, it would not qualify as an interpretation. Beyond that, one would choose the best interpretation that also had the minimal level fit (according to an early version of his interpretation theory of law)[15] or choose the theory that had the best combination of fit and value (according to later versions of his theory).[16]

In *Law's Empire*, Dworkin argues that legal theory may advance from the "pre-interpretive stage" (in which rules of conduct are identified) to the "interpretive stage" (in which the justification for these rules is decided upon) to the "post-interpretive stage" (in which the rules of conduct are reevaluated based on what has been found to justify them). A complete legal theory does not merely identify the rules of a legal system, then, but also interprets and evaluates them.

For Dworkin, a complete legal theory must consider not only the relation between law and coercion (i.e., the force of law), but also the relation between law and rightfulness or justifiability (i.e., the grounds of law). Thus, Dworkin argues that a complete legal theory must address not only the question of whether the rules of a legal system are justified, but also the question of whether there are sufficient grounds for coercing individuals to comply with the rules of the system. In order to accommodate both the force and the grounds of law, he argues that a complete legal theory needs principles of interpretation.

Hart has responded that in any legal system, there may be cases in which existing laws are vague or indeterminate and that judicial discretion may be necessary in order to clarify existing laws in these cases. Hart also argues that by clarifying vague or indeterminate laws, judges may actually make new laws. He asserts that this argument is rejected by Dworkin, who contends that judicial discretion is not an exercise in making new laws but is a means of determining which legal principles are most consistent with existing laws and which legal principles provide the best justification for existing laws.

HART-DWORKIN DEBATE

In the long-running Hart-Dworkin debate, it often seems that the participants do not agree on what they are arguing about. Notoriously, as described above, their debate began on just such a note. Thus, in "The Model of Rules I," Dworkin claimed that the dispute between the two theorists concerned whether the law is a model of rules.[17] This formulation, however, proves misleading, because, as is now generally recognized, Hart never claimed that the law is simply a model of rules (in Dworkin's sense of "rule"), nor is he committed to such a position.[18]

As their debate continued, it has ranged over such disparate issues as: (1) the role of policy in adjudication; (2) the ontological foundations of rules; (3) the possibility of descriptive jurisprudence; (4) the function of law; (5) the objectivity of value; (6) the vagueness of concepts; and (7) the nature of legal inference.

But as I voiced above, the basic debate between Hart and Dworkin essentially has to do with the relation between legality and morality. Dworkin's basic strategy throughout the course of the debate has been to argue that, in one form or another, legality is ultimately determined not by social facts alone, but by moral facts as well. In other words, the existence and content of positive law is, in the final analysis, governed by the existence and content of the moral law. This contention directly challenges and threatens to undermine Hart's positivist picture on the nature of law, in which legality is never determined by morality but rather by social practice. To exemplify their differences, consider the following: when judges consider what morality requires in order to decide what the law requires, social facts alone cannot determine the content of the law. As one might expect, however, Hart argues that this dependence of legality on morality is either merely apparent or does not, in fact, undermine the social foundations of law and legal systems.

NOTES

1. See H.L.A. Hart, *The Concept of Law*, ed. Leslie Green (Oxford: Oxford University Press, 2012), 56–57, 84–91.

2. See chapter 13 *infra,* regarding Hans Kelsen's "Pure Theory of Law."

3. In Hart's system, only one "rule of recognition" is implied.

4. See Joseph Raz, *The Concept of a Legal System* (Oxford: Clarendon Press, 1980), 197–200.

5. See chapter 13, *infra*, regarding Raz's discussion of the criteria of legality and authoritative sources of law.

6. Ronald Dworkin, *Taking Rights Seriously* (Cambridge: Harvard University Press, 1978), 14–45.

7. One of Dworkin's concerns has to do with the compatibility of legal positivism, since positivism, which is deeply conventionalist, provides no plausible mechanism for understanding one of the most important features of law, i.e., disagreement about the grounds of law.

8. See chapters 10 and 14 *infra* regarding Hart's implication that each legal system has only one rule of recognition.

9. See John Rawls, *The Law of Peoples* (Cambridge: Harvard University Press, 1997).

10. See Ronald Dworkin, *Law's Empire* (Cambridge: Harvard University Press, 1986).

11. Ibid., 43–44, regarding Dworkin's "semantic sting" argument.

12. See note 8 above and accompanying text.

13. See Dworkin 1978: 14–45.

14. Ronald Dworkin, "The Model of Rules," *University of Chicago Law Review* 35;1 (1967): 14–46.

15. E.g., see Ronald Dworkin, *Law's Empire* (Cambridge: Harvard University Press, 1986).

16. Hart takes some responsibility for the confusion: "Much credit is due to Dworkin for having shown and illustrated [the] importance [of legal principles] and their role in legal reasoning, and certainly it was a serious mistake on my part not to have stressed their non-conclusive force." He nonetheless goes on to disavow Dworkin's interpretation of his views: "But I certainly did not in my use of the word 'rule' claim that legal systems comprise only 'all or nothing' standards or near conclusive rules." Hart 2012: 263.

17. See note 14 above and accompanying text.

18. See Scott Shapiro, "The 'Hart-Dworkin' Debate," *University of Michigan Law School* 77 (2007): 1–54.

Chapter 13

Legal Positivism

As discussed above, legal positivism embraces a broad range of theories linked insofar as they all deny a necessary connection between law and morals and they all prescribe that the validity of any law be traced to an objectively verifiable source. Law thereby results from social facts and is not of normative value. Accordingly, legal positivists are conventionalists since they believe that there must be agreement about the criteria of legality in order for law to exist.

By contrast, natural law theory contends that law consists of a series of propositions derived from nature, that legal and moral normativity are closely connected, and that law entails a moral determinant. As treated throughout part IV, the dispute between legal positivists and natural law theorists covers an extensive scope of textured debates including contested matters of reason, rules, duty, obligations, and rights.

Early legal positivists focused their analyses on legislative institutions and law-applying institutions such as courts (e.g., Jeremy Bentham) and the role of coercive force in law (e.g., John Austin). Contemporary legal positivists have turned their attention to the systematic and normative character of law, generating a split between inclusive positivists and exclusive positivists. Inclusive legal positivists, like H.L.A. Hart, argue that although any law's existence does not depend on its merits, it can include moral principles, and they allow for the overlap between social and moral facts, as discussed in the preceding chapter.

In this chapter, I examine exclusive legal positivism through the account of Joseph Raz, who insists that the content of law can be understood solely through social facts, thereby ignoring moral principles. Further, I examine the positivist accounts of Hans Kelsen and Scott Shapiro. Writing in the legal positivist tradition, Hans Kelsen's "pure theory of law" defines law as a system of coercive norms, with an underlying basic norm, the *Grundnorm*. In attempting to promote exclusive legal positivism and reject the tenets of natural law theory, Scott Shapiro develops a "planning theory of law." This theory, which equates social facts with facts in planning, may also be viewed as an attempt to create a rapprochement between tenets of legal positivism with those of those of natural law.

EXCLUSIVE LEGAL POSITIVISM

Joseph Raz's argument for a hard or "exclusive" legal positivism is based on the premise that all criteria for legality must stem from what he calls "social sources."[1] That is, Raz argues that the existence and content of the law are determined exclusively by means of factual (social) considerations, without reference to moral considerations. He further contends that each legal system's moral value can be judged independently and that its content is based wholly on contingent facts concerning human beings and their societies.

Critics of Raz's views have pointed out that there are clear contrary examples to his barring of moral sources, including the moral standards found in constitutional provisions and the use of moral reasoning to determine the content of common law norms. Raz, however, denies that these examples are in fact refutations or that they pose examples contrary to his theory. He asserts, rather, that often a judge characterizes opinions using conventions of presentation or that a judge may use somewhat misleading labels so as not to provoke preconceptions such as, for instance, judges do not legislate.[2] Raz's explanation, however, is not wholly satisfactory and sounds more like glib rationalization.

Moreover, Raz rarely discusses law in terms of a rule of recognition, preferring instead to rely upon criteria of legality or of authoritative sources. In contrast, Hart's rule of recognition sets out the criteria for membership in a community's laws, and thus, (a) provides the identity conditions for a legal system, and (b) specifies the criteria of legality that judges may apply. As referenced above, Raz presents three objections to the Hartian rule of recognition:

1. Certain standards of conduct can be binding on officials even if they are not part of the law, so it cannot be that by selecting the criteria of law, the rule of recognition is thereby selecting the set of standards that judges have a duty to apply;
2. Whether a rule of recognition exists in a community always depends not just on facts, but on an account of the individuation of norms or rules; and,
3. The rule of recognition can never specify the identity conditions of a legal system, because the law is always the law of a particular group

or community, and therefore the identity conditions of a legal system depend on the identity conditions of the groups or communities.

Raz further critiques Hart's inclusive legal theory by claiming that the concept of duty carries the same meaning in law as it does in morality. On the contrary, responds Hart, legal duty describes only what is required by law.[3] Other legal scholars challenge Raz's position that a conceptual feature of law is that it necessarily claims morally legitimate authority as well as disputing whether legal authority functions in the manner that Raz describes.[4]

AUTHORITY AND REASON

The linchpin of Raz's account rests in how he conceives of and details the role of authority by means of his practical difference thesis. That is, those subject to authority are given guidance by means of the reasons authorities establish to explain actions. Raz thus develops a service conception of authority, in which the role of authority is to enable subjects conform to reason. To explain this service conception of authority, Raz presents a seeming paradox about the compatibility of authority and reason:

> To be subjected to authority, it is argued, is incompatible with reason, for reason requires that one should always act on the balance of reasons of which one is aware. It is of the nature of authority that it requires submission even when one thinks that what is required is against reason. Therefore, submission to authority is irrational.[5]

In responding to this alleged paradox, Raz observes that one is not necessarily required to act on the balance of all the reasons of which one is aware. Indeed, some reasons exclude other reasons as proper grounds for action.[6] Authoritative orders, he contends, have a compound structure with both first-order reasons to act as an order requires and second-order exclusionary reasons not to act on (at least some) countervailing considerations. Raz captures the exclusionary effect of authoritative orders in his preemption thesis: "The fact than an authority requires performance of an action is a reason for its performance which is not to be added to all other relevant reasons when deciding what to do, but should replace some of them."[7]

In the preemption thesis, Raz positions authority and reason as not incompatible. That is, an authoritative order does not require anything other than acting on the balance of non-excluded reasons. While the preemption thesis may explain what an authoritative order does, it does not address which claims to authority, or which authorities, are legitimate. Thus, while authority may be seen as the right to rule, such that subjects are obligated to obey, there may be disagreements about the qualifications of a certain person to rule.[8]

The answers that Raz provides to this problem include both a normal justification thesis and a dependence thesis. In the normal justification thesis, a person has authority over another if her/his orders would help the person conform better to reason's requirements than s/he otherwise would. Under the dependence thesis, Raz claims that an authority's orders should be based on reasons that independently apply to those persons subject to them. Both theses, Raz concludes, "articulate the service conception of the function of authorities, that is, the view that their role and primary normal function is to serve the governed."[9]

One objection to the normal justification thesis is that it fails to capture the conditions of political authority. That is, the capacity to help subjects conform to reason does not ground political authority because political authorities have other roles to play. Another objection points to its procedural nature, underscoring how helping subjects conform to reason is insufficient to ground either a right to rule or an obligation to obey.[10]

RIGHT TO RULE

It appears that Raz once construed the right to rule as "a moral power to issue obligation—or duty-imposing directives," and not as a claim on subjects to obey.[11] Later, however, Raz argues that authority involves an "appeal to compliance" which "makes sense precisely because it is an invocation of the duty to obey."[12]

Moreover, Raz asserts that having authority over someone is tantamount to having a kind of "normative power" over her/him, and that directions of authoritative persons or institutions provide "protected reasons" for acting according to instructions.[13] But how do laws serve as protected reasons for action? Rather than an independent moral obligation to obey, Raz suggests that law exists only for those who have "respect for the law."[14]

LEGAL SYSTEM

Raz never directly makes the argument for the existence of a legal system, whereby some of its constituents must be morally obligated to obey the law. Instead, he repeatedly refers to his conclusion that there is no general moral obligation to obey the law, without spelling out the consequences of the argument. He further contends that the identity and existence of a legal system may be tested by reference to three elements: efficacy, institutional character, and (social) sources.[15]

Indeed, for Raz, the very existence of any legal system depends on its having the authority it claims, and it does not have authority unless it includes some who are morally obligated to obey its laws by virtue of their respect for the law. Thus, Raz posits a necessary connection between law and moral obligation. The existence of any particular moral obligation, however, is itself contingent upon both the existence of a legal system and the individual's possession of the attitude of respect for the law of that system. This observation attenuates Raz's answer to his central question regarding the nature of law's authority.

KELSEN'S PURE THEORY OF LAW

Hans Kelsen writes in the legal positivist tradition, rejecting claims of natural law. Thus, Kelsen claims that traditional legal philosophies in the early 20th century were hopelessly contaminated by political ideology and moralizing on the one hand or by attempts to reduce the law to natural or social sciences on the other hand. He found both of these reductionist endeavors seriously flawed. In their stead, he proffers a "pure theory of law," which avoids reductionism of any kind and serves "as a 'pure' theory of law because it aims at cognition focused on the law alone," and this purity serves as its "basic methodological principle."[16]

More specifically, Kelsen views traditional jurisprudence as maintaining a dual system comprising subjective law (the rights of a person) and objective law (the system of norms). Throughout history this dualism has proven a useful tool for putting the law in the service of politics, especially by rulers or dominant political parties. In response, Kelsen's pure theory of law aims to replace this dualism with a unitary system of objective positive law that is insulated from political manipulation.

> The Pure Theory describes the positive law as an objectively valid order and states that this interpretation is possible only under the condition that a basic norm is presupposed. . . . The Pure Theory, thereby characterizes this interpretation as possible, not necessary, and presents the objective validity of positive law only as conditional—namely conditioned by the presupposed basic norm.[17]

For Kelsen, that is, the law is basically a scheme of interpretation,[18] whereby an act or an event gains its legal-normative meaning by means of another legal norm that confers this normative meaning.[19] His pure theory of law thus defines law as a system of coercive norms created by the state that rests on the validity of a basic norm, or a generally accepted *Grundnorm*, such as the supremacy of the constitution.

BASIC NORM

Kelsen explains that a legal norm is valid if it has been created in accordance with another, higher norm:

> The general norms so applied are valid because they were created in accordance with the constitution. What is the validity of the constitution? The norm from which the constitution derives its validity is the basic norm of the legal order. The basic norm is responsible for the unity of the legal order.[20]

As such, the basic norm serves three theoretical functions in Kelsen's theory of law. The first function is to ground a non-reductive explanation of legal validity. The second is to ground a non-reductive explanation of the normativity of law. And finally, the third function is to explain the systematic nature of legal norms.

LEGAL SYSTEMS

Kelsen is certainly correct in stating that legal norms necessarily enter into legal systems. But do legal systems exhibit a systematic unity of the kind Kelsen avers? That is, Kelsen postulates that: (1) Every two norms that ultimately derive their validity from one basic norm belong to the same legal system; and, (2) all legal norms of a given legal system ultimately derive their validity from one basic norm.

Raz, for one, contested the accuracy of both postulates. Thus, he argues that two norms can derive their validity from the same basic norm, but nonetheless fail to belong to the same system as, for example, in the case of an orderly secession whereby a new legal system is created by the legal authorization of another. Nor is it necessarily true, according to Raz, that all the legally valid norms of a given system derive their validity from the same basic norm.[21]

In accordance with the importance he gives to a legal system's basic norm, Kelsen further argues that constitutional continuity is both necessary and sufficient for the identity of a legal system.[22] Critics of this view often claim that both the "necessary and sufficient" constitutional continuity claims are false.[23] Yet, Kelsen's main insight about the unity of legal systems appears to be correct. Law is essentially systematic, and it is also true that the idea of legal validity and law's systematic nature are very closely linked. Norms are legally valid within a given system, and they have to form part of a system of norms that is in force in a given place and time. Critically, a norm can only be legally valid if it belongs to a system, a legal order, that is by and large actually practiced by a certain population. And thus, the idea of legal validity, as Kelsen admits, is closely tied to this reality of a social practice; a legal system exists, as it were, only as a social reality, a reality that consists in the fact that people actually follow certain norms.

RELATIVISM

Some scholars argue that Kelsen's thought shifted from a Kantian transcendental argument in order to establish the necessary presuppositions of some categories and modes of perception essential for rational cognition, those which form deep, universal, and necessary features of human cognition.[24] It may be that Kant formulated his transcendental argument in response to Hume's skepticism concerning knowledge. In any event, Kelsen remains much closer to Hume's skeptical views than to Kant's rationalism. In particular, Kelsen himself remains highly skeptical of any objective grounding of morality, Kant's moral theory included. Indeed, Kelsen views morality as relativist all the way down.

This relativism haunts Kelsen's basic theory of law as well. Thus, he explicitly rejects the idea that the basic norm is something like a necessary feature or category of human cognition. Rather, the presupposition of a basic norm is optional. Neither is the acceptance of the normativity of law necessary; anarchism, as a rejection of law's normative validity is certainly an option, Kelsen maintained. The basic norm is presupposed only by those who accept the "ought," that is, the normative validity of the law. But there exists no rational compulsion to support this attitude:

> The Pure Theory describes the positive law as an objectively valid order and states that this interpretation is possible only under the condition that a basic norm is presupposed. . . . The Pure Theory, thereby characterizes this interpretation as possible, not necessary, and presents the objective validity of positive law only as conditional—namely conditioned by the presupposed basic norm.[25]

In suggesting a comparison with religion, Kelsen exacerbates the friction between his stated anti-reductionist approach with his relativistic views. That is, if one presupposes the relevant basic norm is a matter of choice, it is an ideological option, not something governed by reason. Likewise, the normativity of law, presupposed by its basic norm, is optional: "An anarchist, for instance, who denied the validity of the hypothetical basic norm of positive law . . . will view its positive regulation of human relationships . . . as mere power relations."[26] Once Kelsen admits that the content of a basic norm is fully determined by practice, it becomes very difficult to understand how his explication of legal validity may be non-reductive.

NORMATIVITY

The normativity of law, Kelsen asserts, is presupposed by the basic norm. A problem emerges, however, in his basic anti-reductionist approach to legal validity: since we cannot derive an "ought" from an "is," some "ought" must be presupposed in the background that would enable us to interpret certain acts or events as having legal significance. Perhaps Kelsen relies on one of his three theoretical functions of law, that of efficacy, to overcome this problem: efficacy is a condition of the validity of the basic norm, and a basic norm is legally valid if and only if it is actually followed in a given population.

Kelsen's conception of legal normativity may turn out to be a form of natural law completely relativized to a certain point of view, although in Kelsen's theory the relevant point of view is distinctly a legal one, not some general conception of morality or reason. What question remains is whether Kelsen succeeds in providing a non-reductive explanation of legal normativity, given the fact that his account of legal validity turns out to be reductive after all. The trouble here is not simply the relativizing to a point of view; the trouble resides in Kelsen's failure to ground the choice of the relevant point of view in anything like reason. By deliberately avoiding any explanation of what it is that might ground an agent's choice of endorsing a legal point of view, or any given basic norm, Kelsen leaves some of the most pressing questions concerning the normativity of law unanswered.

SHAPIRO'S PLANNING THEORY OF LAW

In *Legality*, Scott Shapiro offers a new theory of the nature of law.[27] His basic claim is that laws are plans for living together, and legal systems are institutions that create certain kinds of plans for societies to follow. He thereby characterizes legal activity as a form of shared planning activity, the fundamental aim of which is to solve moral disagreements that cannot be properly resolved by purely moral deliberation. His further claim is that laws are plans created by planning institutions with a specific moral aim, and that law can be thought of as a set of plans to achieve complex human goals.

The moral aim of Shapiro's legal theory is somewhat surprising, since his stated intention is to defend exclusive legal positivism and to reject the core commitments of natural law theory. Shapiro's objection is that if the function of law is to guide conduct by means of reasoning, then theoretically, every law must be capable of making what he calls a "practical difference." He further argues that rules that are law in virtue of their satisfying moral conditions of legality cannot make a practical difference, because the reason to act that they purport to create is already expressed in the condition of their legality.

Shapiro may be seen as a positivist, but one who tries to bridge the differences between legal positivism and natural law theory, a project whose success has been open to criticism. In his attempt to meld the two, Shapiro rejects inclusive legal positivism, which holds that the function of law is to guide conduct. Rather, his planning theory of law presents a method to solve what he describes as the possibility problem, which queries how law can be authoritative without referring to higher laws. Questions arise, though, about whether his insights positing social facts as facts about plans are sufficiently novel and powerful enough to warrant placing a new label on them, by using an analogy to another human activity to reframe the question.

LAWS AS PLANS

Shapiro refers to the "plans" in his approach as having the same meaning as used in ordinary everyday discourse. More formally, he states that plans are things that "require, permit, or authorize agents to act, or not act in certain ways under certain conditions" which we create by adopting, settling upon, or accepting them.[28] Thus, plans in his legal context are seen as guides to conduct which are created by us through our adopting them. He goes into some detail about the features of plans and planning to make the argument that laws are plans and legal systems are planning organizations.[29]

That is, Shapiro's planning theory claims that what makes a law a law, is that: (a) it is part of a "master plan" adopted by a certain group of officials; or (b) it is a plan which has been created in accordance with, and whose application is required by, such a master plan; or (c) it is a plan-like norm whose application is required by such a master plan. The relevant group of planners should be office-holders, the authority the group claims under the master plan is compulsory, and the planning group is "self-certifying."[30] The group sharing the master plan must also claim to have moral aims to engage in the planning activity.

LAW'S MORAL AIMS

Shapiro argues that the law is self-certifying, insofar as it operates by means of a master plan containing different forms and it operates by means of a presumption of validity from superior planning organizations. But Shapiro also posits a function that he claims is unique to law:

> When a community faces moral problems that are numerous and serious, and whose solutions are complex, contentious, or arbitrary, certain modes of planning such as improvisation, spontaneous ordering, private bargaining, communal consensus, or personalized hierarchies will be costly to engage in, sometimes prohibitively so. Unless the community has a way of reducing the costs and risks of planning, resolving these moral problems will be, at best, expensive and, at worst, impossible. On the Planning Theory, the fundamental aim of the law is to meet this moral demand in an efficient manner. By providing a highly nimble and durable method of social planning, the law enables communities to solve the numerous and serious problems that would otherwise be too costly or risky to resolve.[31]

Thus, the primary function of law for Shapiro is to remedy the moral deficiencies of the circumstances of legality, whereby specific moral problems include such matters as, "questions about ownership, contractual obligations, duties of care to one another, proper levels of taxation, limitations on public power, legitimacy of state coercion."[32]

The distinctive moral aim of Shapiro's planning theory is certainly contentious. Critiques of his theory include the simple point that a "plan" rarely comes into play in legal discourse, while the concept of a "rule" is extremely common. If we think that theories of law should reflect, at least in part, the self-understanding of (certain) participants to the legal system, then this is some reason to doubt whether the idea of a plan is central to the concept of law. Indeed, Hart's view that law is a system of different kinds of rules aligns more closely to the internal point of view of legal officials. The question arises, though, of whether the connections between laws, plans, legal systems, and planning institutions does not present merely an amalgam of Hart's primary and secondary rules.[33]

PLANNING INSTITUTIONS

For Shapiro, "Legal systems are institutions of social planning" whose purpose is "to compensate for the deficiencies of alternate forms of planning in the circumstances of legality."[34] In reviewing his argument to replace the concept of legal systems with that of planning institutions, it becomes evident that for Shapiro, customary rules are not plans. This is because customs are not created by procedures whose intention is to create rules/norms for the guidance of conduct, thereby creating a problem in regard to legal systems whose master "plan"—the fundamental rules setting out who has powers and duties of adjudication and how rules can be created—is wholly customary.

If such legal systems exist, then Shapiro's theory cannot account for them; such systems simply do not have a master plan. At most, they have Hartian rules of recognition, adjudication, and change. As John Gardner and Timothy Macklem point out in their review of *Legality*, this presents a serious problem for Shapiro, since there are such systems whose master rules are largely, if not entirely, customary, as exemplified by England and other countries with a common law constitution. Under Shapiro's theory, then, whether England has a legal system is called into question.[35]

Shapiro's theory is unable to explain law's normativity, an important element in any positivist theory. The creation of a legal norm takes a legal official to create; however, it takes a legal official to create a legal norm—a "chicken and egg" problem. Here, Shapiro attempts to explain what he claims to be a feature of law; namely, that legal officials who depart from the law without "compelling" reasons are open to criticism. He attempts to do so by claiming the officials have adopted a master plan. That is, it is the adopting of the plan that gives officials a compelling reason to adhere to the law and thus opens them to criticism in the event of their departing from it. It is far from clear, however, that the mere adoption of a plan always provides a reason—even a reason which could be outweighed by other reasons—to adhere to it.

In the end, Shapiro's disposition condition on plans seems false. He claims that a plan does not exist unless it was created in such a way as to dispose the subjects of the plan (the persons whom the plan seeks to guide) to adhere to it. This seems false. To make a plan for others, it only seems to be necessary that said subjects have some degree of belief that a plan will influence their conduct. That belief need not, however, be warranted for the plan to exist.

NOTES

1. See Joseph Raz, *The Authority of Law* (Oxford: Oxford University Press, 1994), 201–237. By contrast, H.L.A. Hart views himself as a soft or "inclusive" positivist in the sense that he accepts that some principles may be legally binding by virtue of their value or merit, but morality can be a condition of validity only where his rule of recognition so stipulates.

2. Joseph Raz, *Between Authority and Interpretation* (Oxford: Oxford University Press, 2009), 190–202.

3. H.L.A. Hart, "Legal Duty and Obligation," in *Essays on Bentham* (Oxford: Clarendon Press, 1982), 154.

4. Jules Coleman, *The Practice of Principle* (Oxford: Oxford University Press, 2003), 133.

5. Joseph Raz, *The Authority of Law* (Oxford: Clarendon Press, 1979), 3.

6. This argument concerning reason is reminiscent of Raz's discussion of the relation between reason and incommensurable moral values. In moral decision-making situations that involve incommensurable moral values and where reason is incapable of guiding action, Raz ignores examining the nature of value. Instead, he analyzes the nature of agency and rationality in two kinds of relationships. Thus, he distinguishes human agency, in which reasons require action, from what he terms a classical conception of agency in which the will (which Raz views as separate from desire) chooses "among options that reason merely renders eligible" (*Engaging Reason* [Oxford: Oxford University Press, 1999], 47). In favoring this classical conception of agency, Raz employs rationality in a weak sense (and not in the Aristotelian sense of appealing to practical reasoning), which is the strategy that some value pluralists adopt when attempting to solve the comparison problem among competing moral values.

7. Jospeh Raz, *Ethics in the Public Domain* (Oxford: Clarendon Press, 1994), 214.

8. Joseph Raz, "Authority and Justification," in *Authority*, ed. Joseph Raz (New York: New York University Press, 1990), 115–141.

9. Joseph Raz, *The Morality of Freedom* (Oxford: Clarendon Press, 1986), 56.

10. See Stephen Darwall, *The Second-Person Standpoint* (Cambridge: Harvard University Press, 2009).

11. See Raz 1979: 16–20.

12. Raz 1986: 26.

13. Ibid., 18–19; also see Raz's Chinese cooking example (p. 64).

14. Ibid., 250.

15. See Raz 1979.

16. Hans Kelsen, *Introduction to the Problems of Legal Theory,* trans. Bonnie Litschewski Paulson and Stanley L. Paulson (Oxford: Clarendon Press, 2002), 7.

17. Hans Kelsen, *Pure Theory of Law*, trans. Max Knight (Berkeley: University of California Press, 1967), 217–218.

18. Compare with Ronald Dworkin's discussion on law as interpretation in chapter 12 *infra.*

19. See H.L.A. Hart, *The Concept of Law,* intro. Leslie Green, postscript eds. Joseph Raz and Penelope A. Bulloch (Oxford: Oxford University Press, 2012), 105; compare with H.L.A. Hart's rule of recognition discussion in chapter 12 *infra.*

20. Hans Kelsen, "The Pure Theory of Law and Analytical Jurisprudence," *Harvard Law Review* 55 (1941): 44, 63.

21. Raz 1979: 127–129.

22. See Hans Kelsen, *Pure Theory of*Law, trans. Max Knight (Berkeley: University of California Press, 1967).

23. E.g., Joseph Raz, "Two Views of the Nature of the Theory of Law," *Legal Theory* 4 (1998): 258.

24. Hart rejected Kelsen's transcendentalist Kantian view of authority in favor of an empirical Weberian view.

25. Kelsen 2009: 217–218.

26. Hans Kelsen, *General Theory of Law and State,* trans. Anders Wedberg (New York: Russell & Russell, 1961), 413.

27. Scott Shapiro, *Legality* (Cambridge: Harvard University Press, 2011).

28. Ibid., 127.

29. Ibid., 120–148: (1) plans may be incomplete or partial; (2) plans may have sub-plans; (3) planning has its own inner rationality (plans need to be fleshed out, consistent, and reasonably resistant to reconsideration); (4) plans are created to guide conduct, and by different people; (5) plans are created by processes that dispose people to conform to them; (6) plans can be shared by groups; (7) shared plans are better than improvisation, especially if difficult problems are encountered; (8) the content of plans can be determined independently of the reasons for or against adopting the plan; (8) planning can be bottom up or top down; and (9) the costs of planning can be reduced by adopting policies, customs, and hierarchies.

30. Ibid., 221–223.

31. Ibid., 213.

32. Ibid., 213, 170.

33. See Hart 2012.

34. Shapiro 2011: 171.

35. See John Gardner and Timothy Macklem, "Review of *Legality*," *Notre Dame Philosophical Reviews* 2011: https://ndpr.nd.edu/reviews/legality/.

Chapter 14

Contemporary Theories of Justice

At the outset of this study, I expressed my belief that law should serve the demands of justice and I discussed the classical accounts of Plato and Aristotle, whose concepts of law are subsumed under their views of justice: law in the service of justice. Some of their views have made their way into contemporary theories of justice.[1] Of relevance here, for instance, the Aristotelian concept of particular justice as based on equality finds its way into contemporary distributive theories of justice, including John Rawls' influential theory of justice as fairness. Distributive theories of justice, however, do not account for important social matters such as power, which is not amenable to distribution. Relational theories of justice, on the other hand, attempt to address such social issues.[2] In particular, the theory of justice as right actions is consonant with the legal theory presented in this study.[3]

To avoid misunderstanding, I do not subscribe to either the metaphysical framework of Plato or the insistence on character development found in Aristotle as articulated in their writings. In my view, justice has its underpinnings in morality. Thus, it is the linkage of morality to justice I promote, a linkage that needs to be revisited often since, contrary to Plato and much of Aristotle, I believe that both morality and justice are dependent in large part on social norms. That is, social norms comprise common standards within various social groupings, in effect defining acceptable or appropriate behavior in differing social circumstances. Such social norms vary by community, as do the strength or weakness of such norms within communities, and moreover, they change over time. In other words, social norms represent contingent circumstances, and as such require continual assessment, at least with respect to how morality informs justice.

JUSTICE AS FAIRNESS

Writing in reaction to the then predominant moral theory of utilitarianism, which posits the greatest good for the greatest number of people, John Rawls begins *A Theory of Justice* with the statement that, "Justice is the first virtue of social institutions."[4] With this assertion, Rawls echoes Aristotle and John Stuart Mill while defining justice as fairness as based on a social contract.[5]

More specifically, Rawls sets out to construct a conception of justice that "constitutes the most appropriate moral basis for a democratic society."[6] His moral inquiry results in an egalitarian distributive construct in which justice, generally, requires that primary social goods (liberty and opportunity, income and wealth, and the bases for self-respect) be distributed equally within a society, unless unequal distribution is to everyone's advantage.[7] Under favorable social conditions, then, a special concept of justice as fairness may obtain.[8]

Focusing then on the concept of equality that helps drive his theory, Rawls holds that "[a]ll social primary goods—liberty and opportunity, income, wealth, and the bases of self-respect—are to be distributed equally unless an unequal distribution of any or all of these goods is to the advantage of the least favored."[9]

TWO PRINCIPLES OF JUSTICE AS FAIRNESS

Assuming that society is composed of free and equal, rational moral beings, Rawls articulates two principles of justice as fairness, as follows:[10]

First Principle: Each person is to have an equal right to the most extensive total system of equal basic liberties compatible with a similar system of liberty for all.
Second Principle: Social and economic inequalities are to be arranged so that they are both:

1. To the greatest benefit of the least advantaged, consistent with the just savings principle, and
2. Attached to offices and positions open to all under conditions of fair equality of opportunity.

The first principle of justice as fairness, the basic liberty principle, guarantees the equal basic rights and liberties needed to secure the fundamental interests of free and equal citizens and to pursue a wide range of conceptions of the good, including these basic freedoms: liberty of conscience and freedom of thought, freedom of association, the political liberties, the rights and liberties constituting freedom of the person (including the right to hold personal property), and the rights and liberties of the rule of law. These liberties, Rawls argues, are necessary to develop and exercise moral powers and to pursue a wide range of differing but reasonable conceptions of the good.

Having staked the claim, Rawls formulates a second principle, the difference principle. His second principle regulates differences (inequalities) in primary social goods by providing fair equality of educational and employment opportunities and a guaranteed minimum of the all-purpose means (including income and wealth), so that all individuals can pursue their interests, powers, and prerogatives of office as well as maintain self-respect. Rawls views the individual's pursuit of interests, then, as critical to distributive justice, while, through his second priority rule, establishing the priority of justice over efficiency and welfare (the Pareto distribution), as well as over the ideal of maximizing the sum of advantages in society.

SOCIAL INSTITUTIONS

Fundamentally, Rawls bases his theory of justice on a society whose principles of justice directly structure society's basic institutions, institutions which anchor: a liberal constitutional democracy, including a political constitution; a system of markets and the regulation of economic relations; a legal system of trials, property, and contracts; and the family. Rawls identifies these institutions as basic, since they provide rules that structure the lives of individuals in the larger framework of fundamental rights and duties, while they also determine how to divide advantages of social cooperation. As such, they have a profound influence on who we are as well as on our life prospects and are, accordingly, the first subject of justice.

In sum, a just political constitution upholds Rawls' first principle, the liberty principle, through the claim that the state makes and enforces laws for equal citizens in a government with limited powers, while a just economic order upholds his second principle, the difference principle, providing equal opportunity with regard to education, culture, and income, while preventing monopolies.

In conceiving his just society in a legal framework, Rawls realizes the gap between the ideal and the real and so answers why we should comply with laws by defining injustice and unjust laws. In the end, he argues that while we have a natural duty of justice to comply with the laws of an imperfectly just society, the perpetual violation of the principle of liberty and the exhaustion of legal means of redress may justify civil disobedience, and in extreme circumstances, rebellion.

Realizing the need for further guidance, Rawls proposes that just institutions are determined through a four-stage sequence with hypothetical deliberation principles for deriving and applying principles of justice to institutions: the original position, the constitutional stage, the legislative stage, and the judicial or "last" stage. At each stage beyond the original position, as discussed below, the "veil of ignorance" is incrementally lifted, and the rules agreed to previously act to constrain what is rational in the succeeding stages. More concisely: an ever-narrowing process based on reasoning postulated in the original position determines just rules. In characterizing this sequence, Rawls insists upon just institutions to curb the moral arbitrariness of fortune that determines the social position, physical characteristics, and other natural facts of how one is born into society. Not allowing fate as an appropriate platform for justice, Rawls insists that society's basic institutions must be fair.

In short, it is the justice of the basic structure of society that concerns Rawls. Subordinating fortune's claims to structure, Rawls would support distributions only when the basic structure of society is fair, and only if such claims meet legitimate expectations of the parties. Similar to the static nature of models articulated by Plato and Aristotle, Rawls embraces the ideal of a well-ordered society, one which is perfectly just and in which all citizens openly agree upon the same conception of justice. Not only does such a society enact justice in its laws and institutions, citizens have a sense of justice and a basic willingness to comply with these terms. Heeding reflections from the original position, individuals engage in and desire to seek a conception of justice that will be stable in a well-ordered society generally acceptable to all reasonable and rational persons.

ORIGINAL POSITION

A novel feature in Rawls' argument is a thought experiment, asking us to imagine ourselves in the original position, the position of rational, free, and equal persons who, under a veil of ignorance, jointly agree upon and commit to principles of social and political justice. He further imagines that parties in the original position are presented with a list of the main conceptions of justice drawn from the traditions of social and political philosophy, so that they can choose the conception of justice that best advances their interests. The original position, he further explains, serves as the most effective place to apply the maximin rule, whereby the action whose worst outcome proves better than the worst outcome of all other alternatives should prevail. Rather than the principle of (average) utility, justice as fairness thereby argues for a conservative strategy of choice under uncertainty.[11]

Rawls' theory thereby relies upon human beings to possess a sense of justice, which thus provides a source of moral judgment as well as a source of moral motivation. It is controversial, however, to assume that humans have an intuitive moral sense of justice. Beginning with considered judgments that arise from this sense of justice, Rawls imagines the parties engaging in a deliberative process, reflecting upon and revising their considered beliefs until they are in equilibrium; that is, until the resultant principles of justice are stable and consistent with one another.[12] To posit equilibrium as a workable mechanism, Rawls assumes social norms that would allow cooperation, which, of course, are both possible and necessary in a social contract.

In the end, Rawls contends that the most rational choice for parties in the original position yields his two principles of justice, whereby, as discussed above, the first principle, the liberty principle, is upheld by a just political constitution and second principle, the difference principle, is effected by means of a just economic order.

INDETERMINACY

H. L. A. Hart formulated the widely known criticism of Rawls' first principle, his equal basic liberty principle, as being indeterminate in application, since Rawls includes no reference to external measures or values. Thus, in his essay, "Rawls on Liberty and Its Priority," Hart analyzes Rawls' first principle, the principle of greatest equal liberty, along with the associated priority rule that "liberty can only be restricted for the sake of liberty."[13] Hart finds this principle—which treats only the maximizing and extent of liberty—indeterminate, since in trying to apply it, the concept of greatest liberty cannot be distinguished from judgments about which liberties are more important than others, and just as problematically, determining which liberties are more important than others depends on what ends they serve.[14] Furthermore, where all the conflicting moral values in question are basic liberties, Rawls' explanation of adjusting and regulating basic liberties so that they operate in a central range of application is unpersuasive and unhelpful in moral decision-making.

In *A Theory of Justice*, Rawls attempts to ground a comprehensive liberalism on moral principles rather than on political principles, and he affirms autonomy as an intrinsic human good that must be promoted by institutions of justice in society. Although Rawls holds that justice may not properly serve as a political conception reasonably acceptable to free and equal citizens, he nonetheless dramatically moves his discussion of justice from the moral to the political realm in his later work of *Political Liberalism*.[15]

CRITICISMS

In addition to Hart's charge of indeterminacy, Rawls' theory of justice as fairness has been subject to a number of serious criticisms, including: (1) that the outcome-orientation of Rawls' second principle, his difference principle, moves his theory outside a comfortably deontological approach;[16] (2) that Rawls' argument for the priority of the right over the good is not successful;[17] and, (3) that his adoption of multiple permissible comprehensive conceptions of the good underlying his theory of justice elicits the charge of incommensurability.[18]

DISTRIBUTIVE AND RELATIONAL ACCOUNTS

Among other contemporary distributive theories of justice, prominent ones include: (a) Ronald Dworkin's theory of resource equality whereby resources are distributed through a hypothetical auction-insurance scheme, and which has been viewed as an example of luck egalitarianism;[19] (b) Charles Beitz's cosmopolitan theory of global natural resource equality;[20] and, (c) Derek Parfit's question of whether intergenerational justice can actually exist, along with his utilitarian calculus resulting in his Repugnant Conclusion.[21]

Contemporary debates in justice often assume a liberal political context, in which concepts of liberty and equality, especially various concepts of political equality, come into play. Critically, since distributional views, as mentioned above, tend to ignore important societal issues such as power and that these issues are not amenable to distribution. Of course, individuals do live in groups, and consequently, the political aspect of any formulation of justice may not be ignored. A distributional approach to the question, however, insufficiently treats important societal realities. In other words, I do not view justice, as do many contemporary theorists, as a distributional matter in Aristotelian vein, whereby the task of justice is to develop political institutions, "just institutions," to distribute or redistribute liberties and social goods of society.

Rather, focusing on the individual as responsible for her or his actions, coded as such through social or political norms, I view justice as a relational matter. Critically, when viewing justice as a distributional matter, such individual responsibility is ignored. Rather than assigning justice the task of distributing social goods to those least advantaged in society or otherwise, I view the task of justice as providing normative guidance in an individual's relations to others. The key to such a relational view of justice is communication, both in a substantive sense as a rational, discursive method of resolving disparate conflicting views, but also in an instrumental sense as a conduit to convey ideas, especially the transmission of values through time.

JUSTICE AS RIGHT ACTIONS

My answer to the justice question, looking back to Plato and Aristotle, is to develop a moral framework to inform the political landscape of the times. Thus, I view the proper task of justice as the development of normative guidance in the form of action-guiding principles that may be applied in variable circumstances.[22] Further, the set of principles arrived upon should, critically, be able to be universalized—by which I mean principles that are not self-defeating, that are reversible, and that may be consistently applied.

TWO PRINCIPLES OF JUSTICE AS RIGHT ACTIONS

Thus, I arrive at a formulation of two principles of justice, in lexical priority:

> *The Responsibility Principle*: One is responsible for one's own actions.
>
> *The Equality Principle*: One should act with respect and concern for persons having the same right to act and to respond to one's actions.[23]

I thereby maintain that justice includes responsible actions based on rational and autonomous moral agency, with the individual (not groups) as the proper bearer of rights and responsibilities. In taking an analytical approach, and arguing for the right over the good, I deepen the apparent transparency of the political tenet—*do what is right*—with a morally thick register, one that recognizes the conventions, thought, and richness of moral traditions of various cultures, by framing the concept in a deontological approach.

In viewing justice as right actions, then, I assume that a person owes a duty of justice when her or his actions may affect others. This responsibility for intentional actions is set forth in the first principle of justice as right actions, the Responsibility Principle, as limited by the second principle, the Equality Principle, which advises that we consider how others might act in response to an individual's actions. Thus, the second principle, the Equality Principle, with its reference to other persons, and consequently the external world and experience, works both as a constraint on the first principle of justice as right actions, the Responsibility Principle, as well as a repository of resources for moral decision-making, as it empirically reaches into particular communities in which individuals are situated, along with the laws and customs of such communities. It also provides the touchstone for a priority rule in situations involving conflicting values.

In examining the variability of circumstances, I mention two additional concerns. First, the circumstances or facts of a situation are often not hard and nubby items. Rather, what facts are relevant in a given situation may be open to various shades of interpretation and characterization that may be critical in determining what constitutes just actions in any given event. In addition to interpreting and selecting relevant facts, addressing the question of circumstances themselves must be understood as setting the context for the application of rules of justice.

VALUE PLURALISM

In the approach to justice as right actions, plural values are embraced, although I do not favor a strong value pluralist account, nor one afflicted by the problem of incommensurability. Like Immanuel Kant and John Rawls, and in contrast to both Joseph Raz and John Stuart Mill, I advocate for the right over the good. The priority of the right, which Rawls presents in his theory as neutral and anti-perfectionist, may be seen as placing limits, in the interest of fairness, on differing conceptions of the good.

In arguing for the right over the good, I acknowledge attendant theoretical problems to the deontological approach of justice as right actions, and I propose a thin underlying theory of the good, which comprises four concepts, as follows:[24]

1. rationality;
2. autonomous moral agency;
3. equal concern and respect for others; and
4. plurality of values.

Thus, value pluralism may be seen to enter the account of justice as right actions by means of the second principle, the Equality Principle, which states that in societal interactions, mutual respect and concern between individuals should be normative. This weak value pluralism is further supported by the concepts of tolerance and social diversity, as envisioned in a political context of liberalism. In other words, a politically framed, morally thick concept—*do what is right*—approached from a deontological perspective impels my argument on justice.[25]

NORMS AND CUSTOMS

The cultural contingency implied in the Responsibility Principle may be ameliorated by the Equality Principle's reference to the external world and experience. For instance, as previously discussed, there are moral resources and constraints contained in Tim Scanlon's concept of "parametric universalism," which seek to identify certain deeply embedded, culturally universal concepts that exclude genocide, murder, and totalitarian rule from acceptable moral behavior.[26] While Scanlon's views may be seen as relativistic, they are nonetheless grounded in certain cross-cultural concepts, making external analyses possible while minimizing intuition as a standard.

In further searching for action-guiding moral resources referenced in the Equality Principle, it proves useful as well to identify morally thick concepts. As also referenced above, Bernard Williams in his benign treatment of moral relativism identifies four concepts that are able to bear a substantial amount of cross-cultural weight, including cowardice, truthfulness, brutality, and gratitude.[27]

Finally, for those situations in which a conflict in values is identified under the two principles of justice as right actions, the value which best adheres to or promotes the notion of due respect and concern for persons embedded in this account is the one that should prevail as a priority rule.

THE INDIVIDUAL AND THE POLITY

As discussed, for justice as right actions, the view of liberalism that serves as the political context for the theory includes the concepts of tolerance and social diversity, but not by according power to groups in a manner that diminishes the focus on the individual as a rational and moral agent. That is, while I accept a liberal political context, again, I believe that the individual should be the proper bearer of rights and responsibilities in political society. In other words, the appropriate political context is a liberalism that has components of negative liberty and equality of concern and respect, further including the concepts of tolerance and social diversity, with the equality component acting as both a constraint and as a repository of moral resources.

More explicitly, the component of equality as embedded in the Equality Principle is Kantian in promoting equality of concern and respect while also comprising one of the components of liberalism (along with negative liberty, tolerance, and social diversity) that serves as the political context for my approach. It is equality as well that serves as the touchstone in the priority rule for justice in situations involving conflicting values. Thus, in justice as right actions, equality is deontological in conception and as such serves as both a political measure and as an adjudicating value.

INTERNATIONAL JUSTICE

In justice as right actions, a moral basis for international relations among nations may be found in the Responsibility Principle, which prescribes responsible actions based on rational and moral agency and which further looks to the Equality Principle and its concept of due concern and respect for providing appropriate constraints on actions, as well as a view of the external world and experience for providing resources for moral decision-making. Further, my view of personal identity as largely a social construct, as well as the importance of intentions underlying actions, may map comfortably onto nations as well as individuals, and relations between and among nations. Politically, the moral agency I attribute to nations is supported by the notion that nations and states are commonly understood to be organized for the common good of their people.

In extending justice as right actions internationally, one question posed should be whether moral agency may be properly attributable to nations as actors, followed by the question of what action-guiding principles may be appropriate for nations *inter se,* as well as between nations and individuals. A subsequent question then arises concerning what political order may be appropriate as a framework for justice as right actions internationally, especially in respect to the situation where there is no minimal state binding nations, one which may legitimately use physical coercive power to protect rights or interests of member nations.

For answers to these questions, I focus on international relations and look to communication as the key. I argue that moral agency may indeed be properly attributable to nations, and I contest the realist view that rejects morality and instead offers self-interest as the guiding principle for nations in their relations with other nations.[28] Further, the laws and customs of people constitute part of the empirical landscape that may be reached through the Equality Principle as applied to international matters, carrying with it, in this case, the analogous concept of due concern and respect for other nations.[29] In providing normative guidance to nations, that is, the Equality Principle may be seen as providing constraints to the responsible actions of nations, as well as resources for moral decision-making.[30]

Importantly, in its normative action-guiding function, justice as right actions looks to parametric universalisms, as well as morally thick concepts, included in the laws and customs of various nations and peoples, mindful that with conflicting values, the particular value that best adheres to or promotes due respect and concern for others is preferred over competing values in any given circumstance.[31] Insofar as respect and concern for others receive priority, it follows that global obligations of justice are articulated for nations *inter se,* as well as in the relations among nations, states, and individuals. Clearly, approaching international justice in this manner does not reduce the likelihood of controversial conflicts of values, but in such cases, justice as right actions also adopts a cooperative method of reasoned discourse to arrive at just resolutions of such issues.

In attempting to universalize the concept of fundamental rights, for example, the thirty Articles of the United Nations' Universal Declaration of Human Rights take up much space in trying to avoid specific aberrations of moral behavior. Rather than articulating specific instances that may over time and over cultures may or may not obtain, it may prove more useful to articulate clear, overarching principles.[32] Thus, the four goods identified in the thin theory of the good underlying justice as right actions, especially the good of due concern and respect for others, may provide guidance that not only underscores the intent of the thirty articles, but also instances not covered by them.

Since justice as right actions characterizes the concept of universal human rights as instantiating a culturally contingent debate, negotiated through the Equality Principle, it avoids both Charles Beitz's resorting to what amounts to an exception, as well as the controversial setting of minimum standards as John Rawls would require.[33] Instead, justice as right actions considers human rights as part of the empirical landscape, including the questions of the content and scope of the concept of human rights as well as challenges to their universality.

JUSTICE IN THE FUTURE

Justice as right actions rests on the notion that justice is relational rather than distributive, with a key component being communication that is, as stated above, both substantive in the sense of providing a method for clarifying and resolving disputes through rational discourse, as well as instrumental, especially with regard to the transmission of values.[34] As with international justice, the values to be transmitted into the future are contained in the theory's underlying thin theory of the good outlined earlier, whose concepts bolster both the Responsibility and Equality Principles.

To transmit these values to future generations, the Equality Principle further provides a resource, since it makes empirical reference to the external world and experience, to the laws and customs of societies. Because justice as right actions embraces a relational view, its deontological approach avoids the utilitarian infelicities of Derek Parfit's Repugnant Conclusion and advocates for transmitting values over time in a liberal political framework of negative liberty and equality of respect and concern, together with the concepts of tolerance and diversity. The empirical reliance upon persons and their societies proposed in the Equality Principle, together with the priority rule for conflicting values provided in the theory, thus serves to provide continuing relevance for future obligations of justice.

NOTES

1. See Young Kim, *Justice: Classical Foundations and Contemporary Debates* (Lanham: Lexington Books, 2018); also see chapter 15 *infra* regarding the fit of justice as right actions with the theory of law.
2. E.g., see Iris Marion Young, *Justice and the Politics of Difference* (Oxford: Oxford University Press, 1990); although I disagree with the premise of her related group rights theory.
3. See Young Kim, *Justice as Right Actions* (Lanham: Lexington Books, 2015), ch. 10.
4. See John Rawls, *A Theory of Justice* (Cambridge: Harvard University Press, 1971), 1.
5. See chapter 14 *infra* regarding Rawls' theory of justice.
6. Ibid., viii; but see John Rawls, *Political Liberalism* (New York: Columbia University Press, 1993), where he takes the discussion of justice as fairness from a moral point of view to a political one.
7. Rawls 1971: 62.
8. Among the vast multitude of works on Rawls' theory of justice, the following provide excellent insights: Samuel Freeman, *Rawls* (New York: Routledge, 2007); several essays in Norman Daniels, ed., *Reading Rawls* (New York: Basic Books, 1975); and Chandran Kukathas and Philip Pettit, *Rawls* (Stanford: Stanford University Press, 1990).
9. Rawls 1971: 303.
10. Ibid., 302.
11. For critiques of Rawls' use of a maximin rule, see John Harsanyi, *Essays on Ethics, Social Behavior and Scientific Explanation* (Dordretch: D. Reidel, 1976): 37–63; also see R. M. Hare, *Essays on Political Morality* (Oxford: Oxford University Press, 1998), ch. 14.
12. As such, the selection process entails reflective equilibrium, which has been interpreted as a coherentist method used to justify moral beliefs epistemically. See Norman Daniels, "Reflective Equilibrium," *Stanford Encyclopedia of Philosophy*, https://plato.stanford.edu/entries/reflective-equilibrium (2016).
13. See H. L. A. Hart, "Rawls on Liberty and Its Priority," in ed. Norman Daniels, *Reading Rawls* (Oxford: Blackwell, 1975), 206–229. In the same essay (pp. 238–239), Hart also raises the question of whether there are secondary sets of principles for non-basic liberties. Further, despite Rawls' reformulation into the *basic liberties*

principle in *Political Liberalism,* the principle remains susceptible to the charge of indeterminacy.

14. Ibid., 241: "conflicts between basic liberties will be such that different resolutions of the conflict will correspond to the interests of different people who will diverge over the relative value they set on the conflicting liberties."

15. See Rawls 1993.

16. Rawls' difference principle does not seem deontological at all insofar as his difference principle has an outcome orientation.

17. See discussion of the right and the good in chapter 2 *infra.*

18. See John Gray, *Two Faces of Liberalism (Cambridge: Polity Press*, 2000), 72–75, 92; also see discussion of value pluralism and incommensurability in chapter 3 *infra.*

19. See Ronald Dworkin, *Sovereign Virtue* (Cambridge: Harvard University Press, 2000); also see chapter 3 *infra* regarding Dworkin's theory of resource equality and critiques thereof.

20. See Charles Beitz, *Political Theory and International Relations* (Princeton: Princeton University Press, 1999); also see Charles Beitz "International Liberalism and Distributive Justice," *World Politics* 51;2 (1999): 269–296; further, see chapter 10 *infra* regarding Beitz's world view of international relations.

21. Derek Parfit, *Reasons and Persons* (Oxford: Clarendon Press, 1984); for a rejection of Parfit's Repugnant Conclusion, see Kim 2015: ch. 9.

22. See Kim 2015: ch. 1.

23. Ibid., 3.

24. Ibid., 12–13, 48–50.

25. Ibid., 63–70.

26. Based upon a loose definition of rationality and a contractualist framework, Scanlon develops "[a] view that allows for such variations in what is right, by applying a fixed set of substantive moral principles to varying circumstances, [which] is not relativism but rather what [he calls] 'parametric universalism.'" T. M. Scanlon, *What We Owe to Each Other* (Cambridge: Harvard University Press, 2000), 328.

27. See Bernard Williams, *Ethics and the Limits of Philosophy* (Cambridge: Harvard University Press, 1985), 140.

28. See Charles Beitz, *Political Theory and International Relations* (Princeton: Princeton University Press, 1999), in which Beitz argues for a cosmopolitan approach to international relations, rather than a Hobbesian realist one. However, the grounds for his argument shift from one of interdependence and cooperation, to one based on Kantian moral obligations.

29. See John Rawls, *The Law of Peoples* (Cambridge: Harvard University Press, 1997).

30. See Kim 2015: ch. 8; also see chapter 10 *infra.*

31. See T. M. Scanlon, *What We Owe Each Other* (Cambridge: Harvard University Press, 2000), regarding "parametric universalism" and Bernard Williams, *Ethics and the Limits of Philosophy* (Cambridge: Harvard University Press, 1985) concerning morally thick concepts.

32. By way of example, Saudi Arabia, a member of the United Nations, abstained from signing the Universal Declaration of Human Rights on the grounds that Article 18, which provides for a right to change religions, articulates a view offensive to Islam.

33. See notes 21, 29, and 30 above, with accompanying texts.

34. Parfit's utilitarian view of future lives leads inexorably to his Repugnant Conclusion: "For any perfectly equal Population with very high positive welfare, there is a population with very low positive welfare which is better, other things being equal." Derek Parfit, *Reasons and Persons* (Oxford: Clarendon Press, 1984), 388.

PART V

Justice and Law

Chapter 15

Justice and Law

In the preceding chapter, I outlined a theory of justice as right actions. I've previously expressed my belief that law should be in the service of the demands of justice. The question I address in this chapter is how well the theory of justice as right actions fits the theory of law developed in these pages.

The theory of justice as right actions presents a deontological, normative theory. Rather than taking a distributive approach to the question of justice, it takes a relational approach which is led by moral concerns. This view focuses on the individual and her/his relations with other persons and institutions in society. Thus, the foundation of the theory of justice as right actions is moral, and morality drives the theory and the search for the right thing to do in given circumstances.

By contrast, the theory of law presented here has a political foundation and may be seen to be connected to morality at the top level, as justice as right actions provides the moral framework and resources within which rules of law are made. Law involves attempts to make authoritative political pronouncements to regulate human behavior, and these pronouncements sometimes overlap with moral and normative concerns.

What is law? In my view, law comprises social and normative rules of behavior imposed by a political authority, and thus, the foundation of law is political, including the power to enforce rules. Accordingly, the question of law at the ground level is primarily a question of obedience—whether and in what circumstances it is appropriate to obey the law. Since the question of obedience to the law is a normative question, it follows that the answer is dependent on the contingent content of a society's conventions, and on the relevance and strength of morality in the legal system.

As such, this theory of law accepts that law and the legal system consist of rules and duties that depend on the values and norms of society for their legal validity. More specifically, I present and describe the operation of two principles of law undergirding this study's theory of law. Hence, the nature of obligation, especially legal and moral obligations, is examined here, along with the concept of moral responsibility. In doing so, I also address important questions of values and norms, as they are fundamental to any normative theory of law.

PRINCIPLES OF JUSTICE

The theory of justice as right actions stems from a moral view of the world, and as discussed above, result in two principles in lexical priority:

> *The Responsibility Principle*: One is responsible for one's own actions.
>
> *The Equality Principle*: One should act with respect and concern for persons having the same right to act and to respond to one's actions.

PRINCIPLES OF LAW

This study's normative legal theory has political foundations, and thus may also be stated as two principles in lexical priority, as follows:

> *First Principle*: One should obey those laws of legal-rational political authority that are not otherwise violative of societal norms and customs.
>
> *Second Principle*: Government should only enforce rules of human behavior of legitimate legal-rational political authority.

RELIGIOUS AND METAPHYSICAL BELIEFS

In the search for normative guidance for actions, I reject the ontological bases of religious beliefs (whatever the variety), metaphysical beliefs (universal eternal forms), and epistemological beliefs (*cogito ergo sum*). All three sets of beliefs assume an initial leap of faith, so that much of the reasoning by strong proponents of these views seem more like rationalizations, rather than arising from some unbiased starting point.

RIGHT OVER GOOD

Both the theory of justice as right actions proposed here and the theory of law presented in this study depend on a deontological point of view, with the same underlying thin theory of the good, and both privilege the priority of the right over the good. Further, they both rely on rational, autonomous moral agents in the consideration of responsible actions. As mentioned earlier, I rely on a moderate view of rationality, rather than a more extreme Platonic or Cartesian view, as a precedential method of acquiring knowledge.

RATIONALITY

In my moderate view of rationality, as discussed in chapter 2, I take an Aristotelian stance that practical reasoning starts with the normative question of what is one to do, considers questions of value, and leads to a consideration of intentional actions. Theoretical reasoning, by contrast, may be seen as concerned with matters of fact and their explanation. Examined in this manner, the contrast between practical reason and theoretical reason addresses two different systems of norms: those for the regulation of action (practical reason), and those for the regulation of belief (theoretical reason).

I view practical reason as requiring reflection to resolve the question of what an agent is to do. Thus, issues to be explored from the perspective of practical reason include: whether and how deliberative reflection can give rise to action, what norms for the assessment of action are binding upon us as agents, and whether such norms are purely instrumental. Also discussed in chapter 2, when practical reason weighs such issues, moral responsibility is evoked. In other words, moral responsibility depends upon the rational and autonomous individual to judge, act, and deliberate norms in such a manner that a particular type of reaction—generally speaking, praise or blame—is elicited. It is important to underscore here, as argued in chapter 3, that in deliberating the requisite reaction (e.g., praise or blame), the conditions and objects of moral responsibility intrinsically require analyses that consider norms to some degree.

OPERATION OF PRINCIPLES OF JUSTICE AND LAW

As to how the principles of justice as right actions work together with the principles of the normative legal theory presented in this study, I offer the following:

I. (a) *The Responsibility Principle of Justice as Right Actions* ("One is responsible for one's own actions") focuses on the individual and her/his responsibility as rational and autonomous moral agent for intentional actions that affect others.

(b) *The First Principle of the Theory of Law* articulated in these pages ("One should obey those laws of legal-rational political authority that are not otherwise violative of societal norms and customs") also focuses on the individual, but takes a more political approach, accepting Weberian classifications of the sources of political authority in addressing the permissible ambit of an individual's actions towards others in society. The First Principle thus understands that the question of law is primarily a question of obedience—whether and in what circumstances it is appropriate to obey the law.

II. (a) *The Equality Principle of Justice as Right Actions* ("One should act with respect and concern for persons having the same right to act and to respond to one's actions") extends the moral obligations of justice to the external world through the Kantian concept of due concern and respect.
(b) *The Second Principle of the Theory of Law* presented here ("Government should only enforce rules of human behavior of legitimate legal-rational political authority") addresses the political foundation of law, and the question of political rule and the social institutions which legislate, administer, and enforce the law.

Thus, in deciding upon just actions (within a moral framework), a person should determine whether any applicable law is just or not, in such a way to provide a normative answer to the question of obedience to the law in question.

Conclusion

Normative Principles of Law

In pursuit of the question of law, I have explored foundational political and moral issues, and in so doing, I have developed the normative theory of law presented in these pages. My hope is that the theory presents and explicates two useful and durable principles of law that provide normative guidance as to questions of lawful actions. In this concluding chapter, I summarize my investigation into the question of law, an analysis of the issues presented, the views developed, and arguments advanced in working out these principles of law.

TWO PRINCIPLES OF LAW

Related, the two principles of law discussed in these pages may be stated in lexical priority, as follows:

> *First Principle*: One should obey those laws of legal-rational political authority that do not otherwise violate societal norms and customs.
>
> *Second Principle*: Government should only enforce rules of human behavior of legitimate legal-rational political authority.

This view understands the foundation of law to be political by including the power to enforce rules. Thus, the question of law is seen primarily as a question of obedience—whether and in what circumstances it is appropriate to obey the law.

In attempting to determine whether and under what circumstances the law should be obeyed under the first principle, the norms and customs of the relevant society should be taken into account, thus making the determination a culturally contingent issue. As an example, it may be useful to consider that, for Kant, the operation of the Categorical Imperative resulted in the absolute prohibition against murder, theft, and lying. While the operation of the two principles of law articulated here aligns with Kant's prohibition against murder, theft, and lying, it does so by means of a different approach. That is, in contradistinction to Kant's Categorical Imperative the approach examined in this study takes an empirical view of the external world and experience through the first principle and allows for sanctions through the second principle.

Again like Kant, this approach is also deontological. The theory here, however, attempts to be value-neutral, while also acknowledging an underlying thin theory of the good, including concepts of rationality, autonomous moral agency, equal concern and respect for others, and the plurality of values. Underlying these two principles of law, then, is the Kantian notion of due respect and concern for persons.[1] The legal theory I develop here, however, includes interrogating both moral and political aspects, acknowledging that principles are not universal. That is, the first principle engages moral considerations, as based on the individual and is further designed to provide normative guidance to a person's actions. In designating the individual as responsible for her or his own actions, the first principle creates a relation to political aspects as articulated in the second principle.

That is, to engage in moral considerations, an individual relies upon the external world and experience for limits on appropriate actions. In this manner, the first principle sets the ambit of proper actions for persons in society, based in the caveat that norms and customs need to be taken into account, thus making the determination a culturally contingent matter. Hence, the first principle also points to the political foundation of law, and the question of obedience—whether and in what circumstances it is appropriate to obey the law.

In keying on the individual for this first principle, I express my view of the importance of responsible actions by individuals based on rational and autonomous moral agency. That is, I view persons as responsible, in the sense of accountability, for their intentional actions. The sense of agency that I pursue includes elements of rationality and autonomy although, as mentioned previously, I diverge from Kant's view that rationality entails autonomy. In other words, for rational, autonomous individuals, the first principle states a normative rule for obeying laws in society.

As stated above, the first principle thus sets the parameters for the second principle, which is political and which accedes in lexical priority to the first principle. It corresponds to the first principle in that it sets the proper ambit of societal response to an individual's lawful actions. It directly addresses government and the political foundation of law, addressing the proper treatment of citizens in society.

OBLIGATIONS

The inquiry into moral and legal obligations, or duties, explores normative reasons for action and looks into questions of intention and psychological motivation. In examining these matters, I review concepts of practical reason, due concern and respect, responsibility, moral luck, and moral relativism.[2]

While morality (and moral obligation) may be seen as concerning principles of right and wrong, and of good and bad behavior, laws (and legal obligation) may be seen as rules of conduct or action regulating behavior which are created and enforced by a controlling authority, often social institutions or government. Thus, while one may argue that a person has a prima facie duty to obey the law, if the law at issue offends societal norms and customs, then the question of obedience to the law is evoked. The main question here is often presented as the extent to which legal obligations, simply because they are legal obligations, give rise to moral obligations. Is there a general duty to obey the legal norms of the society in which a person lives?

VALUES AND NORMS

This study has explored critical questions of values and norms, since they underpin normative legal theories: What is the source of values? What shape should a theory of values have? Should there be one overarching value or a plurality of values? If a plurality of values exists, without any overarching value or hierarchal ranking of values in a value theory, what should be made of incommensurable values? What defines the right and the good? What is the rational authority of norms?

RELIGION AND METAPHYSICS

While some interpretations of religious commands, rules and laws are considered in this study for their normative significance, they are examined without delving into their ontological contexts. Likewise, in examining some metaphysical arguments on the nature of law, they are assessed not for their ontological significance, but with respect to their normative characteristics. More specifically, religious approaches often stipulate starting points that require an initial leap of faith and are thereby unsatisfying as neutral rational vantage points for exploring questions of morality and the normative character of law. Similarly, metaphysical approaches start with top-down theoretical assumptions that hinder the analysis and study of the question of law. Consequently, excluded from this study are ontological considerations of religious and metaphysical approaches to the question of law.

CLASSICAL VIEWS OF LAW

In the classical accounts of Plato and Aristotle, concepts of law are subsumed under their respective views of justice, positioning law in service of justice. While both Plato and Aristotle believed in a moral universe, Plato constructed a metaphysical framework with his theory of forms, while Aristotle focused on character development as leading to the good life.[3]

Their theories are included here, because I share their view that law should be in the service of justice. Thus, in the normative theory of law presented in these pages, I examine the fit of the theory of law presented here with a conception of justice—the theory of justice as right actions.

EARLY NATURAL LAW THEORIES

I have also discussed theories of Thomas Aquinas, Thomas Hobbes, and John Locke, with respect to their discussions of natural law.[4] While the term natural law covers a broad range of views, I examined a classic view of natural law in this context, as follows: (1) natural law is given by God; (2) it is naturally knowable and authoritative over humans; and, (3) it holds that the good is prior to the right, although this last proposition has raised controversy as applied to Hobbes' and Locke's theories.

Some scholars have adopted the view that natural law, not natural rights, is primary. They hold that when Locke emphasized the right to life, liberty, and property, he was primarily making a point about the duties we have toward other people: duties not to kill, enslave, or steal. Most scholars also argue that Locke recognized a general duty to assist with the preservation of humankind, including a duty of charity to those who have no other way to procure their subsistence. These scholars regard duties as primary in Locke because rights exist to ensure that we are able to fulfill our duties.

I agree with another group of theorists, however, who take rights to be paramount for Locke, some going so far as to portray Locke's position as essentially similar to that of Hobbes. They point out that Locke defended a hedonist theory of human motivation and argue that he must agree with Hobbes about the essentially self-interested nature of human beings. Locke, they claim, recognizes natural law obligations only in those situations where our own preservation is not in conflict, further emphasizing that our right to preserve ourselves trumps any duties we may have.

EARLY THEORIES OF LEGAL POSITIVISM

While there are differences in their legal theories, both Jeremy Bentham and John Austin starkly distinguish natural law from positive law.[5] As 18th century advocates of legal positivism, Bentham and Austin marginalize natural law theory as comprising a series of propositions derived from nature that closely connects legal and moral normativity, based in the supposition that there is a moral determinant to legality. In both their views, however, legal positivism denies a necessary connection between law and morals. Moreover, they both posit that the validity of any law can be traced to an objectively verifiable source.

POLITICAL SOCIETY AND CIVIL GOVERNMENT

As I have argued, I view law as consisting of social and normative rules of behavior imposed by a legitimate political authority, together with legal principles for interpreting such rules, viewing the foundation of law as political, including the power to enforce rules and positing that law is primarily a question of obedience.

Based in the approach that the foundation of law is political, I proceeded to examine the tensions between the concepts of natural rights and natural law, justifications of political rule, modern concepts of rights, and political legitimacy and civil government. In exploring the question of political legitimacy, I examined the broad contemporary concept of rights, since rights drive discussions of permissible actions and institutions, as well as underlie the concept of political legitimacy.

There are two main contemporary theories of rights: the will theory and the interest theory. A will theorist asserts that the function of a right is to give the holder of the right control over another's duty. Thus, according to H.L.A. Hart, the right-holder is "a small scale sovereign." In this camp, the views of Immanuel Kant and Hans Kelsen link rights and normative control. That is, for will theorists, this link between rights and authority (the authority to control what others may do) is a matter of definition.

By contrast, interest theorists maintain that the function of a right is to further the right-holder's interests.[6] An owner has a right not because owners have choices, but because ownership makes the owner better off, advancing her interests. An individual's rights, claims the interest theorist, are Hohfeldian incidents which benefit the person involved. Jeremy Bentham, John Austin, Joseph Raz, and Matthew Kramer may be included in this camp.

There are weaknesses in both accounts. With regard to will theory, there may be no such thing as an unwaivable right (for instance, a right not to be enslaved). Under the will theory, it is impossible for incompetents to have rights; yet, the concept contradicts what is ordinarily perceived as what should be the case. Further, bare privilege rights (e.g., in a Hobbesian state of nature) do not represent the right of authority over others.

The interest theory also fails what ordinarily would be understood as rights. On the one hand, a person may have an interest in something without having a right to that object. On the other hand, a judge may have an interest in sentencing a convict to life in prison, but the judge's interests cannot justify ascribing such power to affect a convict's normative situation. Joseph Raz, for instance, admits that such important rights such as freedom of expression or freedom of contract are not justified by the interests of the citizens who hold them; rather, such rights advance the common good.

I find the Hohfeldian approach to be useful in analyzing rights in the broad sense. In this sense, natural rights would then appear to be a subset of moral rights, and for the legal theory presented in these pages, the will theory proves helpful for the function of rights with its focus on such concepts as power and duty.

LEGITIMATE DOMINATION

As explicated, I have adopted a Weberian descriptive classification in the two principles of law set forth in these pages. Rather than emphasizing moral goals as such, like justice (e.g., Kant) or freedom (e.g., Hegel), Max Weber accepts a Hobbesian outlook on politics.

The three ideal types of legitimate domination Weber identified are based on charisma, tradition, and legal rationality. The first type of legitimacy claim, charisma, depends largely on how persuasively the leaders prove their qualities, for which they receive personal devotions and emotive investment from those ruled. The second kind of claim, tradition, can be made successfully when certain practices, customs, and mores are institutionalized to produce a stable pattern of domination over a long duration of time. In contrast to these crucial dependences on personality traits and the passage of time, the third type of authority, legal rationality, is unfettered by time, place, and other contingencies as it derives its legitimacy from adherence to impersonal rules and general principles that can only be found by suitable legal-rational reasoning.

LIBERALISM

In political theory, liberalism is typically seen to include the concepts of liberty or freedom and equality. Of course, differing and complex views of these concepts have emerged, according, for example, to the emphasis given one concept over another and additional concepts that may be included in different versions of liberalism.

Classic political liberalism is based on the individual as the bearer of rights. In recent times, however, the equality component of liberalism may be said to be the more dominant element, thus implying the concept of obligations as well as the concept of rights. John Rawls, for example, links the concept of equality to his distributive theory of justice as fairness. Moreover, for Ronald Dworkin, equality is positioned as the political sovereign virtue, and serves as the linchpin of his theory of resource equality.

My view of political liberalism includes consideration of equality as well, but does so in a conceptual framework that promotes the concepts of negative liberty, equality of concern and respect, tolerance, and diversity.[7]

GROUP RIGHTS

While exploring the political foundations of law, I discussed the concept of group rights in the framework of a just or unjust society, since, as I argue, law should be viewed in the service of justice. I have examined various contemporary group rights theories, including approaches based on oppression and domination, communal life, gender, race, and culture.[8] Since these accounts are often framed in the context of just and unjust societies, at a basic level, these group rights theories are antithetical to the classic liberal view that rights should be based on the individual.

INTERNATIONAL RELATIONS

There are about 200 separate nation-states. How may relations between and among these states be guided or regulated? What mechanisms and institutions may be positioned or promoted to secure a peaceful, stable world order? What does just war theory add to the discussion?

In developing his theory of global political justice, Charles Beitz explains that he does not focus on questions of war and peace, one of the central concerns of international relations.[9] He accounts for this omission on two grounds: first, scholarship on just war theory has received considerable philosophical attention in recent years. Second, any just war theory must rest upon a more general theory of international right, which is what he prefers to discuss, as he develops cosmopolitanism view of international relations in rebuttal to a Hobbesian worldview.

INTERNATIONAL LAW

The term "rule of law" has gained currency in contemporary times. The term may be seen as an ideal of political morality and refers to the primacy of laws and institutions of the legal system in the structure of governance. The term, however, has been used in a variety of definitions. One question that arises is whether the rule of law extends to the evaluation of international law, and if so, under what interpretation and with what particular implications.

Legal theorists who explore what the rule of law means can be arranged along a line from thin (formal procedural) to thick (substantive) versions. Thin accounts of the rule of law, for example, emphasize formal-procedural accounts of the rule of law. At the opposite end, thick accounts favor substantive accounts, sometimes concluding that the rule of law does not apply to international law, since it imposes demands that cannot conceivably be made of international, as opposed to domestic, law.

CONTEMPORARY NATURAL LAW THEORIES

Following in the natural law tradition of Aquinas are contemporary legal theorists like John Finnis and Lon L. Fuller. While Finnis pursues the question of what is truly good for individuals, Fuller foregrounds the goal orientation characterizing individual behavior to natural law issues. Fuller also engaged in a well-known debate with the legal positivist H.L.A. Hart. While the debate has focused on Fuller's eight principles of law, the underlying dispute has to do with the conceptual connection between law and morality.

SUBSTANTIVE NATURALISM

In contemporary times, the prominent natural law theorist John Finnis may be viewed as further developing classical natural law theory.[10] To articulate his thoughts on natural law, he adopts two key features of the natural law theory of Thomas Aquinas: (1) God's role as the giver of natural law, and (2) human beings as the recipients of natural law, with natural law comprising principles of practical rationality by which human action may be judged as reasonable or unreasonable. Finnis argues that the purpose of law is to establish, "what is really good for human beings," thereby evoking an Aristotelian version of what constitutes a worthwhile, valuable life (*eudaimonia*): the good over the right.

PROCEDURAL NATURALISM

Like John Finnis, Lon L. Fuller rejects the conceptual naturalist idea that there are necessary substantive moral constraints on the content of law.[11] But unlike Finnis, Fuller believes that law is necessarily subject to a procedural morality. In Fuller's view, human activity is necessarily goal-oriented or purposive in the sense that people engage in a particular activity in order to achieve some end. Insofar as human activity is essentially purposive, according to Fuller, particular human activities can be understood only in terms that make reference to their purposes and ends.

SOCIAL FACTS

A primary thesis of legal positivism extending back to the accounts of Jeremy Bentham and John Austin is that legal facts are fully grounded in social facts. Legal facts hold solely in virtue of social facts, with the exclusion of any moral facts. H.L.A. Hart's contemporary legal theory of social facts has come to be known as inclusive legal positivism, or in his own words, "soft positivism."[12] He uses Austin's command theory of law, and his criticisms of Austin's theory, to construct a platform for his account of law as rules and to articulate an "internal" point of view of the law.

Ronald Dworkin has argued forcefully against Hart's theory of law and his "rule of recognition," as he pursues a "third-way" theorizing of law, one which is neither naturalist nor positivist. Dworkin's concerns about legal positivism have to do not only with Hart's rules of law and whether moral principles can count as authoritative legal texts, but also with the deeply conventionalist views underlying legal positivism.[13]

HART-DWORKIN DEBATE

The long-running Hart-Dworkin debate centers on the relation of, and separability between, legality and morality. It often seems, however, that the participants do not agree on what they are arguing about. Notoriously, their debate began on just such a note. Thus, in "The Model of Rules I," Dworkin claimed that the dispute between the two theorists concerned whether the law is a model of rules. This formulation, however, proves misleading, because, as is now generally recognized, Hart never claimed that the law is simply a model of rules (in Dworkin's sense of "rule"), nor is he committed to such a position.

As their debate continued, it has ranged over such disparate issues as: (1) the role of policy in adjudication; (2) the ontological foundations of rules; (3) the possibility of descriptive jurisprudence; (4) the function of law; (5) the objectivity of value; (6) the vagueness of concepts; and (7) the nature of legal inference. But as I voiced above, the basic debate between Hart and Dworkin essentially has to do with the relation between legality and morality.

CONTEMPORARY LEGAL POSITIVISM

As indicated earlier, legal positivism embraces a broad range of theories linked insofar as they all deny a necessary connection between law and morals and they all prescribe that the validity of any law be traced to an objectively verifiable source. Law thereby results from social facts and is not of normative value. Accordingly, legal positivists are conventionalists since they believe that there must be agreement about the criteria of legality in order for law to exist.

By contrast, natural law theory contends that law consists of a series of propositions derived from nature, that legal and moral normativity are closely connected, and that law entails a moral determinant. The dispute between legal positivists and natural law theorists covers an extensive scope of textured debates including contested matters of reason, rules, duty, obligations, and rights.

Thus, writing in the legal positivist tradition, Hans Kelsen rejects claims of natural law.[14] That is, Kelsen claims that traditional legal philosophies in the early 20th century were hopelessly contaminated by political ideology and moralizing on the one hand or by attempts to reduce the law to natural or social sciences on the other hand. He found both of these reductionist endeavors seriously flawed. In their stead, he proffers a "pure theory of law," which avoids reductionism of any kind and serves "as a 'pure' theory of law because it aims at cognition focused on the law alone," and this purity serves as its "basic methodological principle."

More specifically, Kelsen views traditional jurisprudence as maintaining a dual system comprising subjective law (the rights of a person) and objective law (the system of norms). Throughout history this dualism has proven a useful tool for putting the law in the service of politics, especially by rulers or dominant political parties. In response, Kelsen's pure theory of law aims to replace this dualism with a unitary system of objective positive law that is insulated from political manipulation.

PLANNING THEORY OF LAW

In *Legality*, Scott Shapiro offers a new theory of the nature of law.[15] His basic claim is that laws are plans for living together, and legal systems are institutions that create certain kinds of plans for societies to follow. He thereby characterizes legal activity as a form of shared planning activity, the fundamental aim of which is to solve moral disagreements that cannot be properly resolved by purely moral deliberation. His further claim is that laws are plans created by planning institutions with a specific moral aim, and that law can be thought of as a set of plans to achieve complex human goals.

The moral aim of Shapiro's legal theory is somewhat surprising, since his stated intention is to defend exclusive legal positivism and to reject the core commitments of natural law theory. Shapiro's objection is that if the function of law is to guide conduct by means of reasoning, then theoretically, every law must be capable of making what he calls a "practical difference." He further argues that rules that are law in virtue of their satisfying moral conditions of legality cannot make a practical difference, because the reason to act that they purport to create is already expressed in the condition of their legality.

Shapiro may be seen as a positivist, but one who tries to bridge the differences between legal positivism and natural law theory, a project whose success has been open to criticism. In his attempt to meld the two, Shapiro rejects inclusive legal positivism, which holds that the function of law is to guide conduct. Rather, his planning theory of law presents a method to solve what he describes as the possibility problem, which queries how law can be authoritative without referring to higher laws. Questions arise, though, about whether his insights positing social facts as facts about plans are sufficiently novel and powerful enough to warrant placing a new label on them, by using an analogy to another human activity to reframe the question.

JUSTICE AS RIGHT ACTIONS

Early in this study, I expressed my belief that law should serve the demands of justice. My answer to the justice question is to develop a moral framework to inform the political landscape of the times. Thus, I view the proper task of justice as the development of normative guidance in the form of action-guiding principles that may be applied in variable circumstances.[16] Further, the set of principles arrived upon should, critically, be able to be universalized—by which I mean principles that are not self-defeating, that are reversible, and that may be consistently applied.

Thus, I arrive at a formulation of two principles of justice, in lexical priority:

> *The Responsibility Principle*: One is responsible for one's own actions.
>
> *The Equality Principle*: One should act with respect and concern for persons having the same right to act and to respond to one's actions.[17]

I thereby maintain that justice includes responsible actions based on rational and autonomous moral agency, with the individual (not groups) as the proper bearer of rights and responsibilities. In taking an analytical approach, and arguing for the right over the good, I deepen the apparent transparency of the political tenet—*do what is right*—with a morally thick register, one that recognizes the conventions, thought, and richness of moral traditions of various cultures, by framing the concept in a deontological approach.

In viewing justice as right actions, then, I assume that a person owes a duty of justice when her or his actions may affect others. This responsibility for intentional actions is set forth in the first principle of justice as right actions, the Responsibility Principle, as limited by the second principle, the Equality Principle, which advises that we consider how others might act in response to an individual's actions. Thus, the second principle, the Equality Principle, with its reference to other persons, and consequently the external world and experience, works both as a constraint on the first principle of justice as right actions, the Responsibility Principle, as well as a repository of resources for moral decision-making, as it empirically reaches into particular communities in which individuals are situated, along with the laws and customs of such communities. It also provides the touchstone for a priority rule in situations involving conflicting values.

VALUE PLURALISM

In the approach to justice as right actions, plural values are embraced, although I do not favor a strong value pluralist account, nor one afflicted by the problem of incommensurability. Like Immanuel Kant and John Rawls, and in contrast to both Joseph Raz and John Stuart Mill, I advocate for the right over the good. The priority of the right, which Rawls presents in his theory as neutral and anti-perfectionist, may be seen as placing limits, in the interest of fairness, on differing conceptions of the good.

In arguing for the right over the good, I acknowledge attendant theoretical problems to the deontological approach of justice as right actions, and I propose a thin underlying theory of the good, which comprises four concepts, as follows:

1. rationality;
2. autonomous moral agency;
3. equal concern and respect for others; and
4. plurality of values.

Thus, value pluralism may be seen to enter the account of justice as right actions by means of the second principle, the Equality Principle, which states that in societal interactions, mutual respect and concern between individuals should be normative. This weak value pluralism is further supported by the concepts of tolerance and social diversity, as envisioned in a political context of liberalism. In other words, a politically framed, morally thick concept—*do what is right*—approached from a deontological perspective impels my argument on justice.

NORMS AND CUSTOMS

The cultural contingency implied in the Responsibility Principle may be ameliorated by the Equality Principle's reference to the external world and experience. For instance, as argued above, there are moral resources and constraints contained in Tim Scanlon's concept of "parametric universalism," which seek to identify certain deeply embedded, culturally universal concepts that exclude genocide, murder, and totalitarian rule from acceptable moral behavior.[18] While Scanlon's views may be seen as relativistic, they are nonetheless grounded in certain cross-cultural concepts, making external analyses possible while minimizing intuition as a standard.

In further searching for action-guiding moral resources referenced in the Equality Principle, it proves useful as well to identify morally thick concepts. As also referenced previously, Bernard Williams in his benign treatment of moral relativism identifies four concepts that are able to bear a substantial amount of cross-cultural weight, including cowardice, truthfulness, brutality, and gratitude.[19]

Finally, for those situations in which a conflict in values is identified under the two principles of justice as right actions, the value which best adheres to or promotes the notion of due respect and concern for persons embedded in this account is the one that should prevail as a priority rule.

JUSTICE AND LAW

I have outlined a theory of justice as right actions, expressing my belief that law should serve the demands of justice. The theory of justice as right actions presents a deontological, normative theory. Rather than taking a distributive approach to the question of justice, it takes a relational approach which is led by moral concerns. This view focuses on the individual and her/his relations with other persons and institutions in society. Thus, the foundation of the theory of justice as right actions is moral, and morality drives the theory and the search for the right thing to do in given circumstances.

By contrast, the theory of law presented here has a political foundation and may be seen to be connected to morality at the top level, as these pages' concept of justice provides the moral framework and resources within which rules of law are made. Law involves attempts to make authoritative political pronouncements to regulate human behavior, and these pronouncements sometimes overlap with moral and normative concerns.

RIGHT OVER GOOD

Both the theory of justice as right actions proposed here and the theory of law presented in this study depend on a deontological point of view, with the same underlying thin theory of the good, and both privilege the priority of the right over the good. Further, they both rely on rational, autonomous moral agents in the consideration of responsible actions.

RATIONALITY

As mentioned earlier, I rely on a moderate view of rationality, rather than a more extreme Platonic or Cartesian view, as a precedential method of acquiring knowledge. In my moderate view of rationality, I take an Aristotelian stance that practical reasoning starts with the normative question of what is one to do, considers questions of value, and leads to a consideration of intentional actions. Theoretical reasoning, by contrast, may be seen as concerned with matters of fact and their explanation. Examined in this manner, the contrast between practical reason and theoretical reason addresses two different systems of norms: those for the regulation of action (practical reason), and those for the regulation of belief (theoretical reason).

I view practical reason as requiring reflection to resolve the question of what an agent is to do. Thus, issues to be explored from the perspective of practical reason include: whether and how deliberative reflection can give rise to action, what norms for the assessment of action are binding upon us as agents, and whether such norms are purely instrumental. When practical reason weighs such issues, moral responsibility is evoked. In other words, moral responsibility depends upon the rational and autonomous individual to judge, act, and deliberate norms in such a manner that a particular type of reaction—generally speaking, praise or blame—is elicited. It is important to underscore here that in deliberating the requisite reaction (e.g., praise or blame), the conditions and objects of moral responsibility intrinsically require analyses that consider norms to some degree.

LAW AS NORMATIVE PRINCIPLES

Thus, the theory of law presented in these pages may be articulated through two principles of law, in lexical priority, as follows:

> *First Principle*: One should obey those laws of legal-rational political authority that do not otherwise violate societal norms and customs.
>
> *Second Principle*: Governments should only enforce rules of human behavior of legitimate legal-rational political authority.

NOTES

1. See Immanuel Kant, *Groundwork of the Metaphysic of Morals*, trans. H. J. Paton (New York: HarperCollins, 2009): 88.
2. See chapter 2 *infra.*
3. See Plato, *The Republic*, trans. Desmond Lee, 2nd ed. (London: Penguin Books, 2003), and Aristotle, *The Nicomachean Ethics of Aristotle*, trans. D. Ross, rev. Lesley Brown (Oxford: Oxford University Press, 2009), Book V; see also, Young Kim, *Justice: Classical Foundations and Contemporary Debates* (Lanham: Lexington Books, 2018), chs. 2 and 3.
4. See chapter 5 *infra.*
5. See Jeremy Bentham, *The Works of Jeremy Bentham* (Edinburgh: William Tait, 1843), Vol. I, and John Austin, *Lectures on Jurisprudence or The Philosophy of Positive Law*, 2 vols. Ed. R. Campbell (London: John Murray; reprinted, Bristol: Thoemmes Press, 2002)
6. See Wesley Hohfeld, *Fundamental Legal Conceptions as Applied in Judicial Reasoning*, Eds. P. Campbell and D. Thomas, Intro. N. Simmonds. (London: Routledge, 2016); see also, chapter 7 *infra.*

7. See Young Kim, *Justice as Right Actions* (Lanham: Lexington Books, 2015), ch. 4.

8. See ibid., ch. 10.

9. See Charles Beitz, *Political Theory and International Relations*, 2nd ed. (Princeton: Princeton University Press, 1999).

10. See John Finnis, *Natural Law and Natural Rights*, 2nd ed. (Oxford: Oxford University Press, 2011).

11. See Lon Fuller, *The Morality of Law*, rev. ed. (New Haven: Yale University Press, 1969).

12. See H.L.A. Hart, *The Concept of Law*, 3rd ed., intro. L. Green (Oxford: Oxford University Press, 2012).

13. See Ronald Dworkin, *Law's Empire*, 2nd ed. (Cambridge: Belknap Press, 1986); see also Ronald Dworkin, *Taking Rights Seriously* (London: Bloomsbury Press, 2013).

14. See Hans Kelsen, *Pure Theory of Law*, 2nd ed., trans. M. Knight (Clark: Lawbook Exchange, Ltd., 2009).

15. See Scott Shapiro, *Legality* (Cambridge: Belknap Press, 2013).

16. Young Kim, *Justice as Right Actions* (Lanham; Lexington Books, 2015).

17. Id., 3.

18. See T. M. Scanlon, *What We Owe Each Other* (Cambridge: Belknap Press, 1998).

19. See Bernard Williams, *Moral Luck* (Cambridge: Cambridge University Press, 1981).

Works Cited

Annas, Julia (1981). *An Introduction to Plato's Republic.* Oxford: Oxford University Press.

———. (1976). "Plato's 'Republic' and Feminism." *Philosophy* 51(197): 307–321.

Anscombe, G.E.M. (1958). "Modern Moral Philosophy." *Philosophy* 33(124): 1–19.

Aquinas, Thomas (1920). *Summa Theologica.* Trans. Fathers of the English Dominican Province. Ed. Paul A. Boer Sr. New York: Benziger Brothers.

Aristotle (2009a). *Aristotle's* Nicomachean Ethics, *Book VII.* Ed. Carlo Natali. Oxford: Oxford University Press.

———. (2009b). *The Nichomachean Ethics of Aristotle.* Trans. D. Ross; Rev. Lesley Brown. Oxford: Oxford University Press.

———. (2009c). *The Politics*. Trans. Ernest Baker. Oxford: Oxford University Press.

———. (1992). *The Politics*. Trans. T. A. Sinclair. Rev. Trevor Saunders. London: Penguin.

Arneson, Richard (1995). "Against Complex Equality." In Eds. David Miller and Michael Walzer, *Pluralism, Justice and Equality*: 226–252.

Austin, John (2002). *Lectures on Jurisprudence*, or *The Philosophy of Positive Law*, 2 vols. Ed. R. Campbell. London: John Murray; reprinted, Bristol: Thoemmes Press.

———. (1995). *The Province of Jurisprudence Determined.* Ed. Wilfred Rumble. Cambridge: Cambridge University Press.

Barry, Brian (2001). *Culture and Equality.* Cambridge: Polity Press.

———. (1990). *Political Argument: A Reissue with a New Introduction.* Berkeley: University of California Press.

———. (2002). "Second Thoughts: Some First Thoughts Revived." In Ed. Paul Kelly, *Multiculturalism Reconsidered*: 204–238.

Barry, Rachel, Tad Brennan, and Charles Brittain, eds. (2012). *Plato and the Divided Self.* Cambridge: Cambridge University Press.

Bentham, Jeremy (1977). "*A Comment on the Commentaries and A Fragment of Government.*" In Ed. J. H. Burns and H.L.A. Hart, *The Collected Works of Jeremy Bentham.* London: University of London Press.

———. (1983). *Constitutional Code*. Eds. F. Rosen and J. H. Burns. Oxford: Oxford University Press.

———. (1996). *An Introduction to the Principles of Morals and* Legislation. Eds. J. H. Burns and H.L.A. Hart. Oxford: Clarendon Press.

———. (1990). *Securities Against Misrule and Other Constitutional Writings for Tripoli and Greece*. Eds. P. Schofield and F. Rosen. Oxford: Clarendon Press.

———. (1843). *The Works of Jeremy Bentham*, vol. 1. Edinburgh: William Tait.

Beitz, Charles (1999a). "International Liberalism and Distributive Justice: A Survey of Recent Thought." *World Politics* 51(2): 269–296.

———. (1999b). *Political Theory and International Relations,* 2nd ed. Princeton: Princeton University Press.

Berlin, Isaiah (1969). "Two Concepts of Liberty." In *Four Essays on Liberty*. Oxford: Oxford University Press: 118–172.

Bingham, Tom (2010). *The Rule of Law*. London: Allen Lane.

Blackstone, William (2016). *Commentaries on the Laws of England.* Ed. David Lemmings. Oxford: Oxford University Press.

Cohen, G. A. (2004). "Expensive Taste Rides Again." In Ed. Justine Burley, *Dworkin and His Critics*, Oxford: Blackwell Publishing: 3–29.

———, Ed. (1995). *Self-Ownership, Freedom and Equality*. Cambridge: Cambridge University Press.

Coleman, Jules (2003). *The Practice of Principle: In Defence of a Pragmatist Approach to Legal Theory.* Oxford: Oxford University Press.

Cooper, Kody (2018). *Thomas Hobbes and the Natural Law.* Notre Dame, IN: University of Notre Dame.

Crawford, James (2014). *Chance, Order, Change: The Course in International Law, General Course on Public International Law.* Boston: Martinus Nijhoff.

———. (2006). *The Creation of States in International Law*, 2nd ed. Oxford: Clarendon Press.

Daniels, Norman, Ed. (1975). *Reading Rawls: Critical Studies on John Rawls'* "*A Theory of Justice*." New York: Basic Books.

———. (2011). "Reflective Equilibrium." Ed. Edward Zalta. *Stanford Encyclopedia of Philosophy,* http://plato.stanford.edu/entries/reflective-equilibrium.

Darwall, Stephen (2009). *The Second-Person Standpoint: Morality, Respect, and Accountability.* Cambridge: Harvard University Press.

Delgado, Richard, and Jean Stephancic (2012). *Critical Race Theory: An Introduction*, 2nd ed. New York: New York University Press.

Dworkin, Ronald (1986). *Law's Empire.* Cambridge: Harvard University Press.

———. (1967). "The Model of Rules." *University of Chicago Law Review* 35(1): 14–46.

———. (2013). "A New Philosophy for International Law." *Philosophy & Public Affairs* 41(1): 2–30.

———. (2000). *Sovereign Virtue: The Theory and Practice of Equality*. Cambridge: Harvard University Press.

———. (1978). *Taking Rights Seriously, With a New Appendix, a Response to Critics.* Cambridge: Harvard University Press.

Eshleman, Andrew (2014). "Moral Responsibility." Ed. Edward Zalta. *The Stanford Encyclopedia of Philosophy*, http//plato.standford.edu/archives/sum.2014/entries /moral-responsibility/.
Finnis, John (2013). *The Collected Essays of John Finnis*, 5 vols. Oxford: Oxford University Press.
———. (1980). *Natural Law and Natural Rights*. Oxford: Clarendon Press.
Foot, Philippa (2001). *Natural Goodness*. Oxford: Clarendon Press.
———. (1978). *Virtues and Vices*. Oxford: Blackwell.
Franck, Thomas M. (2017). "The Emerging Right to Democratic Governance." *American Journal of International Law* 86(1): 46–91.
———. (1998). *Fairness in International Law and Institutions.* Oxford: Clarendon Press.
Freeman, Samuel (2007). *Rawls*. The Routledge Philosophers. New York: Routledge.
Fuller, Lon L. (1964). *The Morality of Law*. New Haven: Yale University Press.
———. (1958). "Positivism and Fidelity to Law—A Reply to Professor Hart." *Harvard Law Review* 71(4): 630–672.
———. (1965). "A Reply to Professors Cohen and Dworkin." *Villanova Law Review* 10(4,5): 655–666.
Galston, William (2002). *Liberal Pluralism.* Cambridge: Cambridge University Press.
———. (2005). *The Practice of Liberal Pluralism*. Cambridge: Cambridge University Press.
Gardner, John, and Timothy Macklem. "Review of *Legality*." *Notre Dame Philosophical Reviews*, https://ndpr.nd.edu/reviews/legality/.
Gray, John (1985). *Liberalism*. Minneapolis: University of Minnesota Press.
———. (1996). *Mill on Liberty: A Defence,* 2nd ed. Oxford: Routledge.
———. (2000). *Two Faces of Liberalism*. Cambridge: Polity Press.
Goodin, Robert, and Philip Pettit, eds. (1993). *A Companion to Contemporary Political Philosophy*. Oxford: Blackwell Publishing.
Green, Leslie (2004). "Legal Obligation and Authority." Ed. Edward Zalta. *The Stanford Encyclopedia of Philosophy*, https://plato.stanford.edu/entries/legal -obligation/.
Habermas, Jürgen (1996). *Between Facts and Norms: Contributions to a Discourse Theory of Law and Democracy*. Trans. William Rehg. Cambridge: The MIT Press.
Hare, R. M. (1998). *Essays on Political Morality*. Oxford: Oxford University Press.
———. (1981). *Moral Thinking: Its Levels, Method, and Point*. Oxford: Oxford University Press.
Harman, Gilbert (1996). "Moral Relativism and Moral Objectivity." In Eds. Gilbert Harman and Judith L. Thompson, *Moral Relativism and Moral Objectivity*. Oxford: Blackwell Publishers: 1–19.
Harsanyi, John (1976). *Essays on Ethics, Social Behavior and Scientific Explanation*. Dordrecht: D. Reidel Publishing Company.
Hart, H.L.A. (2012). *The Concept of Law*. 3rd ed. Intro. and Notes Leslie Green. Postscript Eds. Joseph Raz and Penelope A. Bulloch. Oxford: Oxford University Press.

———. (1982). "Legal Duty and Obligation." In *Essays on Bentham: Studies on Jurisprudence and Political Theory.* Oxford: Clarendon Press: 127–161.
———. (1958). "Positivism and the Separation of Law and Morals." *Harvard Law Review* 71(4): 593–629.
———. (1975). "Rawls on Liberty and Its Priority." In Ed. Norman Daniels, *Reading Rawls: Critical Studies on Rawls' "A Theory of Justice."* Oxford: Blackwell: 206–229.
———. (1965–1966). "Review of Lon L. Fuller, *The Morality of Law*." *Tennessee Law Review* 33: 563.
von Hayek, Friedrich (1978). *Law, Legislation and Liberty: The Mirage of Social Justice*, vol. 2. Chicago: University of University Press.
Hobbes, Thomas (2017). *Three-Text Edition of Thomas Hobbes's Political Theory:* The Elements of Law, De Cive, *and* Leviathan. Ed. Deborah Baumgold. Cambridge: Cambridge University Press.
Hohfeld, Wesley (2016). *Fundamental Legal Conceptions as Applied in Judicial Reasoning.* Eds. P. Campbell and D. Thomas. Intro. N. Simmonds. London: Routledge.
Hugo, Victor (1982). *Les Miserables.* Trans. Norman Denny. London: Penguin Books.
Hume, David (2001). *A Treatise of Human Nature*. Eds. David Fate Norton and Mary J. Norton. Oxford: Oxford University Press.
International Court of Justice. Statute: www.icj-cij.org/statute.
Irwin, Terence (1988). *Classical Thought.* Oxford: Oxford University Press.
———. (1995). *Plato's Ethics*. Oxford: Oxford University Press.
Juvenal (2014). Ed. Lindsay Watson and Patricia Watson, vol. II. Cambridge: Cambridge University Press.
Kant, Immanuel (1997). *Critique of Pure Reason.* Trans. and Eds. Paul Guyer and Allen Wood. Cambridge: Cambridge University Press.
———. (2009). *Groundwork of the Metaphysic of Morals*. Trans. H. J. Paton. New York: HarperCollins.
Kelly, Paul (2002). "Introduction: Between Culture and Equality." In Ed. Paul Kelly, *Multiculturalism Reconsidered*: 1–17.
———. (2004). *Liberalism*. Cambridge: Polity Press.
———, Ed. (2002). *Multiculturalism Reconsidered*. Cambridge: Polity Press.
Kelsen, Hans (1961). *General Theory of Law and State*. Trans. Anders Wedberg. New York: Russell & Russell.
———. (1997). *Introduction to the Problems of Legal Theory: A Translation of the First Edition of the* Reine Rechtslehre *or* Pure Theory of Law. Trans. Bonnie Litschewski Paulson and Stanley L. Paulson. Oxford: Clarendon Press.
———. (1967). *Pure Theory of Law*. Trans. Max Knight. Berkeley: University of California Press.
———. (1941). "The Pure Theory of Law and Analytical Jurisprudence." *Harvard Law Review* 55(1): 44–70.
Kleingeld, Pauline (2012). *Kant and Cosmopolitanism: The Philosophical Ideal of World Citizenship.* New York: Cambridge University Press.
Korsgaard, Christine (1986). "Aristotle and Kant on the Source of Value." *Ethics* 96(3): 486–505.

———. (1996). *The Sources of Normativity*. Ed. Onora O'Neill. Cambridge: Cambridge University Press.

Kraut, Richard (2013). "Aristotle on Becoming Good: Habituation, Reflection and Perception." In Ed. Christopher Shields, *The Oxford Handbook of Aristotle*. Oxford: Oxford University Press: 529–557.

———. (1992). "The Defense of Justice in Plato's *Republic*" In Ed. Richard Kraut. *The Cambridge Companion to Plato*. Cambridge: Cambridge University Press.

Kukathas, Chandran, and Philip Pettit (1990). *Rawls: "A Theory of Justice" and Its Critics*. Stanford: Stanford University Press.

Kymlicka, Will (1993). "Community." In Eds. Robert E. Goodin and Philip Pettit, *A Companion to Contemporary Political Philosophy*. Malden: Blackwell Publishing: 366–378.

———. (1995). *Multicultural Citizenship: A Liberal Theory of Minority Rights*. Oxford: Oxford University Press.

von Leyden, W. (1967). "Aristotle and the Concept of Law." *The Journal of the Royal Institute of Philosophy* XLII(159): 1–19.

Locke, John (1996). *An Essay Concerning Human Understanding*. Ed. Kenneth Winkler Indianapolis: Hackett Publishing.

———. (2002). *Essays on the Law of Nature*. Ed. W. von Leyden. Oxford: Oxford University Press.

———. (1980). *Second Treatise of Government*. Ed. Crawford Brough Macpherson. Indianapolis: Hackett Publishing.

———. (1998). *Two Treatises, Two Treatises on Government*. Ed. Peter Laslett. Cambridge: Cambridge University Press.

Machiavelli, Niccolò (2004). *The Prince*. Trans. W. K. Marriot. London: Penguin Books.

MacIntyre, Alasdair (1985). *After Virtue*, 2nd ed. London: Duckworth.

Mill, John Stuart (1998). "On Liberty." In Ed. John Gray, *John Stuart Mill on Liberty and Other Essays*. Oxford: Oxford University Press: 5–130.

Miller, David, and Michael Walzer, eds. (1995). *Pluralism, Justice and Equality*. Oxford: Oxford University Press.

Miller, Fred (1995). *Nature, Justice, and Rights in Aristotle's* Politics. Oxford: Clarendon Press.

Mulhall, Stephen, and Adam Swift (1996). *Liberals and Communitarians*, 2nd ed. Oxford: Blackwell.

Nagel, Thomas (1979). *Mortal Questions*. New York: Cambridge University Press.

Nietzsche, Friedrich (1973). *Beyond Good and Evil*. Trans. R. J. Hollingdale. Harmondsworth: Penguin Books.

Nozick, Robert (1974). *Anarchy, State, and Utopia*. New York: Basic Books.

Okin, Susan (1999). *Is Multiculturalism Bad for Women?* Princeton: Princeton University Press.

Parfit, Derek (1984). *Reasons and Persons*. Oxford: Clarendon Press.

Paul, Jeffrey, Ed. (1991). *Reading Nozick: Essays on Anarchy, State, and Utopia*. Totowa: Rowman and Littlefield.

Pettit, Philip (1993). "The Contribution of Analytical Philosophy." In Eds. Robert E. Goodin and Philip Pettit, *A Companion to Contemporary Political Philosophy.* Malden: Blackwell Publishing: 7–38.

Pettit, Philip, and Michael Smith (1997). "Parfit's P." In Ed. Jonathan Dancy, *Reading Parfit*. Oxford: Blackwell.

Plato (1970). *The Laws*. Trans. Trevor Saunders. London: Penguin Books.

———. (2003). *The Republic*, 2nd ed. Trans. Desmond Lee. London: Penguin Books.

———. (2002). *The Statesman*. Trans. J. B. Skemp. London: Bristol Classical Press.

———. (1992). *Theaetetus*. Ed. Bernard Williams; Trans. M. J. Levett; Rev. Miles Burnyeat. Indianapolis: Hackett Publishing Company.

Popper, Karl (1971). *The Open Society and Its Enemies*. Princeton: Princeton University Press.

Pufendorf, Samuel (1991). *On the Duty of Man and Citizen According to Natural Law.* Ed. James Tully. Trans. Michael Silverthorne. Cambridge: Cambridge University Press.

Rawls, John (1997). *The Law of Peoples*. Cambridge: Harvard University Press.

———. (1993). *Political Liberalism*. New York: Columbia University Press.

———. (1988). "The Priority of the Right and Ideas of the Good." *Philosophy and Public Affairs* 17(4): 251–276

———. (1971). *A Theory of Justice*. Cambridge: Harvard University Press.

Raz, Joseph (1990). "Authority and Justification." In Ed. Joseph Raz, *Authority*. New York: New York University Press: 115–141.

———. (1995). *The Authority of Law: Essays on Law and Morality.* Oxford: Oxford University Press.

———. (2009). *Between Authority and Interpretation: On the Theory of Law and Practical Reason.* Oxford: Oxford University Press.

———. (1980). *The Concept of a Legal System: An Introduction to the Theory of a Legal System*, 2nd ed. Oxford: Clarendon Press.

———. (1999). *Engaging Reason: On the Theory of Value and Action*. Oxford: Oxford University Press.

———. (1994). *Ethics in the Public Domain*. Oxford: Clarendon Press.

———. (1986). *The Morality of Freedom*. Oxford: Oxford University Press.

———. (2003). "The Practice of Value." In Ed. Grethe B. Peterson, *Tanner Lectures on Human Values*. Salt Lake City: University of Utah Press: vol. 11: 113–150.

———. (2006). "The Problem of Authority: Revisiting the Service Conception." *Minnesota Law Review* 90: 1003–1044.

———. (2004). *Reason and Value Themes from the Moral Philosophy of Joseph Raz.* Eds. R. Jay Wallace, Phillip Pettit, Samuel Scheffler, and Michael Smith. Oxford: Clarendon Press.

———. (1998). "Two Views of the Nature of the Theory of Law: A Partial Comparison." *Legal Theory* 4 (1998): 249–282.

Roemer, John (1986). "Equality of Resources Implies Equality of Welfare." *Quarterly Journal of Economics* 101: 751–784.

Sandel, Michael (1998). *Liberalism and the Limits of Justice*, 2nd ed. Cambridge: Cambridge University Press.

Scanlon, T. M. (1991). "Nozick on Rights, Liberty, and Property." In Ed. Jeffrey Paul. *Reading Nozick: Essays on Anarchy, State, and Utopia*. Totowa: Rowman and Littlefield: 107–129.
———. (2000). *What We Owe to Each Other*. Cambridge: Harvard University Press.
Shapiro, Scott (2007). "The 'Hart-Dworkin' Debate: A Short Guide for the Perplexed." *University of Michigan Law School*. Public Law and Legal Theory Working Paper Series 77: 1–54.
———. (2011). *Legality*. Cambridge: Harvard University Press.
Shoemaker, David (2011). "Attributability, Answerability, and Accountability: Toward a Wider Theory of Moral Responsibility." *Ethics* 121: 603–632.
Shields, Christopher, Ed. (2002). *The Oxford Handbook of Aristotle*. Oxford: Oxford University Press.
Smith, Angela (2012). "Attributability, Answerability, and Accountability: In Defense of a Unified Account." *Ethics* 122: 575–589.
Strauss, Leo (2002). *The City and Man*. Chicago: University of Chicago Press.
Strawson, P. F. (2008). "Freedom and Resentment." In *Freedom and Resentment and Other Essays*. New York: Routledge: 1–28.
Thucydides (2009). *History of the Peloponnesian War*. Trans. Martin Hammond. Notes and Intro. P. J. Rhodes. Oxford: Oxford University Press.
United Nations. Charter: www.un.org/en/about-us/un-charter.
———. Universal Declaration of Human Rights: https://www.un.org/en/about-us/universal-declaration-of-human-rights.
Vlastos, Gregory (1997). "Was Plato a Feminist?." In Ed. Richard Kraut, *Plato's Republic: Critical Essays*. Lanham: Rowman & Littlefield Publishers, Inc.
Waldron, Jeremy (1999). *Law and Disagreement*. Oxford: Clarendon Press.
Walzer, Michael. (1995). "Money and Complex Equality." In Eds. David Miller and Michael Walzer (2015). *Just and Unjust Wars: A Moral Argument with Historical Illustrations*, 5th ed. New York: Basic Books.
———. (1995). *Pluralism, Justice and Equality*. Oxford: Oxford University Press.
———. (1995). "Response." In Eds. David Miller and Michael Walzer, *Pluralism, Justice and Equality*: 281–298.
———. (1983). *Spheres of Justice*. New York: Basic Books.
Weber, Max (2013). *Economy and Society*, 2 vols. Eds. Guenter Roth and Claus Wittich. Oakland: University of California Press.
———. *(1997). Political Writings*. Eds. Peter Lassman and Ronald Speirs. Cambridge: Cambridge University Press.
———. *(1997). The Theory of Social and Economic Organization*. Ed. and Trans. Alexander Henderson and Talcott Parsons. New York: Free Press.
Williams, Bernard (1985). *Ethics and the Limits of Philosophy*. Cambridge: Harvard University Press.
———. (2007). Ed. Geoffrey Hawthorn. *In the Beginning Was the Deed: Realism and Moralism in Political Argument*. Princeton: Princeton University Press, 2005
———. (1981). *Moral Luck*. Cambridge: Cambridge University Press.

Young, Iris Marion (1997). "A Multicultural Continuum: A Critique of Will Kymlicka's Ethnic Nation Dichotomy." *Constellation* 4(1): 48–53.

———. (1990). *Justice and the Politics of Difference*. Oxford: Oxford University Press.

Index

Aquinas, Thomas. *See* natural law
Aristotle. *See* classical views

Berlin, Isaiah. *See* value pluralism

civil government, 2, 67–75, 173–74
classical views, 2, 35–49, 87, 103, 149, 152, 155, 161, 172; Aristotle, 2, 8, 9, 12n10, 14, 16, 17, 19, 24, 27, 30, 35, 41–46, 48n34, 49n52, 67, 68, 78, 80, 87, 94, 103, 108, 111–12, 146n6, 149, 150, 152, 155, 161, 172; Plato, 2, 8, 13–14, 17, 18–19, 23, 24–25, 27, 35–40, 41, 42, 43, 46, 47n1, 47n21, 48n24, 48n26, 67, 78, 84, 87, 94, 103, 108, 111–12, 149, 152, 155, 161, 167, 172, 182
communities and communitarianism, 29, 31n24, 39, 42–46, 48n26, 55, 57–58, 73–74, 80, 82, 89–94, 97–99, 118–20, 128–29, 136–37, 144, 149, 155–56, 180
complex equality and distributive justice. *See* equality
cosmopolitanism. *See* international law
constitutions, 2, 35–36, 38–39, 41, 45, 46, 47n7, 59, 73, 87, 111–12, 136, 140, 145, 151–53
conventions. *See* normative theories of law
critical race theory (CRT), 95–97

Dworkin, Ronald, 5, 45, 62, 77, 79, 80, 81–83, 85n17, 110–11, 125, 129, 131–33, 154, 175, 177–78

equality, 39, 42, 44–46, 47n20, 48n23, 49n52, 74, 77, 80–3, 88–94, 98–100, 104, 149, 150–51, 154, 155–60, 166, 168; classical views of equality, 39, 42, 44–46; complex equality and distributive justice, 2, 44–45, 49n52, 51, 77, 80–81, 87, 90–93, 97–100, 105–8, 149–51, 154–55, 159, 165, 175, 182
The Equality Principle, 155–60, 166, 168
exclusive legal positivism. *See* legal positivism

Finnis, John. *See* natural law
Fuller, Lon, 117, 120–23, 176, 177

gender, 87, 88, 93–95, 100, 175; Okin, Susan, 93–95; Young, Iris Marion, 87–89, 93–94, 98–99
Gray, John, 28, 78–79, 84

Hart, H.L.A. 5, 60–62, 71, 110, 117, 122–23, 125–33, 134n16, 135, 136–37, 144, 145, 147n24, 153–54, 160n13, 173, 176–78; *The Concept of Law*, 71, 110, 123, 131; Hart-Dworkin debate, 132–33; Hart–Fuller debate, 122–23
Hobbes, Thomas. *See* natural law
Hohfeld, Wesley, 71–72, 173, 174

inclusive legal positivism. *See* legal positivism
international law, 2, 60, 62, 109–11, 123, 130, 176; cosmopolitanism, 103–6, 154, 161n28; realism, 13, 14, 19, 74, 103–6, 158, 161n28; war, 2, 54–55, 68, 104–5, 108–9, 175–76

justice as distributive, 2, 44–45, 49n52, 77, 80–81, 87, 90–93, 98–100, 105–8, 149, 150–51, 154–55, 159, 165, 175, 182
justice as relational, 1, 2, 87, 149, 154–55, 159, 165, 182

Kant, Immanuel: rationality, 7–9, 10, 14–15, 16, 18–19, 20–21n7, 23–27, 29, 30, 31n8, 35–37, 39, 48n34, 51–52, 54, 58–59, 68, 70, 72, 73, 74, 118, 137, 141, 146n6, 147n29, 150, 152–53, 154, 156, 157, 158, 159, 161n26, 166, 167–68, 169, 170, 171, 174, 176, 181, 182–83
Kelsen, Hans. *See* natural law
Kim, Young: First Principle, 9–11, 18, 25–26, 72, 155–56, 166–68, 169–70, 180, 183; Second Principle, 9–10, 17–18, 72, 155–56, 166–68, 169–70, 180–81, 183; right actions, 1, 2, 6, 8–9, 15, 19, 25, 28–29, 52, 149, 154–60

legal positivism, 57–62, 117, 120, 123, 125, 129, 130–32, 133n7, 135–45, 172–73, 177, 178–79; exclusive, 129, 135, 136–37, 143, 179; inclusive, 123, 125–26, 129, 135, 137, 143, 145n1, 177, 179; social facts, 2, 61–62, 125–33, 135–36, 143, 177, 178–79
legal validity, 1, 2, 9, 30n1, 57, 59, 62n11, 118, 126–30, 131, 135, 139–42, 144, 145n1, 165–66, 173, 178
liberalism, 2, 28, 47n20, 48n23, 73, 77–84, 87, 89–90, 96–99, 106, 153, 156, 157, 175, 181
Locke, John. *See* natural law

Mill, John Stuart, 27–28, 77–80. 84n2, 100, 150, 156, 180; harm principle, 27–28, 31n19, 69, 77–79, 84n2, 100; utilitarianism, 6–7, 14, 25–28, 31n19, 57, 59, 78–79, 150, 154, 159–60, 162n34
morality, 1, 6–8, 13–14, 16, 17, 20, 23, 25, 28, 35, 54, 59, 60, 71, 75n11, 80, 103, 109, 111, 117, 118, 120, 122–23, 125, 126, 130–31, 133, 137, 141, 142, 145n1, 149, 158, 165, 171, 176, 177, 178, 182; moral luck, 13, 17–18, 21n14, 21n17, 171; moral relativism, 11, 13, 18–20, 141–42, 157, 171, 181
multiculturalism, 19, 21n20, 94–95, 97–100

natural law, 2, 51–55, 57, 58, 62, 67–70, 73, 105–6, 117–23, 131, 135–36, 139, 143, 172–74, 176–79; Aquinas, Thomas, 2, 51–54, 68, 117–18, 172, 176; Finnis, John, 5, 117–20, 176–77; Hobbes, Thomas, 2, 38, 51, 52–53, 55, 58, 67–70, 72, 73, 84, 104–5, 161n28, 172, 174, 176; Kelsen, Hans, 62, 71, 127, 135, 139–42, 147n24, 173, 178–79; Locke, John, 2, 51, 53–55, 58–59, 67, 69–71, 105–6, 112, 172

naturalism, 122; procedural, 120–21, 123, 177; substantive, 117–18, 176–77
normative theories of law, 1, 2, 5–10, 12n8, 13, 15, 19, 23, 25, 30, 62, 67, 71–72, 90, 96, 104–6, 110, 120, 125–26, 127, 130, 135–36, 138–40, 141, 154–55, 156, 158, 165–68, 169–83; conventions, 1, 28, 40, 41, 43–44, 60, 73, 123, 129–31, 133n7, 135, 136, 155, 165, 178, 180; norms and customs, 8, 9, 10, 11, 13, 14, 23–30, 42, 72, 73–74, 100, 106–8, 110, 129–31, 145, 147n29, 155–56, 157, 158–59, 166, 168, 169, 170, 171, 174, 180, 181, 183; values, 1, 8–9, 11, 19, 23–30, 59, 78–80, 84, 89, 91, 98, 103, 104, 112, 120–21, 129, 130, 146n6, 153, 155–60, 165–66, 170, 171, 180, 181
norms and customs. *See* normative theories of law
Nozick, Robert, 69–70, 75n9, 80, 92–93

obligations, 5, 8, 13–20, 28, 54–55, 77, 98, 105–6, 108, 110–11, 126–28, 135, 144, 159–60, 161n28, 165–66, 168, 171, 172, 175, 178
Okin, Susan. *See* gender

Plato. *See* classical views
politics, 1, 2, 6–10, 14, 24, 27–30, 35, 37–40, 41, 43–46, 51, 52, 53–55, 58–59, 62, 67–112, 117, 129, 138, 139, 151–60, 165, 166, 168, 169, 170, 173–83; legitimacy, 2, 9, 23–24, 30n1, 54, 67, 70–75, 79, 83–84, 97, 106, 110–11, 123, 126, 137–38, 144, 152, 158, 166, 168, 169, 173, 174, 183
practical reason, 5, 7, 8, 12n8, 13, 14–16, 20n3, 24–26, 30, 51–52, 117–20, 123, 146n6, 167, 171, 176–77, 182–83
Principles, First and Second. *See* Kim, Young
pure theory of law, 135–36, 139, 141, 178–79

Rawls, John, 7, 27, 29, 31n23, 45, 77, 79, 80, 81–82, 90–91, 105–9, 130, 149, 150–56, 159, 161n16, 175, 180; justice as fairness, 29, 31n23, 77, 81, 91, 105–7, 149, 150–54, 156, 160n6, 175, 180; *The Law of Peoples*, 105–8, 130; *Political Liberalism*, 107, 153, 160n6, 161–62n13
Raz, Joseph, 5, 26–28, 62, 72, 79, 110, 128–29, 135–40, 145n1, 146n6, 156, 173, 174, 180
realism. *See* international law
relational justice, 1, 2, 87, 149, 154–55, 159–60, 165, 182
religion and metaphysics, 23, 40, 92, 95, 100, 119, 141, 162n32, 171–72
right actions. *See* Kim, Young
rights, 2, 19, 21n20, 46, 53–55, 58, 61, 67–72, 77, 83, 87–100, 104, 107–12, 113n16, 118, 119–20, 130, 135, 150–51, 158, 159, 160n2, 162n32, 173–75, 178, 180; group rights, 19, 21n20, 87–100, 160n2, 162n32; human rights, 107–12, 113n16; individual rights, 54, 77, 83, 130–31, 139, 155, 157, 175, 180; natural rights, 2, 53, 55, 67–70, 118, 172, 173–74, 178
rule of law, 1, 2, 5, 10, 13, 14, 23, 41, 43–46, 53, 54, 59, 61, 67, 72–74, 111–12, 118, 121–33, 143, 151, 166, 168, 169, 170, 171, 176–79, 182, 183

Scanlon, T. M., 11, 20, 157, 161n26, 181
Shapiro, Scott, 135, 142–45, 179
social contract, 2, 54, 58–59, 70, 150, 153, 161n26
social facts. *See* legal positivism

state of nature, 2, 16, 58–60, 69–72, 103–6, 118–19, 174

value monism, 8–9, 24–25, 37
value pluralism, 9, 25–27, 31n13, 73, 79–80, 83–84, 89, 91–92, 107, 156, 180–81; Berlin, Isaiah, 77, 79–80, 83, 84
values. *See* normative theories of law

Walzer, Michael, 90–93, 109
war. *See* international law
Weber, Max, 72–75, 127, 147n24, 168, 174
Williams, Bernard, 11, 17–20, 26, 73, 157, 181

Young, Iris Marion. *See* gender

About the Author

Young Kim was born in Washington, DC, grew up in Virginia, and was educated at Shimer College, Northwestern University Pritzker School of Law, and The London School of Economics and Political Science. A practicing lawyer, Mr. Kim's teaching interests include corporate and securities law, international law, and legal philosophy. He has taught at the University of Colorado School of Law, on appointment as a Fulbright Senior Specialist at the University of Luxembourg, and at Northwestern University Pritzker School of Law.

The author's research and writing interests include intersections of law, politics, and morality. His current book, *The Question of Law*, investigates the nature of law, and in doing so, develops a normative theory of law. It is the third book of a trilogy. The first book, *Justice as Right Actions* (2015), explores the nature of justice, and advances the eponymous theory of justice as right actions. The second book, *Justice: Classical Foundations and Contemporary Debates* (2018), looks to foundational theories of justice in assessing contemporary theories of justice.

www.ingramcontent.com/pod-product-compliance
Ingram Content Group UK Ltd.
Pitfield, Milton Keynes, MK11 3LW, UK
UKHW041837031026
15587UKWH00002B/840

9 781666 938272